NARRATIVES OF SHIPWRECKS AND DISASTERS,

1586–1860

NARRATIVES OF
SHIPWRECKS AND DISASTERS,
1 5 8 6 – 1 8 6 0

EDITED WITH AN INTRODUCTION AND CHECKLIST OF TITLES

BY

Keith Gibson Huntress

THE IOWA STATE UNIVERSITY PRESS / *Ames*

1974

KEITH G. HUNTRESS, Professor of English and Distinguished Professor in Sciences and Humanities at Iowa State University, is a collector of books in three fields—Western Americana, early American fiction, and maritime history. He holds B.A. and M.A. degrees from Wesleyan University and the Ph.D. degree from the University of Illinois. Dr. Huntress has published poetry and fiction as well as textbooks for freshman English, propaganda analysis, and American history and has also written scholarly articles, chiefly on Melville.

© 1974 The Iowa State University Press, Ames, Iowa 50010
All rights reserved

Composed and printed by The Iowa State University Press

First edition, 1974

Library of Congress Cataloging in Publication Data

Huntress, Keith Gibson, 1913–   comp.
    Narratives of Shipwrecks and Disasters, 1586–1860.
    Bibliography: p.
    1. Shipwrecks.   I. Title.
G525.H898   1974   910'.453   73–12084
ISBN 0–8138–1445–6

FOR IDA,

AND ALSO FOR DEBORAH AND STEVE, CHERIE AND JONATHAN,

ALISON AND BETHANY AND MARGARET

CONTENTS

Introduction, ix

[1] Loss of the Portuguese Vessel *St. James,* 2

[2] Loss of the *Nottingham* Galley, 6

[3] Loss of the French East Indiaman *The Prince,* 18

[4] Loss of the Sloop *Betsy,* 28

[5] Loss of the Brig *Tyrrel,* 38

[6] A Famine in the American Ship *Peggy,* 47

[7] Loss of His Majesty's Ship *Phoenix,* 52

[8] Loss of His Majesty's Ship *Centaur,* 66

[9] Loss of the *Grosvenor* Indiaman, 78

[10] Loss of the *Halsewell* East Indiaman, 106

[11] Loss of His Majesty's Ship *Amphion,* 116

[12] Loss of the French Ship *Droits de L'Homme,* 122

[13] Loss of the *Apollo* Frigate, 126

[14] Loss of the *Earl of Abergavenny* East Indiaman, 131

[15] Loss of the Brig *Polly,* 138

[16] Shipwreck of the French Frigate *Medusa,* 142

[17] Destruction of the *Essex,* 164

[18] Loss of the Ship *Albion,* 172

[19] Loss of the *Frances Mary,* 179

[20] Loss of the *Helen McGregor*, 182

[21] Loss of the *Isabella*, 188

[22] Loss of the *Lady of the Lake*, 194

[23] Destruction of the *Ben Sherod*, 196

[24] Loss of the Steam Packet *Home*, 208

Checklist of Narratives of Shipwrecks and Disasters, 219

INTRODUCTION

I

THE GENESIS of this anthology was the chance purchase twenty-five years ago of a battered copy of R. Thomas's *Remarkable Shipwrecks, Fires, Famines, Calamities, Providential Deliverances, and Lamentable Disasters on the Seas.* Unlike many books, this one lived up to the horrid promise of its ungainly title through forty-three narratives and 354 pages of assorted and fascinating catastrophes. The intrinsic interest of these reports—with their revelation of the almost incredible helplessness of sailing ships, the frequent incompetence of masters and pilots, and the lack of any effective measure of social responsibility in past times—was strengthened by the discovery that they touched upon the lives and works of Wordsworth and Byron, Poe and Melville and Hawthorne. I have read every such book I could lay my hands on and have put together this anthology in the belief that what has been so interesting for me must prove to have some interest for others.

II

THE KIND OF NARRATIVE that appears in these books goes back to the work of Giovanni Ramusio, whose *Navigationi et Viaggi* was published in Venice in 1550 and Richard Hakluyt, of *Principall Navigations, Voiages, and Discoveries of the English Nation* (1589–1600). These compilations naturally included the stories of many shipwrecks as well as of successful voyages. Samuel Purchas's *Hakluytus Posthumus, or Purchas His Pilgrimes* (1625) was a continuation of Hakluyt's work. Other notable collections of voyages and travels were those of Thomas Astley (1745–47), A. and J. Churchill (1752), John Hamilton Moore (1785), and Robert Kerr (1811–24).

These collections were made up from narratives of individual voyages, and the same process was followed to make up collections of narratives of shipwrecks and disasters. A major difference was that stories of shipwrecks and mutinies were more sensational and of less lasting interest than narratives of exploration; consequently the original accounts of disasters were more often taken from newspapers, magazines, and chapbooks than from complete volumes. We know in some detail the way in which the story of one wreck came into the anthologies; this example was probably somewhat typical.

On the night of February 5, 1805, the East Indiaman *Earl of Abergavenny* drifted on the rocks off Portland Bill, costing the lives of almost 250 of the passengers and crew. The master of the ship was Captain John Wordsworth, brother of William Wordsworth. Scholarly investigation has revealed the impact of the death of a loved brother on the poet but also gives in detail, through William Wordsworth's correspondence, the sequence of accounts of the wreck.[1] Reports of the sinking of the *Earl of Abergavenny* and interviews with at least two survivors, Cornet Burgoyne and Fourth-Officer Gilpin, apparently appeared in the *Morning Chronicle* of London a few days after the disaster. A report must also have been made at the East India House, which of course wanted to know all about the wreck of one of the richest ships ever to sail from London to India. On February 13, only eight days after the ship was lost, a forty-nine page pamphlet was published in London by John Stockdale, who claimed that his chapbook was "corrected from the official returns at the East India House." A week later, on February 21, the Minerva Press in London published another pamphlet, *An Authentic Narrative of the Loss of the Earl of Abergavenny . . . by a Gentleman in the East India House*. Probably no gentleman in the East India House was involved with either pamphlet (though some version of the reports to the company was probably included), and the true authors were starveling hack editors relying on the newspaper accounts and possibly on interviews with survivors. Cheap publishers paid little attention to copyright and less to considerations of accuracy and truthfulness, though it must be remembered that for most of these wrecks no other accounts are available. The next year, or perhaps a few years later (the pamphlet is undated), Thomas Tegg of Paternoster Row brought out still another chapbook on the wreck of the *Earl of Abergavenny*. Meanwhile one Archibald Duncan, R.N., had edited an important anthology called *The Mariner's Chronicle*[2] and included the story of the *Earl of Abergavenny*, either condensing the pamphlet narratives or working from the newspapers that were their sources. Some of the wording of the

1. E. L. McAdam, Jr. "Wordsworth's Shipwreck," *PMLA*, June 1962; R. C. Townsend, "John Wordsworth and His Brother's Poetic Development," *PMLA*, Mar. 1966.

2. The publishing history of this book is somewhat difficult. The British Museum Catalogue lists the first edition, published by James Cundee in London, as in six volumes, 1804–[1808]; the second edition, in four volumes, is dated 1804–05. There was another London edition in six volumes in 1810 and two Philadelphia editions, each four volumes, in 1806 and 1810.

Morning Chronicle reports is in the Duncan narrative. Later anthologists stole their accounts from Duncan's collection.

It is interesting to note that almost the same process was followed to much the same result in Portugal almost a century earlier.[3] There had developed in that country in the sixteenth and seventeenth centuries a *literatura de cordel*—"string literature"—a flood of pamphlets on almost any popular subject which were usually displayed in shop doorways strung on a cord. Narratives of shipwrecks were popular, and these early pamphlet treatments were collected in 1735–36 by Bernardo Gomes de Brito in his *Historia tragico-maritima,* the Portuguese equivalent of Duncan's *Mariner's Chronicle.*

The first collection of narratives of shipwrecks that I have been able to locate is James Janeway's *Mr. James Janeway's Legacy to his Friends, containing twenty-seven famous instances of God's Providence in and about Sea-Dangers and Deliverances,* published in London in 1675. The second is the volume in Portuguese, the *Historia tragico-maritima* mentioned above. But the base anthology for most later collections was apparently Archibald Duncan's publication, *The Mariner's Chronicle.* All later collections I have seen copied from Duncan, word for word, or from each other—which means the same thing—and added the narratives of wrecks occurring after 1805–1810 as they could. One notable theft from Duncan was another *Mariner's Chronicle,* published in 1813 in Hartford by Andrus and Starr. Every disaster described is copied from the original *Mariner's Chronicle* except one that occurred in 1809. The popularity of the genre is attested by this volume, which contains the names of about 4,000 subscribers, almost all of New England and New York.

Later collections added accounts from newspapers and magazines and also printed summaries of books devoted to single catastrophes. In 1817, for instance, Captain James Riley published in New York his *Sufferings in Africa: Captain Riley's Narrative,* a full-length book on his captivity in Morocco which became a best seller. The next year Captain Riley, obviously encouraged by the response to his own book, published Judah Paddock's *A Narrative of the Shipwreck of the Ship Oswego,* another account of slavery among the Moors; also in 1818 Archibald Robbins, Captain Riley's mate, told the story of his adventures in another *Journal.* All three books were condensed for readers of anthologies.

Besides newspapers and chapbooks, some magazines were probably also sources of material for anthologists. The *Naval Chronicle* (1799–1818) included narratives of shipwrecks and disasters. William Granger's *New Wonderful Museum and Extraordinary Magazine,* a

---

3. This material on Portugal's literature of wrecks and disasters is condensed from James Duffy's *Shipwreck and Empire* (Cambridge, Mass., 1955), Chapter II.

kind of "string literature" for the English public, has a few such stories. *Chronicles of the Sea* (London, 1838–1840) consisted of 119 weekly numbers, "published every Saturday, price one penny," and was apparently devoted exclusively to maritime disasters. *Gentleman's Magazine* (1731–1868) is cited by one authority as publishing some data on shipwrecks, and *Lloyd's List* (beginning in 1762) provides a bare listing of losses.

Perhaps the most popular of the American collections (I have seen more of these than of any other) was the anthology edited by R. Thomas, A.M., cited in the first paragraph of this introduction. Thomas also published a collection of narratives of naval battles of the War of 1812 and levied on Johnson's *History of the Pirates* for another anthology that was published in a combined volume with the book on shipwrecks. Thomas's book is a completely typical anthology, based on Duncan but including a good many later narratives. His table of contents will give an idea of the scope of these books.

Loss of the Grosvenor Indiaman [Coast of Caffraria, 1782]
Loss of the Fattysalem [Coast of Coromandel, 1761]
Loss of the Ship Hercules [Coast of Caffraria, 1796]
Loss of the Ship Litchfield [Coast of Barbary, 1758]
Loss of the Portuguese Vessel St. James [Coast of Africa, 1586]
Loss of the Ship Centaur [Atlantic, 1782]
Loss of the Sloop Betsy [Coast of Dutch Guiana, 1756]
Loss of the Brig Tyrrel [Atlantic, 1759]
Loss of the Prince, by Fire [Atlantic, 1752]
Loss of the Phoenix [Coast of Cuba, 1780]
Loss of the La Tribune [Coast of Nova Scotia, 1797]
Famine in the American Ship Peggy [Atlantic, 1765]
The Wrecked Seamen [Loss of the *Magpie,* coast of Cuba, n.d.]
Loss of the Peggy [Atlantic, 1785]
Loss of the Halsewell East Indiaman [Bill of Portland, 1786]
Loss of the Nottingham Galley, of London [Boon Island, Maine, 1710]
Loss of the French Ship Droits de L'Homme [Coast of France, 1797]
Loss of the Earl of Abergavenny East Indiaman [Bill of Portland, 1805]
Loss of the Catharine, Venus and Piedmont Transports; and Three Merchant
    Ships [Channel Coast of England, 1795]
Wreck of the British Ship Sidney [Reef off Malaysia, 1806]
Loss of the Ramillies [Atlantic, 1782]
Preservation of Nine Men [Atlantic, n.d., c. 1810]
Loss of the Aeneas Transport [Coast of Newfoundland, 1805]
Loss of the Nautilus Sloop of War [In Greek Archipelago, 1807]
Loss of the Ship Amphion [Blown up at Plymouth, 1796]
Loss of the Helen McGregor [Boiler explosion, Memphis, 1830]
Loss of the Ship Beverly [Burned in the Atlantic, 1826]
Loss of the Frances Mary [Foundered in the Atlantic, 1826]
Loss of the Ship Albion [Coast of Ireland, 1822]

Loss of the Ship Logan by Fire [Atlantic, 1832]
Loss of the Ship Margaret [Atlantic, 1810]
Burning of the Kent [Atlantic, 1827]
Loss of the Ship Boston [Burned in the Atlantic, n.d.]
Loss of the Whale Ship Essex [Stove by a whale in the Pacific, 1820]
Loss of the Isabella [Off Hastings, England, 1833]
Loss of the Rothsay Castle Steamer [Irish Sea, 1831]
Loss of the Brig Sally [Atlantic? 1767]
Sufferings of Ephraim How [Near Cape Sable, Nova Scotia, 1676]
Loss of the Transport Harpooner [Newfoundland, 1818]
Loss of the Brig Polly [Atlantic, 1811]
Loss of the Queen Charlotte [Burned off Leghorn, 1800]
Loss of the Amphitrite Convict Ship [Near Boulogne, 1833]
Loss of the Lady of the Lake [Atlantic, 1833]
Loss of the British Brig Jesse [Atlantic, 1835]

I have located six sizable anthologies of wrecks and disasters published in England between 1675 and 1860, the most important of which
(besides Duncan's) were James Stanier Clarke's two-volume *Naufragia*
of 1805–1806 and Sir J. G. Dalyell's three-volume collection of 1812.
In the United States fifteen anthologies of importance were published
between the pirated Duncan volumes of 1806 and an anonymous collection of 1857. One French anthology, that of De Perthes in 1781,
was translated into English and published by Constable in 1833.

There has been no lack of shipwrecks, of course, since the end of
the age of sail; anthologies of shipwrecks and disasters are still being
published, along with book-length treatments of particular catastrophes. But the sea is no longer the frontier it was in the eighteenth and
nineteenth centuries—and earlier, of course—and this minor genre is of
historical importance only.

III

THE APPEAL of these anthologies, individual narratives, and chapbooks
was probably to the readers of the past much what it is to readers of
the present, but there were certainly some attractions which are no
longer very important though they have interest.

The primary appeal was, and is, that of adventure and suspense
in narrative. The years 1650–1860 made up the peak period for the
wooden sailing ship in commerce and in war. During those years and
earlier these ships served many—almost all—of the purposes of the
present-day warships, cargo ships, cruise ships, liners, airplanes, trains,
trucks, and even automobiles. Sailors made up a significant portion
of the labor force in both England and America, and ship owners and
ship captains were important people of the times. Major sea battles

decided the destinies of nations; major explorations had the same fascination as the moon flights of our own times, with the same sudden extensions of the boundaries of knowledge; and the sea was dangerous and therefore always interesting.

A valuable study could perhaps be made of boredom as a cause of social change. Even in our own day of quite general literacy, comparative affluence, great mobility, and television serials, boredom is a major factor in many lives—as alcohol, drugs, and perhaps the reading of anthologies of shipwrecks all testify. Housman stated a human problem when he wrote:

> Could man be drunk forever
> With liquor, love, or fights,
> Lief would I rise at morning
> And lief lie down at nights.

But that solution, as Housman says in the next stanza, is impossible. If we are bored now, it is depressing to think of the situation of the average citizen of England or the colonies in the eighteenth century, though work and religion certainly took more of their time than they do of ours.

It is a truism here in the United States, at least since Jefferson, that an educated populace is essential for a functioning democracy. We need to be reminded, as Richard Altick reminds us,[4] that during the eighteenth century a majority of the poorer people of England and probably America were absolutely or functionally illiterate, and that many of the members of the ruling class in England felt that this was the proper state of affairs—that literacy meant revolution. They were right, of course, as the history of the last two centuries demonstrates. Altick's books make an extremely interesting point: while many people sought literacy out of intellectual curiosity, or for better understanding of religion,[5] or in hope of political change, or trusting to advance economically, perhaps a large number learned to read in order to take part vicariously in the sensations of the day. *Victorian Studies in Scar-*

---

4. Richard Altick, *The English Common Reader* (Chicago, 1957) and *Victorian Studies in Scarlet* (New York, 1970).

5. The following quotation bears on this point and hits at the kinds of magazines that published accounts of wrecks and disasters:

The countryman was silent. "You Scotch are a strange people," said one of the commercial gentlemen. "When I was in Scotland two years ago, I could hear of scarce anything among you but your church question. What good does all your theology do you?"—"Independently altogether of religious considerations," I replied, "it has done for our people what all your Societies for the Diffusion of Useful Knowledge and all your Penny and Saturday magazines, will never do for yours; it has awakened their intellects, and taught them how to think. The development of the popular mind in Scotland is a result of its theology." (Hugh Miller, *First Impressions of England and Its People*, Boston, 1851, pp. 34–35) *let* deals with murders and murderers—sensational reports of crimes, trials, and executions,[6] which were bought by the millions throughout England and collected in the very popular *Newgate Calendar* (1773, and many later editions), just as the narratives of shipwrecks were collected in *The Mariner's Chronicle*. Murders and shipwrecks were of course not the only sensational events. Altick writes, "So long as there had been newspapers (English journalism had its origins in the late seventeenth century) murders, along with such other evidences of man's depravity or ill-fortune as treason, highway robbery, forgery, piracy, shipwrecks, epidemics, and catastrophic storms, had been news."[7]

As was indicated in the discussion of publishing patterns above, one source for short and frequently faulty reports of shipwrecks and disasters was the penny press—publishers of horrendous, badly written, and frequently lying accounts of anything newsworthy, which sold in the streets for a half-penny, a penny, or even sixpence. James (Jemmy) Catnach, who had a press and shop at Seven Dials,[8] was the chief purveyor of broadsides and pamphlets on murders and trials, but I have located only one narrative of a shipwreck published by him, and that was late—in 1832. The most important publisher of accounts of shipwrecks and disasters at sea was Thomas Tegg, 111 Cheapside, London, who produced around 1805–1810 a whole series of 28-page pamphlets containing the story of one wreck or summaries of two or three catastrophes. Every Tegg pamphlet I have seen has a folding aquatint as frontispiece. Since Tegg published a number of prints by Thomas Rowlandson in about this period, and since so great an artist as George Cruikshank is known to have done some cuts for cheap pamphlets of murder trials,[9] it is possible that some of these aquatints are the work of Rowlandson.

That American readers had the same interest in violence and danger as the English is proved by the popularity here of narratives of shipwrecks, of piracies, and of our own peculiar genre—Indian captivities.

---

6. Dr. Altick would probably be pleased to know that Herman Melville paid half a crown for standing room at the execution of the Mannings in 1849 and sent to Chief Justice Lemuel Shaw of Massachusetts, his father-in-law, a broadside:

LIFE CONFESSION & EXECUTION, of Mr. and Mrs. Manning,
For the Murder of Mr. O'Connor, with Copies of the Letters.
Jay Leyda, *The Melville Log*, New York, 1951, I:330–31.

This was probably the only time that Dickens, Thackeray, and Melville were in the same company—and for what a purpose!

7. Altick, *Victorian Studies in Scarlet*, p. 55.

8. Arthur Bryant, in *The Age of Elegance* (New York, 1951), states that Seven Dials was so dangerous an area that London's rudimentary police force refused to patrol it.

9. Altick, *Victorian Studies in Scarlet*, p. 50.

This preoccupation with violence and danger, coming as it did at a time when literacy was growing—perhaps helping that growth—makes an interesting parallel with the programming of television in our own time. Reading and writing go back 3,000 years or so; but in England and America ability, time, and material did not come together for any large number of people until about 1800. Much of what those people chose to read was on about the same level as our horror movies, television crime serials, and sagas of Western gun-slinging. The media change, but the desire to escape from our own lives into others more exciting is apparently a timeless phenomenon.

Many stories of shipwrecks and disasters were told in the first person by survivors, and identification with their sufferings is easy. Furthermore, there is an obvious appeal in the exotic scenes, language, and circumstances of every tragedy. The problems of navigation in uncharted seas, of seamanship in unimagined straits, of character under lethal stresses, all had and have their fascination. When the Portuguese *St. James,* for instance, struck a reef off Madagascar in 1586, about ninety people crowded into a damaged pinnace. Deciding that someone had to take command, they chose a nobleman as captain. "He instantly employed his authority in causing the weakest, whom he merely pointed out with his finger, to be thrown overboard. In the number of these was a carpenter, who had assisted in repairing the pinnace; the only favor he requested was a little wine, after which he suffered himself to be thrown into the sea without uttering a word."

A second contemporary appeal lay in the religious and moral lessons to be learned—lessens frequently stressed by the narrators. Like survivors of present-day disasters—"Somebody up there loves me!"—they saw the hand of God at work in their deliverances. Such a reading of circumstance automatically entails the assumption that those who did not survive were not intended to, but that assumption seldom troubles the fortunate. Simpler conclusions were the underlining of the necessity for helping others and the occasional demonstration of the rewards of perseverance, of not giving up no matter how hopeless the situation seemed to be. Perhaps the most vivid underlining of a moral lesson came from the source of the dying confessions and statements of murderers cited by Altick—some hack writer wringing the last penny from the careers of two pirates, Gibbs and Wansley, who were hanged in New York in 1830:

> Youths! by their example learn to shun their fate
> (How wretched is the man who's wise too late!)
> Ere innocence, and fame, and life be lost,
> Here purchase wisdom cheaply at their cost!

Rather surprisingly, a fine Melville-like symbolism and Aristotelian catharsis are claimed by one anonymous editor. Of sailors he wrote, "So like the vicissitudes of a whole life, are all his voyages, that we read the details of his route, even his dry log-book, with a fellow-feeling of interest and anxiety. Then we have the enjoyment of his adventures without their dangers. It is pleasant to listen to perils we do not share—to feel our hearts beat, not from fear, but from interest and excitement."[10]

A fourth appeal was a pragmatic one. Sailors, reading of the disasters of others, were supposed to learn caution and responsibility. The need for better-found ships, for better charts and navigational aids, for better lifeboats, for better selection of officers should have been obvious to any reader.

Finally, these editors catered to nationalistic biases. Cyrus Redding, writing in 1833, told his readers: "Here may be seen that courage in danger, defiance in suffering, and unflinching perseverance, which, when applied in defence of the national honour, have cast upon the annals of England the more unsullied portion of their glory."[11] Another editor, writing of the loss of the French frigate *Medusa*, stated: "There is also something peculiarly gratifying to an Englishman in the reflection, that such a disaster could not have befallen almost any British crew. It was evidently nothing but the utter and thorough selfishness which actuated the leaders and most of those on board both the ship and the raft, which rendered the affair at all very serious."[12] The loss of the *Medusa* was certainly a tragedy of incompetence and cowardice, but any reader of these narratives must conclude that those characteristics know no nationality. I have seen no editorial comment on the conduct of Captain Inglefield of the British warship *Centaur*, who was one of the first to leave that doomed vessel, and little about any of the almost numberless examples of weakness of American and British character under the threat of death.

These secondary appeals of the narratives have some interest for the present-day reader as examples of social history, but there is no doubt at all about the primary purpose of the writers and compilers— "I wants to make your flesh creep!" One anthology, titled *The Terrors of the Sea*, lured readers by details on the title page:

. . .
and narratives of
poor wretches forced to abandon their
floating homes without food or
water, thus compelling
them to resort to
CANNIBALISM, WITH ITS ATTENDANT HORRORS

We tend to be a little proud and a little shocked at the freedom of modern literature, with its sex and its homo-sex and its spade a

10. *The Mariner's Chronicle* (New Haven, 1834), p. vi.
11. *A History of Shipwrecks and Disasters at Sea* (London, 1833), p. vi.
12. *Perils and Captivity* (Edinburgh, 1827), p. iv.

bloody shovel. But sex is not the only shocking subject; a moment's thought will convince anyone that people of the early nineteenth century, to say nothing of those of the eighteenth—with Indians and whites at each others' scalps, plagues, infant mortality, scant medical knowledge, lack of sanitation, and sailing ships—were on intimate terms with horrors. One example will perhaps suffice.

The *Frances Mary,* loaded with lumber, sailed from St. Johns, New Brunswick,[13] for Liverpool on January 18, 1826. The ship ran into a series of storms and became a dismasted hulk, afloat only because the cargo was unsinkable. By the middle of February the ship was drifting helpless across the North Atlantic. Passengers and crew were starving.

> Feb. 22, John Wilson, seaman, died at 10 a.m., preserved the body of the deceased, cut him up in quarters, washed them overboard, and hung them up on pins. Feb. 23, J. Moore died, and was thrown overboard, having eaten part of him, such as the liver and heart. . . .
>
> . . . James Frier was working his passage home, under a promise of marriage to Ann Saunders, the female passenger who attended the master's wife, and who, when she heard of Frier's death, shrieked a loud yell, then snatching a cup from Clerk, the mate, cut her late intended husband's throat and drank his blood! insisting that she had the greatest right to it. A scuffle ensued, but the heroine got the better of her adversary, and then allowed him to drink one cup to her two. . . .
>
> . . . Ann Saunders, the other female, had more strength in her calamity than most of the men. She performed the duty of cutting, and cleaning the dead bodies, keeping two knives for the purpose in her monkey jacket, and when the breath was announced to have flown, she would sharpen her knives, bleed the deceased in the neck, drink his blood, and cut him up as usual.

The few survivors were finally taken off the wreck and carried to London. There the story ends, but one wonders about the future career of the indomitable Ann Saunders, and about some putative husband of hers, successor to the unfortunate James Frier. What were his thoughts, of nights, when he lay by her in their quiet English bed, with that right arm about him?

IV

SHIPS OF VARIOUS TYPES have sailed for thousands of years, and whenever and wherever they sailed many of them have been lost. As I pointed out earlier, for a fair share of man's history ships fulfilled

---

13. Melville may well have had this narrative in mind when he wrote of a derelict (*Redburn,* chapter xxii) "passing on our course, without so much as learning the schooner's name, though everyone supposed her to be a New Brunswick lumberman."

most of the functions now carried out by many different forms of transportation; it is a truism of traffic that the larger the number of units involved, the larger will be the number of failures. But when a train breaks down, it simply stops; when a truck fails, it pulls over to the side of the road; when a car grown old in commuting strips its transmission, it is towed off to the wrecker. Ships, like these other means of transportation, grew old and failed; but for a ship there was usually no comfortable road-shoulder to stop on, no tow truck or AAA garage at hand. The weaknesses of ships were revealed under conditions of stress, in storms and while facing unexpected hazards of cold and current. Airplanes are in a similar situation; the medium through which they move has built-in hazards.

Captains and pilots and sailing masters had all the weaknesses of present-day drivers and faced greater difficulties. For centuries there were no real standards to be met, and incompetents were quite regularly put in charge of vessels carrying hundreds of people. The Portuguese *St. James* and the French *Medusa* were only among the worst of many examples. Navigation was a complicated, difficult, and only partly known science; seamanship took a long time to learn. There were never enough men skilled in these areas and with the qualities of character needed to meet the hazards of the sea. The crews were frequently no better at their jobs than the captains were at theirs, and sometimes worse.

People of our century must still face up to the traditional Acts of God which are a part of human fate; we cannot predict earthquakes, volcanic eruptions, floods, or tidal waves well enough to avoid their consequences completely—though progress is being made, and improved communications let us warn more people and do more for survivors. Seamen of the past could not avoid icebergs or wracking series of storms. Violent hurricanes and typhoons—simply too powerful for any ship to withstand—spelled death for the incompetent or the able, the coward or the brave man. Figures are hard to come by, but a compilation of wrecks and disasters published in the 1860s states: "In England it is calculated that about 5,000 natives of the British Isles yearly perish at sea."[14]

The first great navigators for whom there are records available were the Portuguese. It is apparently impossible to be at all accurate, but an authority on the voyages through which Portugal kept functioning its links with its small Indian Empire states that about 130 ships were lost on the Indies run between 1550 and 1650. He concludes, "A reasonable estimate, based on all the information available, would be about a 12 per cent loss for the first fifty years of the sixteenth century and about 16 to 18 per cent loss in the following

14. *The Book of the Ocean* (New York, n.d.), II:vi.

hundred years."[15] The increase in the percentage of losses—unexpected since the route, winds, and currents should have become more familiar—came about (Duffy believes) because of lack of facilities for repairs, an inefficient increase in the size of ships, and lack of enough capable pilots and seamen.

The Spanish fleets for the West Indies and American routes of about the same time were somewhat more efficient than the Portuguese ships—their voyages were shorter—though the losses were still staggering. Robert Marx, who is interested in shipwrecks primarily as sources of treasure and artifacts, writes of this route: "Shipwrecks were the greatest danger. During the three centuries [1500–1800] slightly more than five per cent of the ships in the Indies navigation were shipwrecked, mostly due to bad weather but also to incompetent navigators. A small percentage were lost due to capsizing because of overloading and to fires on board."[16]

William O. S. Gilly published in 1851 a *Shipwrecks of the Royal Navy, 1793–1849,* in which he used the official records to tell in some detail the stories of the losses of thirty-eight ships; he records a total of 471 vessels lost from the Royal Navy during these years. His material includes the period of the Napoleonic Wars, but he does not list vessels lost in combat. The Royal Navy in wartime was forced to keep ships on dangerous stations in all weathers; these records cannot be taken as typical of other types of vessels. On the other hand, the Navy's ships, in spite of many exceptions, were probably much better kept up and better manned than the merchant ships of the same period. Warships had to be prepared to sail and fight at the same time, and that took manpower. A telling example of the hazards of merchantmen in wartime is the loss of twenty-nine of sixty-nine West Indiamen near Figuera, Portugal, in 1804, when the *Apollo* frigate, shepherding a convoy, went ashore. The narrator of the loss of the *Apollo* had no doubt about who was at fault: "This fatal and unprecedented calamity is universally ascribed to the carelessness and inattention of the Commodore: and it is asserted, that had it been dark a quarter of an hour longer, the *whole convoy* would have shared the same fate."[17]

Seventy-one of the 471 losses listed by Gilly (slightly more than one-sixth) cost the lives of all on board. The *Blenheim,* with 590 men, and the *Java,* with about 280, were lost in one typhoon in the Indian Ocean in 1807; the *Hero,* also with 590 men, was lost off

15. Duffy, p. 63.
16. Robert Marx, *Shipwrecks of the Western Hemisphere* (New York, 1971), p. 17. Marx claims to have compiled data on 28,500 shipwrecks around the world, and this book lists approximately 7,000 wrecks in the Western Hemisphere between 1492 and 1825.
17. *Remarkable Shipwrecks* (New Haven, 1813), p. 270.

Jutland in 1811. Among the major wrecks listed by Gilly in which there were survivors were the following:

SHIP	DATE	PLACE	DEAD
Resistance	1798	Blown up in the Straits of Banca	290 of 294
Sceptre	1799	Lost in Table Bay	300 of 491
Queen Charlotte	1800	Burnt off Leghorn	673 of 859
Invincible	1801	Lost near Yarmouth	400 of 590
St. George	1803	Lost off Jutland	731 of 738
Defence	1811	Lost off Jutland	587 of 593

A surprising number of these ships were lost off the coast of Jutland and on the Haak Sands off Holland. The ends of the earth were dangerous, but so were the very home waters of the Royal Navy and the familiar North Sea. Again, most ships sank where most ships were.

Gilly did not cover the period of the American Revolution, in which perhaps the greatest sea disaster of all time occurred. In 1782 the Royal Navy had achieved a major victory under Rodney at the Battle of the Saints. Five French ships of war were captured, including the *Ville de Paris,* the largest warship in the world at that time. Albion states the succeeding events succinctly:

Rodney thought that the ships could stand a summer passage, but the September "line storm" struck them on the Grand Banks of Newfoundland. The *Canada,* 74, partially dismasted, was the only one of the nine ships of the line to reach England with part of the shattered convoy. The great *Ville de Paris,* 110, foundered with her entire crew of 800; the *Centaur,* 74, *Hector,* 74, and *Glorieux,* 74, also sank with most of the men on board; the flagship, *Ramillies,* 74, was abandoned and blown up at sea; and three sixty-fours captured from the French put into American ports with masts badly damaged and hulls leaking like sieves. . . . The total loss of life from that equinoctial gale off Newfoundland was more than 3,500—exceeding the total number killed in the Navy during the whole war.[18]

An example of the difficulty of arriving at accurate figures on losses and of the vagueness of popular history can be seen by comparing Albion's account with a probably contemporary summary. No source is given for "The Loss of the Ramillies" in R. Thomas's *Remarkable Shipwrecks* (and in other anthologies as well), but that account of the same storm ends, "It was calculated that by the destruction of the fleet, upwards of twenty one thousand and five hundred persons perished. The loss of property has been estimated by the British government to be upwards of £20,000,000. The gale,

18. Robert G. Albion, *Forests and Sea Power, the Timber Problem of the Royal Navy, 1652–1852* (Cambridge, Mass., 1926), pp. 312–13.

which continued for six days, was the most tremendous one on record."[19]

Ironically, ships could sink and hundreds could drown on a day fit for canoeing. In that same year 1782 the *Royal George* sank at her moorings at Spithead with the loss of almost 900 lives because the officer of the day could not believe that the mere loading of a few hogsheads of rum at the low side of the ship, which was canted for a minor repair, could endanger the largest and oldest first-rate in the Royal Navy. As Cowper wrote in his "Lines," these people died because

> A land breeze shook the shrouds
> And she was overset;
> Down went the Royal George
> With all her crew complete.

Cowper used poetic license about losses—three hundred people actually survived the sinking—but he was probably correct in blaming a slight gust of wind, which would not have bothered a dory. The *Royal George* was canted enough to bring her open ports to the water level, the breeze heeled her farther over, the shipped water unbalanced her still more, and she sank in thirteen fathoms.

Alexander Starbuck in his *History of Nantucket* made an exhaustive study of the whalers which sailed from that island port. According to his figures, 1,386 cruises were made between 1788 and 1869. Forty-two vessels were shipwrecked and three burned (between 2.5 and 3 percent). Whalers went around Cape Horn, edged into the Arctic and Antarctic, and did a good deal of cruising that was genuine exploration, chancing unknown reefs and currents. They took risks that other vessels were able to avoid. Whalers, however, were on no timetable, had little incentive to make speedy passages, and carried larger crews than most merchantmen.

A few other scattered examples of the hazards of the sea may be of interest. When the American author Margaret Fuller Ossoli was planning to return to the United States from Italy with her husband and child, she wrote in a last note,

I had intended if I went by way of France to take the packet ship *Argo* from Havre . . . I read of the wreck of the *Argo* returning from America to France. There were also notices of the wreck of the *Royal Adelaide*, a fine English steamer, and of the *John Skiddy*, one of the fine American packets. Thus it seems safety is not to be found in the wisest calculation. I shall embark more composedly in my merchant ship; praying, indeed fervently, that it may not be my lot to lose my babe at sea, either by unsolaced sickness, or

19. R. Thomas, *Remarkable Shipwrecks* (New York, 1835), p. 258.

amid the howling waves. Or that, if I should, it may be brief anguish, and Ossoli, he and I go together.[20]

She was prescient. The ship she finally chose was wrecked on Fire Island, and all three were drowned.

Captain Samuels, of the famous *Dreadnought* packet, tells an interesting story of his own line:

The old adage that "misfortunes never come singly" was exemplified in the case of Mr. Ogden, our agent and part owner, who lost six first-class ships in rapid succession, leaving the *Dreadnought* solitary in the Red Cross Line. The first ship lost was the *St. George,* which was burned in the Chops of the British Channel. The second was the *St. Patrick,* wrecked on the Jersey coast —but no lives lost. The third was the *Highflyer,* from San Francisco, bound to Shanghai. She was never heard from. It was supposed that she was burned by Chinese pirates off Formosa, and that they murdered her crew. Our Government sent a vessel of war to the island to investigate the matter, but she failed to discover any trustworthy data. The captain's spyglass was found, and also the wreck of a vessel which had been run ashore and burned. The fourth vessel lost was the *Driver,* bound to New York from Liverpool; the crew and six hundred emigrants were never heard from. The fifth was the *Racer,* lost on Blackwater Bank, in the Irish Channel; no lives lost. The sixth was the *Andrew Forster,* lost by collision in the Irish Channel; two lives were lost.[21]

The early years of steam showed hardly any improvement over the age of sail and even brought new hazards of explosion and fire. Travel on the Mississippi and its tributaries was particularly dangerous, with racing and drunken captains, collisions, and running on snags. General Jubal Early was perhaps not exaggerating greatly when he wrote, "After improving a little I started back to Mexico, and on my way I had the luck to meet with that fate which is very common to Americans who travel much, that is, I was on a steamboat which was blown up, the 8th of January, 1848, on the Ohio River, a few miles below the mouth of the Kanawha. I had a very narrow escape."[22] His statement about the fate "very common to Americans who travel much" is supported by a story of a collision between the steamers *Wisconsin* and *Tiskilwa* on the Illinois River in 1837:

This melancholy occurrence took place on Saturday about five miles from the mouth of the river,—where, through the obstinacy of the captains of two steamboats, one of the boats was sunk, and upwards of twenty lives lost.

20. Joseph Jay Deiss, *The Roman Years of Margaret Fuller* (New York, 1969), p. 306.
21. Captain S. Samuels, *From the Forecastle to the Cabin* (New York, 1887), pp. 250–53.
22. Jubal A. Early, *Autobiographical Sketch and Narrative of the War Between the States* (Philadelphia and London, 1912), p. xxii.

The captain of the steamer Wisconsin, which was then ascending the river, had repeatedly stated, that if he should meet the Tiskilwa, and her captain would not give him a clear channel, he would run her down. This, it seemed, provoked the captain of the other boat, and he became obstinately determined not to turn out of his course. Both boats met, about five o'clock in the morning,—at a time when all the passengers were in their berths,—and steered directly for each other till within only a few rods, when the captain of the Tiskilwa endeavored, but too late, to avoid the concussion; and by turning a little out of his course, gave a fair broadside to the ascending boat, which took her just behind the wheel, and she sunk in less than three minutes after she was struck.[23]

The game of "chicken" was not invented by the young motorists of the twentieth century.

Perhaps a bit of the folklore of the sea should be mentioned. Sailors were frequently hardy, ignorant, careless of the future, almost fatalistic in their acceptance of risks which seem appalling in our times. Charles Nordhoff, author of *Man of War Life, The Merchant Vessel,* and *Whaling and Fishing*—one of the best authorities on the ordinary sailor's life of the nineteenth century—tells in *The Merchant Vessel* of setting out on a voyage from Mobile to Maine in the dead of winter in a ship so leaky and ill-found that only one man on board believed she would reach port. She did, but a kind of pride in taking chances sent many men to their deaths. W. H. Macy, in his fictional *There She Blows!,* has two sailors talking of leaky ships:

"Then you mean to say that both pumps were going all the time?" said Mr. Bunker.

"Certainly," returned the cooper. "And she leaked at the same rate all the time; no more when pitching in a gale of wind than when lying becalmed in smooth water; and no more at the end of the voyage than when six weeks out from home, which was the time that the leak first started. Why, she leaked so that when we were crossing the tropical latitudes, we used frequently to pump live flying fish! and once or twice the pumps got completely choked with Portuguese men-of-war!"

"That's nothing at all!" put in the second mate, who happened to be within hearing. "I've heard say that, on board the old Yorkshire, they used to take off the lower-deck hatches, sit on the combings, and fish for skipjacks and albicore in the hold!"[24]

I was startled to discover how far back this story went—three hundred years. "One of the most famous of Albuquerque's ships, the *Cirne,* leaked so badly on one occasion that fish reportedly could be seen swimming in the hold."[25]

23. *Steamboat Disasters and Railroad Accidents in the United States* (Worcester, Mass., 1846), p. 174.

24. W. H. Macy, *There She Blows! or, the Log of the Arethusa* (Boston and New York, 1877), p. 171.

25. Duffy, p. 58.

V

So far as I know, these narratives of shipwrecks and disasters have been used by only five writers as sources for scholarly research,[26] but a number of authors of the last two centuries owned them, used them, or were connected with them in curious and interesting ways.

WILLIAM WORDSWORTH

Wordsworth was the poet laureate of the Lake District, Helvellyn his symbol, Rydal Water and Windermere his pygmy oceans. But his uncle had been the captain of an East Indiaman and apparently used his influence to help the poet's brother John to a place in the company's service. After the usual apprenticeship and working up through the ranks at sea, John Wordsworth became captain of the *Earl of Abergavenny,* one of the largest and best of the East India Company's ships. I have told part of the story of the loss of this vessel earlier in the Introduction, as a part of the publishing history of these narratives; most of the rest of the story follows in comments on the reprinted material, but a quick summary is needed here.

The *Earl of Abergavenny* sailed from Portsmouth on February 1, 1805, with 402 passengers, troops, and crew on board. She carried a very rich cargo for India and was part of a convoy of four ships and a man-of-war. There was difficulty in keeping the ships together from the first—February in the English Channel—and a rendezvous in Portland Roads was ordered. A pilot was on board the *Earl of Abergavenny;* Captain Wordsworth was not primarily responsible. The story is a familiar one. The ship bore up for Portland Roads with a steady wind when suddenly the wind slackened, the incoming tide fastened upon the vessel, and she drifted rapidly on the Shambles—a reef off Portland Bill. For an hour she hammered out her bottom on the reef and then drove over into relatively calm water, holed and sinking. The pumps could not keep the water down, there was not wind enough to beach the ship, and she sank two miles off Weymouth Beach in twelve fathoms of water. About 150 persons were saved. John Wordsworth was among those drowned, and the news was relayed to his brother.

The impact of his brother's unexpected death was at first shattering to the poet. John Wordsworth was, by all accounts, a gentle and affectionate man—perhaps a little too gentle and a little too in-

26. E. L. McAdam and R. C. Townsend (note 1); Robert Albion (note 18); D. M. McKeithan, "Two Sources of Poe's *Narrative of Arthur Gordon Pym,*" University of Texas Bulletin No. 13 (1933), pp. 127–37; and my "Another Source for Poe's *Narrative of Arthur Gordon Pym,*" *American Literature* XVI (1944):19–25, and "A Note on Melville's *Redburn,*" *New England Quarterly* XVIII (1945):259–60.

decisive to be an adequate captain of an Indiaman in trouble. He had hoped to make a fortune in his profession (captains were allowed to make small trading ventures of their own) and to be able to subsidize his poet brother. That dream was over. William Wordsworth grieved, defended his brother's competence, denied with little evidence and some heat that he had sought death, and sublimated his sorrow in verse. He wrote three poems about John's death and his own responses—the remarkable "Elegiac Stanzas," the less effective but still moving "Elegiac Verses," and "To the Daisy" (1805). We owe to the loss of the *Earl of Abergavenny* the lines of "Elegiac Stanzas:"

> Ah! then, if mine had been the painter's hand,
> To express what then I saw; and add the gleam,
> The light that never was, on sea or land,
> The consecration, and the poet's dream;

GEORGE GORDON, LORD BYRON

Though more of Byron's ancestors were connected with the Army than with the Navy (seven Byron brothers fought for the King at Edgehill), he came reasonably by an interest in the sea. His grandfather was "Foulweather Jack" Byron, Admiral in the Royal Navy; his granduncle, who preceded him as Baron, owned a yacht which, by one account,[27] was used to smuggle Hollands gin into Scotland. The Honorable John Byron (the Admiral) wrote the story of his circumnavigation of the world and was a major figure in the narrative of the loss of the *Wager*.

When Byron was planning *Don Juan* he decided to include a shipwreck in Canto II. Since he himself knew little of the sea (though he had read his grandfather's book), he was forced into research to learn the concrete details of dealing with maritime disaster. Much earlier, according to Thomas Moore,[28] he had almost certainly read William Mackey's *Narrative of the Shipwreck of the Juno on the Coast of Arracan in the Year 1795* at the school of Dr. Glennie at Dulwich. Perhaps he recalled that story and found the pamphlet again. He also acquired Sir J. G. Dalyell's *Shipwrecks and Disasters at Sea* and read closely a number of the narratives. Stanzas 24–108 of *Don Juan*, Canto II, are a mosaic of his borrowings. Four stanzas, 87–90, are straight from the *Juno* narrative.

The *Monthly Magazine* (Vol. VIII, Aug. 1821) printed examples

27. Hugh Miller, *Tales and Sketches* (Boston, 1865), pp. 343–45.
28. Thomas Moore, *Life of Lord Byron* (London, 1854), pp. 49–51.

of borrowings in parallel columns and accused Byron of plagiarism.[29] The poet, far from denying his borrowings, wrote his publisher, "With regard to the charges about the Shipwreck, I think that I told you and Mr. Hobhouse, years ago, that there was not a circumstance of it not taken from fact; not, indeed, from any single shipwreck, but all from actual facts of different wrecks."[30]

Byron borrowed from the narratives of the loss of the *Juno* for the deaths of two young boys, the wreck of the *Earl of Abergavenny* for the incident of the spirit-room, the famine in the *Peggy* for the drawing of lots and cannibalism, and the loss of the *Betsy* for the killing and eating of a dog. One small detail seems to me to show Byron's dependence on Dalyell and to prove that, like Poe, he really knew very little of vessels and their management. In stanza 32 of Canto II appears the line, "Foremast and bowsprit were cut down . . ." The *down* is a revealing word; any sailor would have written *cut away*. And I believe that I have never seen a reference to cutting away the bowsprit to relieve a ship on her beam-ends. I suspect that Byron thought that masts were cut like trees. In fact, masts have very little strength by themselves and have to be supported by a complicated network of shrouds and stays. When masts had to be cut away, a man was sent into the chains with an axe (see the narrative of the loss of the *Phoenix*) where he cut the lanyards. The force of the wind and the mast's own weight would break off the spar and allow the ship to settle back on an even keel. The bowsprit of a ship was so low as to be unimportant as a weight to overbalance a ship; when a foremast went by the board the bowsprit was frequently torn out or broken, but there would have been little point in cutting it *down*.

Byron's telling of the wreck of the *Trinidada* is a beautiful example of fast-moving narrative in verse, dependent on Dalyell for facts and anecdotes and possibly on Falconer's *The Shipwreck* for the original idea. It is interesting to note that Keats reacted strongly

29. Cited in L. A. Marchand, ed., *Don Juan* (Cambridge, Mass., 1958), p. 466. One example of parallel passages probably cited is as follows:

"Loss of the Earl of Abergavenny"	*Don Juan*, Canto II, Stanza 36
One of the officers, who was stationed at the door of the spiritroom . . . was much importuned by a sailor. . . . The man said he was convinced "it would be all one with them in an hour hence." . . . The officer . . . bid him go, observing "that if it was God's will they should perish, they should die like men."	"Give us more grog," they cried, "for it will be All one an hour hence." Juan answer'd "No! Tis true that death awaits both you and me, But let us die like men, not sink below Like brutes."

30. Byron, letter to Murray, Aug. 23, 1821. Cited in *Complete Poetical Works of Lord Byron* (Boston and New York, 1933), p. 1035.

against Byron's mocking cynicism, objecting especially to the heartlessness and the low estimate of human sympathy in *Don Juan:*

. . .

And the poor little cutter quickly swamped.

LXI

Nine souls more went in her: the long-boat still
Kept above water, with an oar for mast,
Two blankets stitched together, answering ill
Instead of sail, were to the oar made fast;
Though every wave rolled menacing to fill,
And present peril all before surpassed,
They grieved for those who perished with the cutter,
And also for the biscuit-casks and butter.

EDGAR ALLEN POE

In Marie Bonaparte's *Edgar Poe* (1933), a psychoanalytic study of the author using his works as evidence, the French psychiatrist concluded that Poe was a "sado-necrophile." More recently Patrick J. Quinn called *The Narrative of Arthur Gordon Pym* "a profoundly oneiric drama."[31] Neither writer seems to have known (and probably would not have cared to know) that *Pym*, at least, is a mosaic of borrowings from narratives of shipwrecks and piracies, and that most of the evidence in this novel for sado-necrophilism and nightmare came really from sober sea captains and hard-bitten sailors. An author's choice of material may of course be significant and may tell a great deal about the man himself, but it is a little difficult to accept analyses of Poe and his work based on his hurried rewriting of narratives that were being read with eagerness by hundreds of thousands of his fellow Americans.

The Narrative of Arthur Gordon Pym levied heavily on R. Thomas's *Remarkable Events* (reports of piracies) and *Remarkable Shipwrecks*, published in one volume in 1835—a year or two before Poe began his only novel. Poe may also have used Duncan's *Mariner's Chronicle*. He copied from narratives of the wrecks of the *Polly*, the *Peggy*, the *Betsy*, the *Nottingham* galley, the *Centaur*, and the *Sidney*. He probably also used accounts of Gibbs and Wansley, two pirates who mutinied and murdered aboard the brig *Vineyard*, and of Samuel Comstock, "the terrible whaleman," who murdered the officers of the *Globe*. Other borrowings have been traced to Captain Benjamin Morell's *Narrative of Four Voyages*, to J. N.

---

31. Recent scholarship on *Pym* is conveniently summarized in Sidney Kaplan's "Introduction" to *The Narrative of Arthur Gordon Pym* (New York, 1960), from which I have drawn the above quotations.

Reynolds's *Address on the Subject of a Surveying Exploring Expedition,* and to Rees's *Cyclopaedia.* Finally, the major theme of the novel (never fully developed) was almost certainly based on Captain Adam Seaborn's *Symzonia,* an early Utopian novel based on the theory of "Symmes' holes."[32] Poe must have been so busy copying that he could hardly have spent much time enjoying sado-necrophilism or looking up the spelling of *oneiric.*

My own belief is that in *Pym* we have a crudely written first draft of a pot-boiler—written by a genius and therefore both easy to read and of considerable interest, but a pot-boiler nonetheless. It is so full of undigested borrowings and structural and technical absurdities that it comes close to being what Poe himself called it—"a very silly book."

In 1836 Poe submitted a collection of short pieces to Harper's. They were refused in a letter which contained the statement that readers in the United States "have a decided and strong preference for works (especially fiction) in which a single and connected story occupies the whole volume."[33] With this urging Poe set to work, probably unwillingly, probably despising the novel and himself. He could have said, with Melville, "Dollars damn me." Poe knew almost nothing of the sea, but he was a "quick study" and, with some justification, rather scornful of his readers. As reviewer for the *Southern Literary Messenger* he received most new books, and in 1835–37 he must have seen close to a dozen reports of harrowing shipwrecks—probably including anthologies edited by R. Thomas and Charles Ellms. He had evidence that these books were popular, and when he set out to write "a single and connected story" he chose to present a sensational novel of the sea disguised as a real experience. The very title is straight from the genre—*The Narrative of Robert Adams, The Narrative of the Shipwreck and Unparalleled Sufferings of Mrs. Sarah Allen, The Narrative of Arthur Gordon Pym.*

There is no point in listing all the errors and examples of carelessness to be found in *Pym,* but most readers and critics of the book have known no more of the sea than Poe did and have been so caught up by the speed and compelling details of the story that they have ignored absurdities. I list a few examples to bolster my contention that we have in *Pym* a carelessly written first draft.

32. The above material is based on the cited articles by McKeithan and myself (note 26); R. L. Rhea's "Some Observations on Poe's Origins," *Studies in English,* University of Texas Bulletin No. 10 (1930), pp. 135–43; and J. O. Bailey's excellent "Sources for Poe's *Arthur Gordon Pym,* 'Hans Pfaal,' and Other Pieces," *PMLA* (June 1942), pp. 513–35. Sidney Kaplan (note 31), mentions the importance of *Symzonia* in *Pym* but does not refer to Bailey's article where Poe's indebtedness was first pointed out.
33. Quoted in A. H. Quinn, *Edgar Allan Poe* (New York, 1941), p. 251.

1. Early in the book Poe has the mast of a catboat carried short off by the board, and ". . . under the jib only, I now boomed along . . ." The jib, of course, stretched from the mast to a jib-boom or the bow and, once the mast was gone, would have been in the water with the mainsail.

2. Stowage on a whaler was a complicated and time-consuming business. Poe has the *Grampus* set sail for a three- or four-year cruise with a hold full of empty packing boxes, straw matting, and old lumber.

3. Poe has Pym's dog Tiger drink all the water in a *jug;* then, after the dog has killed the villainous mate Jones, Poe forgot all about him and never mentioned him again. Note the sentence, "The dog was still growling over Jones; but, upon examination, we found *him completely dead,* the blood issuing in a stream from a deep wound in the throat, inflicted, *no doubt, by the sharp teeth* of the animal." (My italics)

4. Bailey noted a shift in the characterization of Peters, the half-breed; the same kind of shift occurs in the characterization of Pym himself, who starts as a mere boy dominated by his friend Augustus and ends as a leader bossing and ridiculing the British captain of the *Jane Guy.*

5. I do not think anyone has pointed out that there are just sixteen direct speeches in the whole of *Pym.* One of these is "Ay ay," and the last four are different utterances of "Tekeli-li! Tekeli-li!"

The last pages of the book are effective, but still the novel ends in the air; the many hints of marvels to come and the promised adventures of "nine long years" in a new world are thrown away. Bailey guessed that the book ends as it does because of "exhaustion, confusion, or need of money"; there seems little doubt that he was right.

The Narrative of Arthur Gordon Pym is the best example of really thorough use of the shipwrecks and disasters genre for literary purposes. It is a pity that Poe's haste and carelessness destroyed the effectiveness of his attempt. A finished and polished *Pym* might have been as popular as Captain James Riley's best-selling *Sufferings in Africa: Captain Riley's Narrative;* sales like those could have made Poe independent of editing and hackwork and could have changed the development of American literature.

HERMAN MELVILLE AND NATHANIEL HAWTHORNE

Melville's borrowings from and references to narratives of shipwrecks and disasters are quite fully covered in the introductions to the reprinted stories. He was a reader as well as a sailor and probably knew more of the history of the sea than any other first-rate novelist.

Melville's first mention of narratives in this genre appears in *Redburn* where he wrote, "I had already read two books loaned to me by Max, to whose share they had fallen, in dividing the effects of the sailor who had jumped overboard. One was an account of Shipwrecks and Disasters at Sea."[34] But earlier (late in 1841) he had met a son of Owen Chase, author of the narrative of the wreck of the *Essex,* and had borrowed from him and read Chase's narrative only a short distance from the scene of the tragedy. Melville's father-in-law in 1851 obtained from Thomas Macy of Nantucket a copy of the Chase narrative and gave it to Melville, who was building the climax of *Moby-Dick* out of the memories of Chase. Melville visited Nantucket and talked briefly with Captain Pollard of the *Essex.*

Much earlier (in 1814) Richard Manning, uncle of Nathaniel Hawthorne, wrote his name in a copy of Archibald Duncan's *Mariner's Chronicle,* published in Philadelphia in 1806 in four volumes. Manning either gave or bequeathed the book to Hawthorne, who added his name below his uncle's in 1832. Below Hawthorne's name is written "To H. Melville Pittsfield March 14, 1851" in Melville's hand. This copy of the *Mariner's Chronicle* has perhaps as distinguished a provenance as any book in American literature.[35]

Other books of similar interest owned and read by Melville were the Lay and Hussey story of the mutiny on the *Globe,* Obed Macy's *History of Nantucket* (which included a narrative of the loss of the *Essex*), *A Voyage to the North Pacific* by John D'Wolf (a relative), and three narratives of Admiral John Byron's voyages.

Melville's use of the *Essex* tragedy in *Moby-Dick* is discussed in most studies of that masterpiece, perhaps most fully in Howard Vincent's *The Trying-Out of Moby Dick* and in Charles Olson's *Call Me Ishmael.* The importance of the *Essex* story for Melville is emphasized by the fact that, years after the appearance of *Moby-Dick,* the story of Captain Pollard appeared again in the long philosophical poem *Clarel.*

Billy Budd, left in manuscript at Melville's death and not published until 1924, is based partly on the *Somers* mutiny in the United States Navy and partly on the history of the mutiny at the Nore during the Napoleonic Wars in 1797. In the novel Billy Budd was impressed off the ship *Rights-of-Man,* an ironic touch. I believe no one has pointed out before that there was a real ship, *Droits de l'Homme,* which Melville could have read about in the book Hawthorne gave him.

34. Herman Melville, *Redburn* (Evanston and Chicago, 1969), p. 85.
35. Condensed from M. M. Sealts, *Melville's Reading* (Madison, Milwaukee and London, 1966).

Another modern instance of the use of narratives of wrecks and disasters for fictional purposes is Kenneth Roberts's *Boon Island*, 1956. Roberts lived and wrote at Kennebunkport, Maine, only a few miles from Boon Island, a bare ledge of rock north of the Isles of Shoals. Roberts, doubtless familiar with the story of the wreck of the *Nottingham* galley there in 1710, based his novel on the two narratives of the wreck by John Dean, Master, and Christopher Langman, Mate. The novel, like the original narratives, is primarily a story of man against nature, with nature having much the better of the struggle; but Roberts also gets a little conflict out of disagreements between Dean and Langman, who had no love for each other. *Boon Island* is not one of Roberts's better novels.

VI

I HAVE TRIED to select interesting and representative narratives from anthologies of shipwrecks and disasters, but I have felt free to emphasize connections with the work of major writers because their choices and involvements have value in themselves. I have written introductions for the selections and included quotations and citations of literary interest.

I have included also a checklist of books, pamphlets, and broadsides concerning shipwrecks and disasters. I have set the year 1860 as an arbitrary final date, primarily because public interest in ships and their catastrophes seemed to lessen about that time. The Civil War resulted in the destruction of most of the American whaling fleet and a great reduction in the size of the merchant fleet, steam finally began taking over from sail, and internal development in this country absorbed the major energies and interests of its people. Obviously, this list is only a beginning, but it is considerably longer than any other I have seen and may save time for some future worker in this small field. I shall be pleased if any reader feels

". . . that the good craft Huntress of Nantucket had had the honor of originally bringing him around on that side of the globe."

MELVILLE, *Redburn*, p. 312.

THESE SELECTED NARRATIVES are reprinted from several anthologies of shipwrecks and disasters. I have retained archaic forms of spellings (haulyard for halyard, eat for ate, champered for chamfered) and even some probable mistakes, but obvious typographical errors have been corrected. In a few cases names have been corrected in brackets where they first appear, but the wrong forms have been retained in the text.

NARRATIVES OF SHIPWRECKS AND DISASTERS,

1586–1860

[1]

Loss of the Portuguese Vessel *St. James*

THE WRECK of the *St. James (Santiago)* was an early example of probably thousands of wrecks caused by the stupidity and pride of ships' captains and pilots. The captain of the *St. James* received his deserts eventually, but how many decent people died that he might have his way! One might also comment on the advantages of being a member of an hereditary aristocracy and wonder whether the nobleman who pointed out the useful carpenter with his finger survived the cruise of the pinnace and the depredations of the Caffres.

This narrative came originally from a two-volume *Historia tragico-maritima* compiled by Bernardo Gomes de Brito and published in Lisbon in 1735–36. Gomes de Brito himself found his narratives in pamphlets published anonymously or by survivors of these disasters. The loss of the *St. James* was one of a whole series of similar catastrophes which were probably evidence of and cause for slackening energies and accomplishments that resulted in the loss of the Portuguese empire in the East. James Duffy's *Shipwreck and Empire* (Cambridge, Mass., 1955) deals quite fully with these losses and provides evidence for an almost unbelievable record of unwillingness to learn from experience. The sufferings of the survivors of the *St. James* after they reached the African mainland were much like those of the survivors of the *Grosvenor.*

This account is taken from R. Thomas's *Remarkable Shipwrecks* (1836).

PORTUGUESE VESSEL THE ST. JAMES

Off the Coast of Africa, in 1586.

In the month of May, 1586, intelligence was received at Goa of the loss of the admiral's ship, the St. James. The account of this disaster stated, that after doubling the cape of Good Hope, the captain, conceiving he had neither rocks nor other dangers to dread, proceeded under full sail, without observing his charts, or at least not with the attention he ought. Having a favorable wind, he made his way in a short time, but was driven out of his course towards the rocks called Bassas de India, distant about fifty leagues from the island of Madagascar, and seventy from the continent.

Perceiving they were so near these rocks, and in imminent danger of striking upon them, several of the passengers, who had frequently traversed those seas, were much alarmed. They represented to the captain, that being in the midst of the rocks, it was extremely dangerous to suffer the ship to run under full sail, particularly during the night, and in a season when tempests were very frequent. The captain, regardless of their prudent remonstrances, exerted his authority, ordered the pilots to follow his commands, adding, that the king's commission entitled him to obedience, and that his opinion ought to be taken in preference. However, between eleven and twelve o'clock the same night the vessel was driven towards the rocks, and struck without a possibility of being got off. A confused cry of distress resounded, in every direction, from a multitude composed of about five hundred men and thirty women, who, having no other prospect before their eyes but inevitable destruction, bewailed their fate with the bitterest lamentations. Every effort to save the ship proved ineffectual. The admiral, Fernando Mendoza, the captain, the first pilot, and ten or twelve other persons, instantly threw themselves into the boat, saying they would seek upon the rocks a proper place for collecting the wreck of the ship, with which they might afterwards construct a vessel large enough to convey the whole of the crew to the continent. With this view they actually landed on the rock, but being unable to find a spot proper for the execution of their design, they did not think proper to return to the ship, but resolved to steer towards the African coast. Some provisions which had been thrown in haste into the boat were distributed among them; they then directed their course towards the continent of Africa, where they arrived in safety, after a voyage of seventeen days, and enduring all the horrors of famine and tempestuous weather.

Those who remained on board, finding that the boat did not return, began to despair of saving their lives. To add to their distress, the vessel parted between the two decks, and the pinnace was much damaged by the repeated shocks she sustained from the fury of the waves. The workmen, though very expert, despaired of being able to repair her, when an Italian, named Cypriano Grimaldi, leaped into her, accompanied by ninety of the crew, and, assisted by most of those who had followed him, instantly fell to work to put her into a condition to keep the sea.

Those who could not get on board the pinnace beheld her bearing away from the wreck with tears and lamentations. Several who could swim threw themselves into the sea, in the hope of overtaking her; and some were on the point of getting on board, when their more fortunate comrades, fearing they should be sunk with the weight of all those who endeavored to obtain admittance, pushed them back into the sea, and with their sabres and hatchets cut, without mercy, the hands of such as would not quit their hold. It is impossible to describe the anguish of those who remained on the floating fragments of the wreck, and witnessed this barbarous scene. Seeing themselves cut off from every resource, their cries and lamentations would have melted the hardest heart. The situation of those in the pinnace was not much better; their great number, the want of provisions, their distance from the land, and the bad condition of the crazy bark that bore them, contributed to fill them with gloomy presentiments. Some of the most resolute, however, to prevent the anarchy and confusion which would have aggravated their misery, proposed to their companions to submit to the authority of a captain. To this they all agreed, and immediately chose a nobleman of Portuguese extraction, but born in India, to command them, investing him with absolute power. He instantly employed his authority, in causing the weakest, whom he merely pointed out with his finger, to be thrown overboard. In the number of these was a carpenter, who had assisted in repairing the pinnace; the only favor he requested was a little wine, after which he suffered himself to be thrown into the sea without uttering a word. Another, who was proscribed in the same manner, was saved by an uncommon exertion of fraternal affection. He was already seized and on the point of being sacrificed to an imperious necessity, when his younger brother demanded a moment's delay. He observed that his brother was skilled in his profession, that his father and mother were very old, and his sisters not yet settled in life; that he could not be of that service to them which his brother might, and as circumstances required the sacrifice of one of the two, he begged to die in his stead. His request was complied with, and he was accordingly thrown into the sea. But this courageous youth followed the bark upwards of six hours, making incessant efforts to get on board, sometimes on one side, sometimes on the other, while those who had thrown him over endeavored to keep him off with their swords. But that which appeared likely to accelerate his end proved his preservation. The young man snatched at a sword, seized it by the blade, and neither the pain, nor the exertions made by him who held it, could make him quit his grasp. The others, admiring his resolution, and moved with the proof of fraternal affection which he had displayed, unanimously agreed to permit him to enter the pinnace. At length, after having endured hunger and thirst, and encountered the dangers of several tempests, they landed on the coast of Africa, on the twentieth day after their shipwreck, and there met their companions who had escaped in the first boat.

The rest of the crew and passengers left on the wreck likewise attempted to reach the land. Collecting some loose rafters and planks, they formed a kind of raft, but were overwhelmed by the first sea, and all perished, excepting two who gained the shore. Those who had reached the coast of Africa had not arrived at the end of their sufferings; they had scarcely disembarked when they fell into the hands of the Caffres, a savage and inhuman people, who stripped and left them in the most deplorable state. However, mustering up their courage and the little strength they had left, they arrived at the place where the agent of the Portuguese, at Sofala and Mozambique, resided. By him they were received with the utmost humanity, and after reposing a few days, after their fatigues, they reached Mozambique, and repaired from thence to India. Only sixty survived out of all those who had embarked on the St. James; all the rest perished, either at sea, of fatigue, or hunger. Thus the imprudence of an individual occasioned the loss of a fine vessel, and the lives of above four hundred and fifty persons.

Upon the captain's return to Europe, the widows and orphans of the unfortunate sufferers raised such loud complaints against him that he was apprehended and put in prison; but he was soon afterwards released. The former catastrophe was not a sufficient lesson for this self-sufficient and obstinate man. He undertook the command of another vessel in 1588, and had nearly lost her in the same manner, and in the same place. Fortunately, at sunrise he discovered the rocks, towards which he was running with the same imprudence as in his former voyage. But on his return from India to Portugal he was lost, together with the vessel he was on board of; thus meeting with the just punishment of his culpable obstinacy and misconduct.

[2]

Loss of the *Nottingham* Galley

Boon Island is a mere barren rock east of Portsmouth, New Hampshire, and a little north of the Isles of Shoals. There are only two reasons for anyone to remember it: the *Nottingham* galley was cast away on this rock in December, 1710; and Kenneth Roberts in 1956 built one of his weaker novels out of the narratives of John Dean and Christopher Langman, captain and mate. Dean's story is a minor epic of suffering and survival through twenty-four days of a Maine coast December on a naked rock with little food and no fire. One reason for the popularity of the narrative, reprinted in most of the anthologies I have seen, was doubtless its matter-of-fact treatment of cannibalism; for our own times, Roberts makes rather grisly play with the survivors' reactions to the plump children and stout-haunched matrons of Portsmouth. The *Nottingham* ran on the rocks in an intermittent snowstorm; but there is in the story an implicit criticism of the lookout, probably sheltering under the bulwarks, who failed to see breakers and left their discovery to the captain.

Langman's account, which I have not seen, apparently blamed the wreck on Captain Dean. Roberts's *Boon Island* is partly built on antagonism between the two men. A survivor named Moses Butler, according to Roberts, became a captain at the siege of Louisburg in 1745 and married a New Hampshire Wentworth. John Dean became His Majesty's Consul at Ostend.

This narrative is also taken from Thomas's *Remarkable Shipwrecks.*

NOTTINGHAM GALLEY, OF LONDON.

THE Nottingham Galley, of and from London, of 120 tons, ten guns, fourteen men, John Dean, commander, having taken in cordage in England, and butter, cheese, &c. in Ireland, sailed for Boston in New-England, the 25th of September, 1710. Meeting with contrary winds and bad weather, it was the beginning of December, when we first made land to the eastward of Piscataqua, and proceeding southward for the bay of Massachusetts, under a hard gale of wind at northeast, accompanied with rain, hail and snow; having no observation for ten or twelve days, we, on the 11th, handed all our sails, excepting our fore-sail and maintop sail double reefed, ordering one hand forward to look out. Between eight and nine o'clock, going forward myself, I saw the breakers starboard, but before the ship could wear, we struck upon the east end of the rock, called Boon Island, four leagues to the Eastward of Piscataqua.

The second or third sea heaved the ship alongside of it; running likewise so very high, and the ship laboring so excessively, that we were not able to stand upon deck; and though it was not distant above thirty or forty yards, yet the weather was so thick and dark, that we could not see the rock, so that we were justly thrown into consternation at the melancholy prospect of immediately perishing in the sea. I presently called all hands down to the cabin, where we continued a few minutes, earnestly supplicating the mercy of heaven; but knowing that prayers, alone, are vain, I ordered all up again to cut the masts by the board, but several were so oppressed by the terrors of conscience that they were incapable of any exertion. We, however, went upon deck, cut the weathermost shrouds, and the ship heeling toward the rocks, the force of the sea soon broke the masts, so that they fell towards the shore.

One of the men went out on the bowsprit, and returning, told me he saw something black ahead, and would venture to go on shore, accompanied with any other person: upon which I desired some of the best swimmers (my mate and one more) to go with him, and if they gained the rock, to give notice by their calls, and direct us to the most secure place. Recollecting some money and papers that might be of use, also ammunition, brandy, &c., I then went down and opened the place in which they were; but the ship bilging, her decks opened, her back broke, and her beams gave way, so that the stern sank under water. I therefore hastened forward to escape instant death, and having heard nothing of the men who had gone before,

7

concluded that they were lost. Notwithstanding, I was under the necessity of making the same adventure upon the foremast, moving gradually forward betwixt every sea, till at last quitting it, I threw myself with all the strength I had, toward the rock; but it being low water, and the rock extremely slippery, I could get no hold, and tore my fingers, hands, and arms, in the most deplorable manner, every sea fetching me off again, so that it was with the utmost peril and difficulty that I got safe on shore at last. The rest of the men ran the same hazards, but through the mercy of Providence we all escaped with our lives.

After endeavoring to discharge the salt water and creeping a little way up the rock, I heard the voices of the three men above mentioned, and by ten o'clock we all met together, when, with grateful hearts, we returned thanks to Providence for our deliverance from such imminent danger. We then endeavored to gain shelter to the leeward of the rock, but found it so small and inconsiderable, that it would afford none, (being about one hundred yards long and fifty broad,) and so very craggy that we could not walk to keep ourselves warm, the weather still continuing extremely cold, with snow and rain.

As soon as day light appeared I went toward the place where we came on shore, not doubting but that we should meet with provisions enough from the wreck for our support, but found only some pieces of the masts and yards among some old junk and cables heaped together, which the anchors had prevented from being carried away, and kept moving about the rock at some distance. Part of the ship's stores with some pieces of plank and timber, old sails, canvas, &c. drove on shore, but nothing eatable, excepting three small cheeses which we picked up among the rock-weed.

We used our utmost endeavors to get fire, having a steel and flint with us, and also by a drill, with a very swift motion; but having nothing which had not been water-soaked, all our attempts proved ineffectual.

At night we stowed ourselves under our canvas, in the best manner possible, to keep each other warm. The next day the weather clearing a little, and inclining to a frost, I went out, and perceiving the main land, I knew where we were, and encouraged my men with the hope of being discovered by fishing shallops, desiring them to search for and bring up any planks, carpenter's tools, and stores they could find, in order to build a tent and a boat. The cook then complained that he was almost starved, and his countenance discovering his illness, I ordered him to remain behind with two or three more the frost had seized. About noon the men acquainted me that he was dead; we therefore laid him in a convenient place for the sea to carry him away. None mentioned eating him, though several, with myself, afterwards acknowledged that they thought of it.

After we had been in this situation two or three days, the frost being very severe, and the weather extremely cold, it affected most of our hands and feet to such a degree as to take away the sense of feeling, and render them almost useless; so benumbing and discoloring them as gave us just reason to apprehend mortification. We pulled off our shoes, and cut off our boots; but in getting off our stockings, many, whose legs were blistered, pulled off skin and all, and some, the nails of their toes. We then wrapped up our legs and feet as warmly as we could in oakum and canvas.

Now we began to build our tent in a triangular form, each side being about eight feet, covered it with the old sails and canvas that came on shore, having just room for each to lie down on one side, so that none could turn, unless all turned, which was about every two hours, when notice was given. We also fixed a staff to the top of our tent, upon which, as often as the weather would permit, we hoisted a piece of cloth in the form of a flag, in order to discover ourselves to any vessel that might approach.

We then commenced the building of our boat with planks and timber belonging to the wreck. Our only tools were the blade of a cutlass, made into a saw with our knives, a hammer, and a caulking mallet. We found some nails in the clefts of the rock, and obtained others from the sheathing. We laid three planks flat for the bottom, and two up each side, fixed to stanchions and let into the bottom timbers, with two short pieces at each end, and one breadth of new Holland duck round the sides to keep out the spray of the sea. We caulked all we could with oakum drawn from the old junk, and in other places filled up the spaces with long pieces of canvas, all of which we secured in the best manner possible. We found also some sheet lead and pump-leather, which proved of use. We fixed a short mast and square sail, with seven paddles to row, and a longer one to steer with. But our carpenter, whose services were now most wanted was, on account of illness, scarcely capable of affording us either assistance or advice; and all the rest, excepting myself and two others, were so benumbed and feeble as to be unable to move. The weather, too, was so extremely cold, that we could seldom stay out of the tent more than four hours in the day, and some days we could do nothing at all.

When we had been upon the rock about a week, without any kind of provisions, excepting the cheese above-mentioned, and some beef bones, which we eat, after beating them to pieces, we saw three boats, about five leagues from us, which, as may easily be imagined, rejoiced us not a little, believing that the period of our deliverance had arrived. I directed all the men to creep out of the tent and halloo together, as loud as their strength would permit. We likewise made all the signals we could, but in vain, for they neither heard nor saw us. We, however, received no small encouragement from the sight of them, as they came from the south-west; and the wind being at north-east when we were cast away, we had reason to suppose that our distress might have been made known by the wreck driving on the shore, and to presume that they had come out in search of us, and would daily do so when the weather should permit. Thus we flattered ourselves with the pleasing but delusive hope of deliverance.

Just before we had finished our boat, the carpenter's axe was cast upon the rock, by which we were enabled to complete our work, but then we had scarcely strength sufficient to get her into the water.

About the 21st of December, the boat being finished, the day fine, and the water smoother than I had yet seen it since we came there, we consulted who should attempt to launch her; I offered myself as one to venture in her; this was agreed to, as I was the strongest, and therefore the fittest to undergo the extremities to which we might possibly be reduced. My mate also offered himself, and desiring to accompany me, I was permitted to take him, together with my brother and four more. Thus commending our enterprize to Providence, all that were able came out, and with much difficulty, got our poor patched-up boat to the water-side. The surf running very high, we were obliged to wade very deep to launch her, upon which I and another got into her. The swell of the sea heaved her along the shore and overset upon us, whereby we again narrowly escaped drowning. Our poor boat was staved to pieces, our enterprize totally disappointed, and our hopes utterly destroyed.

What heightened our afflictions, and served to aggravate our miserable prospects, and render our deliverance less practicable, we lost, with our boat, both our axe and hammer, which would have been of great use to us if we should afterwards have attempted to construct a raft. Yet we had reason to admire the goodness of God in producing our disappointment for our safety; for, that afternoon, the wind springing up, it blew so hard, insomuch that, had we been at sea in that imitation of a boat, we must, in all probability, have perished, and those left behind, being unable to help themselves, must doubtless soon have shared a similar fate.

We were now reduced to the most melancholy and deplorable situation imaginable; almost every man but myself was weak to an extremity, nearly starved with hunger and perishing with cold; their hands and feet frozen and mortified; large and deep ulcers in their legs; the smell of which was highly offensive to those who could not creep into the air, and nothing to dress them with but a piece of linen that was cast on shore. We had no fire: our small stock of

cheese was exhausted, and we had nothing to support our feeble
bodies but rock-weed and a few muscles, scarce and difficult to be
procured, at most not above two or three for each man a day; so that
our miserable bodies were perishing, and our disconsolate spirits over-
powered by the deplorable prospect of starving, without any appearance of relief. To aggravate our situation, if possible, we had reason
to apprehend, lest the approaching springtide if accompanied with
high winds, should entirely overflow us. The horrors of such a situation it is impossible to describe; the pinching cold and hunger; extremity of weakness and pain; racking and horrors of conscience in
many; and the prospect of a certain, painful, and lingering death,
without even the most remote views of deliverance! This is, indeed,
the height of misery; yet such alas! was our deplorable case: insomuch
that the greater part of our company were ready to die of horror and
despair.

For my part, I did my utmost to encourage myself, exhort the
rest to trust in God, and patiently await their deliverance. As a slight
alleviation of our fate, Providence directed towards our quarters a
sea-gull, which my mate struck down and joyfully brought to me. I
divided it into equal portions, and though raw, and scarcely affording
a mouthful for each, yet we received and eat it thankfully.

The last method of rescuing ourselves we could possibly devise,
was to construct a raft capable of carrying two men. This proposal
was strongly supported by a Swede, one of our men, a stout, brave
fellow, who, since our disaster, had lost the use of both his feet by
the frost. He frequently importuned me to attempt our deliverance
in that way, offering himself to accompany me, or, if I refused, to go
alone. After deliberate consideration we resolved upon a raft, but
found great difficulty in clearing the fore-yard, of which it was chiefly
to be made, from the junk, as our working hands were so few and
weak.

This done, we split the yard, and with the two parts made side-
pieces, fixing others, and adding some of the lightest planks we could
find, first spiking, and afterwards making them firm. The raft was
four feet in breadth. We fixed up a mast, and out of two hammocks
that were driven on shore we made a sail, with a paddle for each
man, and a spare one in case of necessity. This difficulty being thus
surmounted, the Swede frequently asked me whether I designed to
accompany him, giving me to understand, that if I declined, there was
another ready to offer himself for the enterprise.

About this time we saw a sail come out of Piscataqua river, about
seven leagues to the westward. We again made all the signals we
could, but the wind being northwest, and the ship standing to the
eastward, she was presently out of sight, without ever coming near
us, which proved an extreme mortification to our hopes. The next

day, being moderate, with a small breeze toward the shore in the afternoon, and the raft being wholly finished, the two men were very anxious to have it launched; but this was as strenuously opposed by the mate, because it was so late, being two in the afternoon. They, however, urged the lightness of the nights, begged me to suffer them to proceed, and I at length consented. They both got upon the raft, when the swell, rolling very high, soon overset them, as it did our boat. The Swede not daunted by this accident, swam on shore, but the other being no swimmer, continued some time under water; as soon as he appeared, I caught hold of and saved him, but he was so discouraged that he was afraid to make a second attempt. I desired the Swede to wait for a more favorable opportunity, but he continued resolute, begged me to go with him, or help him to turn the raft, and he would go alone.

By this time another man came down and offered to adventure; when they were upon the raft, I launched them off, they desiring us to go to prayers, and also to watch what became of them. I did so, and by sunset judged them half-way to the mainland and supposed that they might reach the shore by two in the morning. They, however, probably fell in with some breakers, or were overset by the violence of the sea and perished; for, two days afterwards, the raft was found on shore, and one man dead about a mile from it, with a paddle fastened to his wrist; but the Swede, who was so very forward to adventure, was never heard of more.

We who were left on the desolate island, ignorant of what had befallen them, waited daily for deliverance. Our expectations were the more raised by a smoke we observed, two days afterwards in the woods, which was the signal appointed to be made if they arrived safely. This continued every day, and we were willing to believe that it was made on our account, though we saw no appearance of any thing toward our relief. We supposed that the delay was occasioned because they were not able to procure a vessel so soon as we desired, and this idea served to bear up our spirits and to support us greatly.

Still our principal want was that of provision, having nothing to eat but rockweed, and a very few muscles; indeed, when the spring-tide was over, we could scarcely get any at all. I went myself as no other person was able, several days at low water, and could find no more than two or three apiece. I was frequently in danger of losing my hands and arms, by putting them so often into the water after the muscles, and when obtained, my stomach refused them, and preferred rockweed.

Upon our first arrival we saw several seals upon the rocks, and supposing they might harbor there in the night, I walked round at midnight, but could never meet with any thing. We saw likewise, a great number of birds, which perceiving us daily there, would never lodge upon the rock, so that we caught none.

This disappointment was severe, and tended to aggravate our miseries still more; but it was particularly afflicting to a brother I had with me, and another young gentleman, neither of whom had before been at sea, or endured any kind of hardship. They were now reduced to the last extremity, having no assistance but what they received from me.

Part of a green hide, fastened to a piece of the mainyard, being thrown up by the sea, the men importuned me to bring it to the tent, which being done, we minced it small and swallowed it.

About this time I set the men to open junk, and when the weather would permit I thatched the tent with the rope yarn in the best manner I was able, that it might shelter us the better from the extremities of the weather. This proved of so much service as to turn two or three hours rain, and preserve us from the cold, pinching winds which were always very severe upon us.

Toward the latter part of December, our carpenter, a fat man, and naturally of a dull, heavy, phlegmatic disposition, aged about forty-seven, who, from our first coming on shore, had been constantly very ill, and lost the use of his feet, complained of excessive pain in his back, and stiffness in his neck. He was likewise almost choked with phlegm, for want of strength to discharge it, and appeared to draw near his end. We prayed over him, and used our utmost endeavors to be serviceable to him in his last moments; he showed himself sensible, though speechless, and died that night. We suffered the body to remain till morning, when I desired those who were most able, to remove it; creeping out myself to see whether Providence had sent us any thing to satisfy the excessive cravings of our appetites. Returning before noon, and not seeing the dead body without the tent, I inquired why they had not removed it, and received for answer, they were not all of them able; upon which, fastening a rope to the body, I gave the utmost of my assistance, and with some difficulty we dragged it out of the tent. But fatigue, and the consideration of our misery, so overcame my spirits, that being ready to faint, I crept into the tent, and was no sooner there, than, to add to my trouble, the men began to request my permission to eat the dead body, the better to support their lives.

This circumstance was, of all the trials I had encountered, the most grievous and shocking:—to see myself and company, who came hither laden with provisions but three weeks before, now reduced to such a deplorable situation; two of us having been absolutely starved to death, while, ignorant of the fate of two others, the rest, though still living, were reduced to the last extremity, and requiring to eat the dead for their support.

After mature consideration of the lawfulness or sinfulness, on the one hand, and absolute necessity on the other, judgment and conscience were obliged to submit to the more prevailing arguments of our craving appetites. We, at length, determined to satisfy our hunger, and support our feeble bodies with the carcass of our deceased companion. I first ordered his skin, head, hands, feet, and bowels, to be buried in the sea, and the body to be quartered, for the convenience of drying and carriage, but again received for answer, that none of them being able, they intreated I would perform that labor for them. This was a hard task; but their incessant prayers and entreaties at last prevailed over my reluctance, and by night I had completed the operation.

I cut part of the flesh into thin slices, and washing it in salt water, brought it to the tent and obliged the men to eat rock-weed with it instead of bread. My mate and two others refused to eat any that night, but the next morning they complied, and earnestly desired to partake with the rest.

I found that they all eat with the utmost avidity, so that I was obliged to carry the quarters farther from the tent, out of their reach, lest they should injure themselves by eating too much, and likewise expend our small stock too soon.

I also limited each man to an equal portion, that they might not quarrel or have cause to reflect on me or one another. This method I was the more obliged to adopt, because, in a few days, I found their dispositions entirely changed, and that affectionate, peaceable temper they had hitherto manifested, totally lost. Their eyes looked wild and staring, their countenances fierce and barbarous. Instead of obeying my commands, as they had universally and cheerfully done before, I now found even prayers and entreaties vain and fruitless; nothing was now to be heard but brutal quarrels, with horrid oaths and imprecations, instead of that quiet submissive spirit of prayer and supplication they had before manifested.

This, together with the dismal prospect of future want, obliged me to keep a strict watch over the rest of the body, lest any of them, if able, should get to it, and if that were spent we should be compelled to feed upon the living, which we certainly must have done, had we remained in that situation a few days longer.

The goodness of God now began to appear, and to make provision for our deliverance, by putting it into the hearts of the good people on the shore to which our raft was driven, to come out in search of us, which they did on the 2d of January, in the morning.

Just as I was creeping out of the tent I saw a shallop half way from the shore, standing directly toward us, Our joy and satisfaction, at the prospect of such speedy and unexpected deliverance, no tongue is able to express, nor thought to conceive.

Our good and welcome friends came to an anchor to the south-west, at the distance of about one hundred yards, the swell preventing them from approaching nearer; but their anchor coming home obliged them to stand off till about noon, waiting for smoother water upon the flood. Meanwhile our passions were differently agitated; our expectations of deliverance, and fears of miscarriage, harried our weak and disordered spirits strangely.

I gave them an account of all our miseries, excepting the want of provisions, which I did not mention, lest the fear of being constrained by the weather to remain with us, might have prevented them from coming on shore. I earnestly entreated them to attempt our immediate deliverance, or at least to furnish us with fire, which, with the utmost hazard and difficulty they at last accomplished, by sending a small canoe, with one man, who, after great exertion, got on shore.

After helping him up with his canoe, and seeing nothing to eat, I asked him if he could give us fire:—he answered in the affirmative, but was so affrighted by my thin and meagre appearance that, at first, he could scarcely return me an answer. However, recollecting himself, after several questions asked on both sides, he went with me to the tent, where he was surprised to see so many of us in such a deplorable condition. Our flesh was so wasted, and our looks were so ghastly and frightful, that it was really a very dismal spectacle.

With some difficulty we made a fire, after which, determining to go on board myself with the man, and to send for the rest, one or two at a time, we both got into the canoe; but the sea immediately drove us against the rock with such violence that we were overset, and being very weak, it was considerable time before I could recover myself, so that I had again a very narrow escape from drowning. The good man with great difficulty got on board without me, designing to return the next day with better conveniences, if the weather should permit.

It was an afflicting sight to observe our friends in the shallop, standing away for the shore without us. But, God who orders every thing for the best, doubtless had designs of preservation in denying us the appearance of present deliverance: for the wind coming about to southeast, it blew so hard that the shallop was lost, and the crew with extreme difficulty, saved their lives. Had we been with them it is more than probable that we should all have perished, not having strength sufficient to help ourselves.

When they had reached the shore they immediately sent an express to Portsmouth, in Piscataqua, where the good people made no delay in hastening to our deliverance as soon as the weather would allow. To our great sorrow, and as a farther trial of our patience, the next day continued very stormy, and though we doubted not but the people on shore knew our condition, and would assist us as soon as possible, yet our flesh being nearly consumed, being without fresh water, and uncertain how long the unfavorable weather might continue, our situation was extremly miserable. We, however, received great benefit from our fire, as we could both warm ourselves and broil our meat.

The next day, the men being very importunate for flesh, I gave them rather more than usual, but not to their satisfaction. They would certainly have eaten up the whole at once, had I not carefully watched them, with the intention of sharing the rest next morning, if the weather continued bad. The wind, however, abated that night, and early next morning a shallop came for us, with my much esteemed friends captain Long and captain Purver, and three other men, who brought a large canoe, and in two hours got us all on board, being obliged to carry almost all of us upon their backs from the tent to the canoe, and fetch us off by two or three at a time.

When we first came on board the shallop, each of us eat a piece of bread, and drank a dram of rum, and most of us were extremely sea-sick: but after we had cleansed our stomachs and tasted warm nourishing food, we became so exceeding hungry and ravenous, that had not our friends dieted us, and limited the quantity for two or three days, we should certainly have destroyed ourselves with eating.

Two days after our coming on shore, my apprentice lost the greater part of one foot; all the rest recovered their limbs, but not their perfect use; very few, excepting myself, escaping without losing the benefit of fingers or toes, though otherwise all were in perfect health.

[3]

Loss of the French East Indiaman *The Prince*

When storms, reefs, and negligent captains did not threaten, sailors and passengers still had to face the possibility of fire at sea. This narrative, taken from Thomas's anthology, relates how ten men alone survived out of almost three hundred who had put to sea in *The Prince*.

THE PRINCE,

By one of the lieutenants of that Ship.

T HE French East India Company's ship, The Prince, commanded by M. Morin, and bound to Pondicherry, weighed anchor on
the 19th of February, 1752, from the harbor of L'Orient. She had
scarcely passed the island of St. Michael, when the wind shifting, it
was found impossible to double the Turk bank. The utmost efforts,
and the greatest precautions, could not prevent her from striking on
the bank, in such a manner that the mouths of the guns were im-
mersed in the water. We announced our misfortune by signals of distress, when M. de Godeheu, the commander of the port of L'Orient,
came on board to animate the crew by his presence and his orders. All
the chests, and other articles, of the greatest value, were removed safely
into smaller vessels to lighten the ship; the whole night was occupied
with the most laborious exertions. At length the tide, in the morning,
relieved us from our dangerous situation, and enabled us to reach the
road of Port Louis: we owed the preservation of the ship entirely to
the prudent directions of M. de Godeheu, and the measures adopted
in consequence. The ship had sprung several leaks, but fortunately
our pumps kept the water under: half the cargo was taken out of the
vessel, and in about a week we returned to L'Orient, where she was
entirely unloaded. She was then careened and caulked afresh. These
precautions seemed to promise a successful voyage, and the misfortune
we had already experienced showed the strength of the vessel, which
fire alone appeared capable of destroying.

On the 10th of June, 1752, a favorable wind carried us out of the
port, but after a fortunate navigation we met with a disaster of which
the strongest expressions can convey but a faint idea. In this narrative
I shall confine myself to a brief detail, as it is impossible to recollect
all the circumstances.

The 26th of July, 1752, being in the latitude of eight degrees
thirty minutes south, and in longitude five degrees west, the wind
being S.W. just at the moment of taking the observation of the meridian, I had repaired to the quarter, where I was going to command,
when a man informed me that a smoke was seen to issue from the
panel of the greater hatchway.

Upon this information the first lieutenant, who kept the keys of the hold, opened all the hatchways, to discover the cause of an accident, the slightest suspicion of which frequently causes the most intrepid to tremble. The captain, who was at dinner in the great cabin, went upon deck and gave orders for extinguishing the fire. I had already directed several sails to be thrown overboard, and the hatchways to be covered with them, hoping, by these means, to prevent the air from penetrating into the hold. I had even proposed, for the greater security, to let in the water between decks, to the height of a foot; but the air, which had already obtained a free passage through the opening of the hatchways, produced a very thick smoke, that issued forth in abundance, and the fire continued gradually to gain ground.

The captain ordered sixty or eighty of the soldiers under arms to restrain the crew, and prevent the confusion likely to ensue in such a critical moment. These precautions were seconded by M. de la Touche, with his usual fortitude and prudence. That hero deserved a better opportunity of signalizing himself, and had destined his soldiers for other operations more useful to his country.

All hands were now employed in getting water; not only the buckets, but likewise all the pumps were kept at work, and pipes were carried from them into the hold; even the water in the jars was emptied out. The rapidity of the fire, however, baffled our efforts and augmented the general consternation.

The captain had already ordered the yawl to be hoisted overboard, merely because it was in the way; four men, among whom was the boatswain, took possession of it. They had no oars, but called out for some, when three sailors jumped overboard and carried them what they stood so much in need of. The fortunate fugitives were required to return; they cried out that they had no rudder, and desired a rope to be thrown them; perceiving that the progress of the flames left them no other resource, they endeavored to remove to a distance from the ship, which passed them in consequence of a breeze that sprang up.

All hands were still busy on board; the impossibility of escaping seemed to increase the courage of the men. The master boldly ventured down into the hold, but the heat obliged him to return; he would have been burned if a great quantity of water had not been thrown over him. Immediately afterwards, the flames were seen to issue with great impetuosity from the great pannel. The captain ordered the boats overboard, but fear had exhausted the strength of the most intrepid. The jolly-boat was fastened at a certain height, and preparations were made for hoisting her over; but, to complete our misfortunes, the fire, which increased every moment, ascended the main-mast with such violence and rapidity as to burn the tackle; the boat pitching upon the starboard guns, fell bottom upwards, and we lost all hopes of raising her again.

We now perceived that we had nothing to hope from human aid, but only from the mercy of the Almighty. Dejection filled every mind; the consternation became general; nothing but sighs and groans were heard; even the animals we had on board uttered the most dreadful cries. Every one began to raise his heart and hands towards heaven; and in the certainty of a speedy death each was occupied only with the melancholy alternative between the two elements ready to devour us.

The chaplain, who was on the quarter-deck, gave the general absolution, and went into the gallery to impart the same to the unhappy wretches who had already committed themselves to the mercy of the waves. What a horrid spectacle! Each was occupied only in throwing overboard whatever promised a momentary preservation; coops, yards, spars, every thing that came to hand was seized in despair and disposed of in the same manner. The confusion was extreme; some seemed to anticipate death by jumping into the sea, others, by swimming, gained the fragments of the vessel; while the shrouds, the yards, and ropes, along the side of the ship were covered with the crew who were suspended from them, as if hesitating between two extremes, equally imminent and equally terrible.

Uncertain for what fate Providence intended me, I saw a father snatch his son from the flames, embrace him, throw him into the sea then following himself, they perished in each other's embrace. I had ordered the helm to be turned to starboard; the vessel heeled, and this manoeuvre preserved us for some time on that side, while the fire raged on the larboard side from stem to stern.

Till this moment, I had been so engaged that my thoughts were directed only to the preservation of the ship; now, however, the horrors of a twofold death presented themselves; but through the kindness of heaven, my fortitude never forsook me. I looked round and found myself alone upon the deck. I went into the round-house, where I met M. de la Touche, who regarded death with the same heroism that procured him success in India. "Farewell, my brother and my friend," said he, embracing me—"Why, where are you going?" replied I. "I am going, (said he,) to comfort my friend Morin." He spoke of the captain, who was overwhelmed with grief at the melancholy fate of his female cousins, who were passengers on board his ship, and whom he had persuaded to trust themselves to sea in hen-coops, after having hastily stripped off their clothes, while some of the sailors, swimming with one hand, endeavored to support them with the other.

The yards and masts were covered with men struggling with the waves around the vessel; many of them perished every moment by the balls discharged by the guns in consequence of the flames; a third species of death, that augmented the horrors by which we were surrounded. With a heart oppressed with anguish, I turned my eyes away from the sea. A moment afterwards I entered the starboard gallery, and saw the flames rushing with a horrid noise through the windows of the great cabin and the round-house. The fire approached, and was ready to consume me; my presence was then entirely useless for the preservation of the vessel, or the relief of my fellow sufferers.

In this dreadful situation I thought it my duty to prolong my life a few hours, in order to devote them to my God. I stripped off my clothes with the intention of rolling down a yard, one end of which touched the water; but it was so covered with unfortunate wretches, whom the fear of drowning kept in that situation, that I tumbled over them and fell into the sea, recommending myself to the mercy of Providence. A stout soldier who was drowning caught hold of me in this extremity; I employed every exertion to disengage myself from him, but without effect, I suffered myself to sink under the water, but he did not quit his hold; I plunged a second time, and he still held me firmly in his grasp; he was incapable of reflecting that my death would rather hasten his own than be of service to him. At length, after struggling a considerable time, his strength was exhausted in consequence of the quantity of water he had swallowed, and perceiving that I was sinking the third time, and fearing lest I should drag him to the bottom along with me, he loosed his hold. That he might not catch me again I dived, and rose a considerable distance from the spot.

This first adventure rendered me more cautious in future; I even shunned the dead bodies, which were so numerous, that, to make a free passage, I was obliged to push them aside with one hand, while I kept myself above water with the other. I imagined that each of them was a man who would assuredly seize and involve me in his own destruction. My strength began to fail, and I was convinced of the necessity of resting, when I met a piece of the flag staff. To secure it I put my arm through the noose of the rope, and swam as well as I was able; I perceived a yard floating before me, when I approached and seized it by the end. At the other extremity I saw a young man, scarcely able to support himself, and speedily relinquished this feeble assistance that announced a certain death. The sprit-sail yard next appeared in sight; it was covered with people, and I durst not take a place upon it without asking permission, which my unfortunate companions cheerfully granted. Some were quite naked, and others in their shirts; they expressed their pity at my situation, and their misfortune put my sensibility to the severest test.

M. Morin and M. de la Touche, both so worthy of a better fate, never quitted the vessel, and were doubtless buried in its ruins. Whichever way I turned my eyes, the most dismal sights presented themselves. The main-mast, burnt away at the bottom, fell overboard, killing some, and affording to others a precarious resource. This mast I observed covered with people, and abandoned to the impulse of the waves; at the same moment I perceived two sailors upon a hen-coop with some planks, and cried out to them, "My lads, bring the planks, and swim to me." They approached me, accompanied by several others; and each taking a plank, which we used as oars, we paddled along upon the yard, and joined those who had taken possession of the main-mast.

So many changes of situation presented only new spectacles of horror. I fortunately here met with our chaplain, who gave me absolution. We were in number about eighty persons, who were incessantly threatened with destruction by the balls from the ship's guns. I saw likewise on the mast two young ladies, by whose piety I was much edified; there were six females on board, and the other four were, in all probability, already drowned or burned. Our chaplain, in this dreadful situation, melted the most obdurate hearts by his discourse and the example he gave of patience and resignation. Seeing him slip from the mast and fall into the sea, as I was behind him, I lifted him up again. "Let me go, (said he,) I am full of water, and it is only a prolongation of my sufferings." "No, my friend, (said I,) we will die together when my strength forsakes me." In his pious company I awaited death with perfect resignation. I remained in this situation three hours, and saw one of the ladies fall off the mast with fatigue, and perish; she was too far distant for me to give her any assistance.

When I least expected it, I perceived the yawl close to us; it was then five o'clock, P.M. I cried out to the men in her that I was their lieutenant, and begged permission to share our misfortune with them. They gave me leave to come on board, upon condition that I would swim to them. It was their interest to have a conductor, in order to discover land; and for this reason my company was too necessary for them to refuse my request. The condition they imposed upon me was perfectly reasonable; they acted prudently not to approach, as the others would have been equally anxious to enter their little bark; and we should all have been buried together in a watery grave. Mustering, therefore, all my strength, I was so fortunate as to reach the boat. Soon afterwards I observed the pilot and master, whom I had left on the main-mast, follow my example; they swam to the yawl, and we took them in. This little bark was the means of saving the ten persons who alone escaped, out of nearly three hundred.

The flames still continued to consume our ship, from which we were not more than half a league distant; our too great proximity might prove pernicious, and we, therefore, proceeded to windward. Not long after, the fire communicated to the powder-room, and it is impossible to describe the noise with which our vessel blew up. A thick cloud intercepted the light of the sun; amidst this horrible darkness we could perceive nothing but large pieces of flaming wood projected into the air, and whose fall threatened to dash to pieces numbers of unhappy wretches still struggling with the agonies of death. We, ourselves, were not quite out of danger; it was not impossible but that one of the flaming fragments might reach us, and precipitate our frail vessel to the bottom. The Almighty, however, preserved us from that misfortune; but what a spectacle now presented itself! The vessel had disappeared; its fragments covered the sea to a great distance, and floated in all directions with our unfortunate companions, whose despair and whose lives, had been terminated together by their fall. We saw some completely suffocated, others mangled, half burned, and still preserving sufficient life to be sensible of the accumulated horrors of their fate.

Through the mercy of heaven, I retained my fortitude, and proposed to make towards the fragments of the wreck to seek provisions, and to pick up any other articles we might want. We were totally unprovided, and were in danger of perishing with famine; a death more tedious and more painful than that of our companions. We found several barrels, in which we hoped to find a resource against this pressing necessity, but discovered to our mortification that it was part of the powder which had been thrown overboard during the conflagration.

Night approached; but we providentially found a cask of brandy, about fifteen pounds of salt pork, a piece of scarlet cloth, twenty yards of linen, a dozen of pipe staves, and a few ropes. It grew dark, and we could not wait till daylight in our present situation, without exposing ourselves a hundred times to destruction among the fragments of the wreck, from which we had not yet been able to disengage ourselves. We therefore rowed away from them as speedily as possible, in order to attend to the equipment of our new vessel. Every one fell to work with the utmost assiduity; we employed every thing, and took off the inner sheathing of our boat for the sake of planks and nails; we drew from the linen what thread we wanted; fortunately one of the sailors had two needles; our scarlet cloth served us for a sail, an oar for a mast, and a plank for a rudder. Notwithstanding the darkness, our equipment was in a short time as complete as circumstances would permit. The only difficulty that remained was, how to direct our course; we had neither charts nor instruments, and were nearly two hundred leagues from land. We resigned ourselves to the mercy of the Almighty, whose assistance we implored in fervent prayers.

At length we raised our sail, and a favorable wind removed us forever from the floating corpses of our unfortunate companions. In this manner we proceeded eight days and eight nights, without perceiving land, exposed stark naked to the burning rays of the sun by day, and to intense cold by night. The sixth day, a shower of rain inspired us with the hope of some relief from the thirst by which we were tormented: we endeavored to catch the little water that fell in our mouths and hands. We sucked our sail, but having been before soaked in sea-water, it communicated the bitter taste of the latter to the rain which it received. If, however, the rain had been more violent, it might have abated the wind that impelled us, and a calm would have been attended with inevitable destruction.

That we might steer our course with the greater certainty, we consulted, every day, the rising and setting of the sun and moon; and the stars showed us what wind we ought to take. A very small piece of salt pork furnished us one meal in the twenty-four hours: and from even this we were obliged to desist on the fourth day, on account of the irritation of the blood which it occasioned. Our only beverage was a glass of brandy, from time to time; but that liquor burned our stomachs without allaying our thirst. We saw abundance of flying-fish, but the impossibility of catching them rendered our misery still more acute; we were, therefore, obliged to be contented with our provisions. The uncertainty with respect to our fate, the want of food, and the agitation of the sea, combined to deprive us of rest, and almost plunged us into despair. Nature seemed to have abandoned her functions; a feeble ray of hope alone cheered our minds and prevented us from envying the fate of our deceased companions.

I passed the eighth night at the helm: I remained at my post more than ten hours, frequently desiring to be relieved, till at length I sank down with fatigue. My miserable comrades were equally exhausted, and despair began to take possession of our souls. At last, when just perishing with fatigue, misery, hunger, and thirst, we discovered land, by the first rays of the sun, on Wednesday, the 3d of August, 1752. Only those who have experienced similar misfortunes can form an adequate conception of the change which this discovery produced in our minds. Our strength returned, and we took precautions not to be carried away by the currents. At two P.M. we reached the coast of Brazil, and entered the bay of Tresson, in latitude six degrees.

Our first care, upon setting foot on shore, was to thank the Almighty for his favors; we threw ourselves upon the ground, and, in the transports of our joy, rolled ourselves in the sand. Our appearance was truly frightful, our figures preserved nothing human that did not more forcibly announce our misfortunes. Some were perfectly naked, others had nothing but shirts that were rotten and torn to rags, and I had fastened round my waist a piece of scarlet cloth, in order to appear at the head of my companions. We had not yet, however, arrived at the end of all our hardships; although rescued from the greatest of our dangers, that of an uncertain navigation, we were still tormented by hunger and thirst, and in cruel suspense, whether we should find this coast inhabited by men susceptible of sentiments of compassion.

We were deliberating which way we should direct our course, when about fifty Portuguese, most of whom were armed, advanced towards us, and inquired the reason of our landing. The recital of our misfortunes was a sufficient answer, at once announced our wants, and strongly claimed the sacred rights of hospitality. Their treasures were not the object of our desire, the necessaries of life were all that we wanted. Touched by our misfortunes, they blessed the power that had preserved us, and hastened to conduct us to their habitations. Upon the way we came to a river, into which all my companions ran to throw themselves, in order to allay their thirst; they rolled in the water with extreme delight; and bathing was in the sequel one of the remedies of which we made the most frequent use, and which, at the same time, contributed most to the restoration of our health.

The principal person of the place came and conducted us to his house, about half a league distant from the place of our landing. Our charitable host gave us linen shirts and trousers, and boiled some fish, the water of which served us for broth, and seemed delicious. After this frugal repast, though sleep was equally necessary, yet we prepared to render solemn thanks to the Almighty. Hearing that, at the distance of half a league, there was a church dedicated to St. Michael, we repaired thither, singing praises to the Lord, while we presented the homage of our gratitude to Him to whom we were so evidently indebted for our preservation. The badness of the road had fatigued us so much that we were obliged to rest in the village; our misfortunes, together with such an edifying spectacle, drew all the inhabitants around us, and every one hastened to fetch us refreshments. After resting a short time, we returned to our kind host who, at night, furnished us with another repast of fresh fish. As we wanted more invigorating food, we purchased an ox, which we had in exchange for twenty-five quarts of brandy.

We had to go to Paraibo, a journey of fifteen leagues, barefoot, and without any hope of meeting with good provisions on the way; we therefore took the precaution of smoke-drying our meat, and added to it a provision of flour. After resting three days, we departed under an escort of three soldiers. We proceeded seven leagues the first day, and passed the night at the house of a man, who received us kindly. The next evening, a sergeant, accompanied by twenty-nine soldiers, came to meet us for the purpose of conducting and presenting us to the commandant of the fortress; that worthy officer received us graciously, gave us an entertainment, and a boat to go to Paraibo. It was midnight when we arrived at that town; a Portuguese captain was waiting to present us to the governor, who gave us a gracious reception, and furnished us with all the comforts of life. We there reposed for three days, but being desirous of reaching Fernambuc to take advantage of a Portuguese fleet that was expected to sail every day, in order to return to Europe, the governor ordered a corporal to conduct us thither. My feet were so lacerated that I could scarcely stand, and a horse was therefore provided for me.

At length after a journey of four days, we entered the town of of Fernambuc. My first business was to go, with my people, to present myself to the general, Joseph de Correa, who condescended to give me an audience; after which Don Francisco Miguel, a captain of a king's ship, took us in a boat to procure us the advantage of saluting the admiral of the fleet, Don Juan d'Acosta de Porito. During the fifty days that we remained at Fernambuc that gentleman never ceased to load me with new favors and civilities. His generosity extended to all my companions in misfortune, to some of whom he even gave appointments in the vessels of his fleet.

On the fifth of October we set sail, and arrived without any accident, at Lisbon, on the 17th of December. On the second of January, our consul, M. du Vernay, procured me a passage in a vessel bound to Morlaix. The master and myself went on board together, the rest of my companions being distributed among other ships. I arrived at Morlaix on the 2d of February. My fatigues obliged me to take a few days rest in that place, from whence I repaired on the 10th to l'Orient, overwhelmed with poverty, having lost all that I possessed in the world, after a service of twenty-eight years, and with my health greatly impaired by the hardships I had endured.

[4]

Loss of the Sloop *Betsy*

THE *Betsy*, like the *Nottingham* galley, was a small trading vessel, one of thousands that sank not far from land. The chief interest of this account (from Thomas's *Remarkable Shipwrecks*) lies in the good treatment accorded the survivors by the Carib (Caraib in text) Indians, whose soup and fruits seemed to do more good than the London doctors could at that time. Nevertheless, Captain Aubin doubtless went to his grave feeling that ass's milk, warm goat milk at dawn, and bits of chicken wing had saved his life.

This is one of the narratives Poe may have used in writing *The Narrative of Arthur Gordon Pym*. In that first draft of a novel Poe probably planned to have his survivors on the wreck of the *Grampus* kill and eat the faithful Newfoundland dog Tiger as Captain Aubin did his dog, but Poe forgot all about the dog and hustled the manuscript off to the publishers.

LOSS OF THE

SLOOP BETSY,

On the Coast of Dutch Guiana, August 5, 1756.

ON the 1st of August, 1756, says captain Aubin, I set sail for Surinam, from Carlisle bay, in the island of Barbadoes. My sloop, of about eighty tons burthen, was built entirely of cedar, and freighted by Messrs. Roscoe and Nyles, merchants of Bridgetown. The cargo consisted of provisions of every kind, and horses. The Dutch colony being in want of a supply of those animals, passed a law that no English vessel should be permitted to enter there, if horses did not constitute part of her cargo. The Dutch were so rigid in enforcing this condition, that if the horses chanced to die on their passage, the master of the vessel was obliged to preserve the ears and hoofs of the animals, and to swear upon entering the port of Surinam, that when he embarked they were alive, and destined for that colony.

The coasts of Surinam, Berbice, Demarara, Oronoko, and all the adjacent parts, are low lands, and inundated by large rivers, which discharge themselves into the sea. The bottom all along this coast is composed of a kind of mud, or clay, in which the anchors sink to the depth of three or four fathoms, and upon which the keel sometimes strikes without stopping the vessel. The sloop being at anchor three leagues and a half from the shore in five fathoms water, the mouth of the Demarara river bearing S.S.W. and it being the rainy season, my crew drew up water from the sea for their use, which was just as sweet as good river water. The current occasioned by the trade winds, and the numerous rivers which fall into the sea, carried us at the rate of four miles an hour towards the west and north-west.

In the evening of the 4th of August, I was tacking about, between the latitude of ten and twelve degrees north, with a fresh breeze, which obliged me to reef my sails. At midnight, finding that the wind increased in proportion as the moon, then on the wane, rose above the horizon, and that my bark, which was deeply laden, labored excessively, I would not retire to rest till the weather became more moderate. I told my mate, whose name was Williams, to bring me a bottle of beer, and both sitting down, I upon a hen-coop, and Williams upon the deck, we began to tell stories to pass the time, according to the mariners of every country. The vessel suddenly turned with her broadside to windward: I called to one of the seamen to put the helm a weather, but he replied it had been so for some time. I directed my mate to see if the cords were not entangled; he informed me that they were not. At this moment the vessel swung round with her head to the sea, and plunged; her head filled in such a manner that she could not rise above the surf, which broke over us to the height of the anchor stocks, and we were presently up to our necks in water; every thing in the cabin was washed away. Some of the crew, which consisted of nine men, were drowned in their hammocks, without a cry or groan. When the wave had passed, I took the hatchet that was hanging up near the fireplace, to cut away the shrouds to prevent the ship from upsetting, but in vain. She upset, and turned over again, with her masts and sails in the water; the horses rolled one over the other and were drowned, forming altogether a most melancholy spectacle.

I had but one small boat, about twelve or thirteen feet long; she was fixed, with a cable coiled inside of her, between the pump and the side of the ship. Providentially for our preservation there was no occasion to lash her fast; but we at this time entertained no hope of seeing her again, as the large cable within her, together with the weight of the horses, and their stalls entangled one among another, prevented her from rising to the surface of the water.

In this dreadful situation, holding by the shrouds, and stripping off my clothes, I looked round me for some plank or empty box to preserve my life as long as it should please the Almighty, when I perceived my mate and two seamen hanging by a rope, and imploring God to receive their souls. I told them that the man who was not resigned to die when it pleased the Creator to call him out of the world was not fit to live. I advised them to undress as I had done, and to endeavor to seize the first object that could assist them in preserving their lives. Williams followed my advice, stripped himself quite naked, and betook himself to swimming, looking out for whatever he could find. A moment afterwards he cried out, "Here is the boat, keel uppermost!" I immediately swam to him, and found him holding the boat by the keel. We then set to work to turn her, but in vain; at length, however, Williams, who was the heaviest and strongest of the two, contrived to set his feet against the gunwale of the boat, laying hold of the keel with his hands, and with a violent effort nearly succeeding in overturning her. I being to windward, pushed and lifted her up with my shoulders on the opposite side. At length, with the assistance of the surf, we turned her over, but she was full of water. I got into her, and endeavored by the means of a rope belonging to the rigging to draw her to the mast of the vessel. In the intervals between the waves the mast always rose to the height of fifteen or twenty feet above the water. I passed the end of the rope fastened to the boat once around the head of the mast, keeping hold of the end; each time that the mast rose out of the water, it lifted up both the boat and me; I then let go the rope, and by this expedient the boat was three-fourths emptied; but having nothing to enable me to disengage her from the mast and shrouds, they fell down upon me, driving the boat and me again under water.

After repeated attempts to empty her, in which I was cruelly wounded and bruised, I began to haul the boat, filled with water, towards the vessel, by the shrouds; but the bark had sunk by this time to such a depth, that only a small part of her stern was to be seen, upon which my mate and two other seamen were holding fast by a rope. I threw myself into the water, with the rope of the boat in the mouth, and swam towards them to give them the end to lay hold of, hoping, by our united strength, that we should be able to haul the boat over the stern of the vessel; we everted our utmost efforts, and at this moment I nearly had my thigh broken by a shock of the boat, being between her and the ship. At length we succeeded in hauling her over the stern, but had the misfortune to break a hole in her bottom in this manoeuvre. As soon as my thigh was a little recovered from the blow, I jumped into her with one of the men, and stopped the leak with a piece of his coarse shirt. It was extremely fortunate for us that this man did not know how to swim; it will soon be seen what benefit we derived from his ignorance; had it not been for this we must all have perished. Being unable to swim, he had not stripped, and had thus preserved his coarse shirt, a knife that was in his pocket, and an enormous hat, in the Dutch fashion. The boat being fastened to the rigging, was no sooner cleared of the greatest part of the water than a dog of mine came to me, running along the gunwale; I took him in, thanking Providence for having thus sent provision for a time of necessity. A moment after the dog had entered, the rope broke with a jerk of the vessel, and I found myself drifting away. I called my mate and the other man, who swam to me: the former had fortunately found a small spare top-mast, which served us for a rudder. We assisted the two others to get into the boat, and soon lost sight of our ill-fated bark.

It was then four o'clock in the morning, as I judged by the dawn of day, which began to appear, so that about two hours had elapsed since we were obliged to abandon her. What prevented her from foundering sooner was my having taken on board about one hundred and fifty barrels of biscuit, as many or more casks of flour, and three hundred firkins of butter, all which substances float upon the water, and are soaked through but slowly and by degrees. As soon as we were clear of the wreck, we kept the boat before the wind as well as we could, and when it grew light I perceived several articles that had floated from the vessel. I perceived my box of clothes and linen, which had been carried out of the cabin by the violence of the waves. I felt an emotion of joy. The box contained some bottles of orange and lime water, a few pounds of chocolate, sugar, &c. Reaching over the gunwale of our boat we laid hold of the box, and used every effort to open it on the water, for we could not think of getting it into the boat, being of a size and weight sufficient to sink her. In spite of all our endeavors we could not force open the lid; we were obliged to leave it behind, with all the good things it contained, and to increase our distress we had by this effort almost filled our boat with water, and had more than once nearly sunk her.

We, however, had the good fortune to pick up thirteen onions; we saw many more, but were unable to reach them. These thirteen onions and my dog, without a single drop of fresh water, or any liquor whatever, were all that we had to subsist upon. We were, according to my computation, above fifty leagues from land, having neither mast, sails, nor oars, to direct us, nor any kind of articles besides the knife of the sailor who could not swim, his shirt, a piece of which we already used to stop the leak in our boat, and his wide trousers. We this day cut the remainder of his shirt into strips, which we twisted for rigging, and then fell to work alternately to loosen the planks with which the boat was lined, cutting, by dint of time and patience, all round the heads of the nails that fastened them. Of these planks we made a kind of mast, which we tied to the foremast bench; a piece of board was substituted for a yard, to which we fastened the two parts of the trousers, which served for sails, and assisted us in keeping the boat before the wind, steering with the top-mast as mentioned before.

As the pieces of plank which we had detached from the inside of the boat were too short, and were not sufficient to go quite round the edge, when the sea ran very high, we were obliged, in order to prevent the waves from entering the boat, to lie down several times along the gunwale on each side, with our backs to the water, and thus with our bodies to repel the surf, while the other, with the Dutch hat, was incessantly employed in bailing out the water; besides which the boat continued to make water at the leak, which we were unable entirely to stop.

It was in this melancholy situation, and stark naked, that we kept the boat before the wind as well as we could. The night of the first day after our shipwreck arrived before we had well completed our sail; it grew dark, and we contrived to keep our boat running before the wind, at the rate of about a league an hour. The second day was more calm: we each eat an onion, at different times, and began to feel thirst. In the night of the second day the wind became violent and variable, and sometimes blowing from the north, which caused me great uneasiness, being obliged to steer south, in order to keep the boat before the wind, whereas we could only hope to be saved by proceeding from east to west.

The third day we began to suffer exceedingly, not only from hunger and thirst, but likewise from the heat of the sun, which scorched us in such a manner, that from the neck to the feet our skin was as red and as full of blisters as if we had been burned by a fire. I then seized my dog and plunged the knife in his throat. I cannot even now refrain from weeping at the thought of it; but at the moment I felt not the least compassion for him. We caught his blood in the hat, receiving in our hands and drinking what ran over: we afterwards drank in turn out of the hat, and felt ourselves refreshed. The fourth day the wind was extremely violent, and the sea ran very high, so that we were more than once on the point of perishing; it was on this day in particular that we were obliged to make a rampart of our bodies in order to repel the waves. About noon a ray of hope dawned upon us, but soon vanished.

We perceived a sloop, commanded by captain Southey, which, like my vessel, belonged to the island of Barbadoes, and was bound to Demarara; we could see the crew walking upon the deck, and shouted to them, but were never seen nor heard. Being obliged, by the violence of the gale, to keep our boat before the wind, for fear of foundering, we had passed her a great distance before she crossed us; she steered direct south, and we bearing away to the west. Captain Southey was one of my particular friends. This disappointment so discouraged my two seamen that they refused to endeavor any longer to save their lives. In spite of all I could say, one of them would do nothing, not even bail out the water which gained upon us; I had recourse to entreaties; fell at his knees, but he remained unmoved.

My mate and I, at length, prevailed upon him, by threatening to kill him instantly with the top-mast, which we used to steer by, and to kill ourselves afterwards, to put a period to our misery. This menace made some impression on him, and he resumed his employment of bailing as before.

On this day I set the others the example of eating a piece of the dog with some onions; it was with difficulty that I swallowed a few mouthfuls; but in an hour I felt that this morsel of food had given me vigor. My mate, who was of a much stronger constitution, eat more, which gave me great pleasure; one of the two men likewise tasted it, but the other, whose name was Comings, either would not or could not swallow a morsel.

The fifth day was more calm, and the sea much smoother. At daybreak we perceived an enormous shark, as large as our boat, which followed us several hours, as a prey that was destined for him. We also found in our boat a flying-fish, which had dropped there during the night; we divided it into four parts, which we chewed to moisten our mouths. It was on this day that, when pressed with hunger and despair, my mate, Williams, had the generosity to exhort us to cut off a piece of his thigh to refresh ourselves with the blood, and to support life. In the night we had several showers, with some wind. We tried to get some rain water by wringing the trousers which served us for a sail, but when we caught it in our mouths it proved to be as salt as that of the sea; the trousers having been so often soaked with sea-water, that they, as well as the hat, were quite impregnated with salt. Thus we had no other resource but to open our mouths and catch the drops of rain upon our tongues, in order to cool them: after the shower was over we again fastened the trousers to the mast.

On the sixth day the two seamen, notwithstanding all my remonstrances, drank sea-water, which purged them so excessively that they fell into a kind of delirium, and were of no more service to Williams and me. Both he and I kept a nail in our mouths, and often sprinkled our heads with water to cool them. I perceived myself the better for these ablutions, and that my head was more easy. We tried several times to eat of the dog's flesh, with a morsel of onion; but I thought myself rather fortunate if I could get down three or four mouthfuls. My mate always eat rather more than I could.

The seventh day was fine, with a moderate breeze, and the sea perfectly calm. About noon the two men who had drank sea-water grew so weak that they began to talk wildly, like people who are light-headed, not knowing any longer whether they were at sea or on shore. My mate and I were so weak too that we could scarcely stand on our legs, or steer the boat in our turns, or bail the water from the boat, which made a great deal at the leak.

In the morning of the eighth day, John Comings died, and three hours afterwards George Simpson likewise expired. The same evening, at sunset, we had the inexpressible satisfaction of discovering the high lands on the west point of the island of Tobago. Hope gave us strength. We kept the head of the boat towards the land all night, with a light breeze, and a current which was in our favor. Williams and I were that night in an extraordinary situation, our two comrades lying dead before us, with the land in sight, having very little wind to approach it, and being assisted only by the current, which drove strongly to the westward. In the morning we were not, according to my computation, more than five or six leagues from the land. That happy day was the last of our sufferings at sea. We kept steering the boat the whole day towards the shore, though we were no longer able to stand. In the evening the wind lulled, and it fell calm; but about two o'clock in the morning the current cast us on the beach of the island of Tobago, at the foot of a high shore, between little Tobago and Man-of-War bay, which is the easternmost part of the island. The boat soon bilged with the shock; my unfortunate companion and I crawled to the shore, leaving the bodies of our two comrades in the boat, and the remainder of the dog, which was quite putrid.

We clambered, as well as we could, on all fours, along the high coast, which rose almost perpendicularly to the height of three or four hundred feet. A great quantity of leaves had dropped down to the place where we were, from the numerous trees over our heads; these we collected, and lay down upon them to wait for daylight. When it began to dawn we sought about for water, and found some in the holes of the rocks, but it was brackish, and not fit to drink. We perceived on the rocks around us several kinds of shell-fish, some of which we broke open with a stone, and chewed them to moisten our mouths.

Between eight and nine o'clock we were perceived by a young Caraib, who was sometimes walking and at others swimming towards the boat. As soon as he had reached it he called his companions with loud shouts, making signs of the greatest compassion. His comrades instantly followed him, and swam towards us, having perceived us almost at the same time.

The oldest, who was about sixty, approached us, with the two youngest, whom we afterwards found to be his son and son-in-law. At the sight of us the tears flowed from their eyes; I endeavored by words and signs to make them comprehend that we had been nine days at sea, in want of every thing. They understood a few French words, and signified that they would fetch a boat to convey us to their hut. The old man took a handkerchief from his head and tied it round mine, and one of the young Caraibs gave Williams his straw hat; the other swam round the projecting rock and brought us a calabash of fresh water, some cakes of cassava, and a piece of broiled fish, but we could not eat. The two others took the two corpses out of the boat, and laid them upon the rock, after which all three of them hauled the boat out of the water. They then left us, with marks of the utmost compassion, and went to fetch their canoe.

About noon they returned in their canoe, to the number of six, and brought with them, in an earthen pot, some soup which we thought delicious. We took a little, but my stomach was so weak that I immediately cast it up again. Williams did not vomit at all. In less than two hours we arrived at Man-of-War bay, where the huts of the Caraibs are situated. They had only one hammock, in which they laid me and the women made us a very agreeable mess of herbs and broth of quatracas and pigeons. They bathed my wounds, which were full of worms, with a decoction of tobacco and other plants. Every morning the man lifted me out of the hammock, and carried me in his arms beneath a lemon tree, where he covered me with plantain leaves to screen me from the sun. There they anointed our bodies with a kind of oil to cure the blisters raised by the sun. Our compassionate hosts even had the generosity to give each of us a shirt and a pair of trousers, which they had procured from ships that came from time to time to trade with them for turtles and tortoise shell.

After they had cleansed my wounds of the vermin, they kept me with my legs suspended in the air, and anointed them morning and evening with an oil extracted from the tail of a small crab, resembling what the English call the soldier-crab, because its shell is red. They take a certain quantity of these crabs, bruise the ends of their tails, and put them to digest in a large shell upon the fire. It was with this ointment that they healed my wounds, covering them with nothing but plantain leaves.

Thanks to the nourishing food procured us by the Caraibs, and their humane attention, I was able, in about three weeks, to support myself upon crutches, like a person recovering from a severe illness. The natives flocked from all parts of the island to see us, and never came empty handed; sometimes bringing eggs, and at others fowls, which were given with pleasure, and accepted with gratitude. We even had visiters from the island of Trinidad. I cut my name with a knife upon several boards, and gave them to different Caraibs, to show them to any ships which chance might conduct to the coast. We almost despaired of seeing any arrive, when a sloop from Oronoko, laden with mules and bound to St. Pierre, in the island of Martinique, touched at the sandy point on the west side of Tobago. The Indians showed the crew a plank upon which my name was carved, and acquainted them with our situation. Upon the arrival of this vessel

at St. Pierre, those on board related the circumstance. Several merchants of my acquaintance, who traded under Dutch colors, happened
to be there; they transmitted the information to my owners, Messrs.
Roscoe and Nyles, who instantly despatched a small vessel in quest of
us. After living about nine weeks with this benevolent and charitable
tribe of savages, I embarked and left them, when my regret was
equal to the joy and surprise I had experienced at meeting with them.

When we were ready to depart they furnished us with an abun-
dant supply of bananas, figs, yams, fowls, fish, and fruits; particularly
oranges and lemons. I had nothing to give them as an acknowledgment
of their generous treatment but my boat, which they had repaired,
and used for occasionally visiting the nests of turtles: being larger
than their canoes, it was much more fit for that purpose. Of this I
made them a present, and would have given them my blood. My
friend, captain Young, assisted me to remunerate my benefactors. He
gave me all the rum he had with him, being about seven or eight
bottles, which I likewise presented to them. He also gave them several
shirts and trousers, some knives, fish-hooks, sail-cloth for the boat,
with needles and ropes.

At length, after two days spent in preparations for our departure,
we were obliged to separate. They came down to the beach to the
number of about thirty, men, women and children, and all appeared
to feel the sincerest sorrow, especially the old man, who had acted
like a father to me. When the vessel left the bay, the tears flowed
from our eyes, which still continued fixed upon them. They remained
standing in a line upon the shore till they lost sight of us. As we
set sail about nine o'clock in the morning, steering north-east, and
as Man-of-War bay is situated at the north-east point of the island,
we were a long time in sight of each other. I still recollect the moment
when they disappeared from my sight, and the profound regret which
filled my heart. I feared that I should never again be so happy as I
had been among them. I loved them, and will continue to love my
dear Caraibs as long as I live; I would shed my blood for the first of
those benevolent savages that might stand in need of my assistance,
if chance should ever bring one of them to Europe, or my destiny
should again conduct me to their island.

In three days we arrived at Barbadoes. I continued to have a
violent oppression on my breast, which checked respiration, and was
not yet able to go without crutches. We received from the whole
island marks of the most tender interest, and the most generous
compassion; the benevolence of the inhabitants was unbounded. The
celebrated Dr. Hilery, the author of a treatise on the diseases peculiar
to that island, came to see me, together with Dr. Lilihorn. They
prescribed various remedies, but without effect. Both Williams and
myself were unable to speak without the greatest difficulty. Williams

remained at Barbadoes, but I, being more affected, and less robust, was advised to return to Europe. In compliance with their advice I went to London, where I was attended by doctors Reeves, Akenside, Schomberg, and the most celebrated physicians of that metropolis, who gave me all the assistance within the power of their art, from which I received scarcely any relief. At length, after I had been about a week in London, Dr. Alexander Russell, on his return from Bath, heard my case mentioned. He came to see me, and with his accustomed humanity promised to undertake my cure, without any fee; but he candidly acknowledged that it would be both tedious and expensive. I replied that the generosity of the inhabitants of Barbadoes had rendered me easy on that head, entreating him to prescribe for me, and thanking him for his obliging offers.

As he had practised for a long time at Aleppo, he had there seen great numbers afflicted with the same malady as myself, produced by long thirst in traversing the deserts of Africa. He ordered me to leave town to enjoy a more wholesome air. I took a lodging at Homerton, near Hackney; there he ordered me to be bathed every morning, confining me to asses' milk as my only food, excepting a few new-laid eggs, together with moderate exercise, and a ride on horseback every day. After about a month of this regimen he ordered a goat to be brought every morning to my bedside; about five o'clock I drank a glass of her milk, quite hot, and slept upon it. He then allowed me to take some light chicken broth, with a morsel of the wing. By means of this diet my malady was in a great degree removed in the space of about five months, and I was in a state to resume any occupation I pleased; but my constitution has ever since been extremely delicate, and my stomach in particular very weak.

[5]

Loss of the Brig *Tyrrel*

THIS STORY of the loss of an unimportant brigantine and the deaths of a few obscure men illustrates the accidents through which we learn of minor incidents of the past. Mate Purnell, the only survivor of the wreck of the *Tyrrel,* published an eight-page account of his experience in London in 1766. Compilers of anthologies were interested in horrors and in widely known tragedies, but the most important point of all was availability; Purnell's short report found its way into Archibald Duncan's *Mariner's Chronicle* and thence into almost all the other anthologies.

This narrative is taken from Thomas.

LOSS OF THE

BRIG TYRREL.

IN addition to the many dreadful shipwrecks already narrated, the following, which is a circumstantial account given by T. Purnell, chief mate of the brig Tyrrel, Arthur Cochlan, commander, and the only person among the whole crew who had the good fortune to escape, claims our particular attention.

On Saturday, June 28th, 1759, they sailed from New York to Sandy Hook, and came to an anchor, waiting for the captain's coming down with a new boat, and some other articles. Accordingly he came on board early the succeeding morning, and the boat was cleared, hoisted in, stowed, and lashed. At eight o'clock A.M. they weighed anchor, sailed out of Sandy Hook, and the same day, at noon, took their departure from the highland Neversink, and proceeded on their passage to Antigua. As soon as they made sail, the captain ordered the boat to be cast loose, in order that she might be painted, with the oars, rudder, and tiller, which job he (the captain) undertook to do himself.

At four P.M. they found the vessel made a little more water than usual; but as it did not cause much additional labor at the pump, nothing was thought of it. At eight, the leak did not seem to increase. At twelve, it began to blow hard in squalls, which caused the vessel to lie down very much, whereby it was apprehended she wanted more ballast. Thereupon the captain came on deck, being the starboard watch; and close-reefed both top-sails.

At four A.M. the weather moderated—let out both reefs. At eight it became still more moderate, and they made more sail, and set the top-gallant sails; the weather was still thick and hazy. There was no further observation taken at present, except that the vessel made more water. The captain was now chiefly employed in painting the boat, oars, rudder, and tiller.

On Monday, June 30th, at four P.M., the wind was at E.N.E., freshened very much, and blew so very hard as occasioned the brig to lie along in such a manner as caused general alarm. The captain was now earnestly entreated to put for New York, or steer for the capes of Virginia. At eight, took in top-gallant sail, and close reefed both top-sails, still making more weather. Afterwards the weather became still more moderate and fair, and they made more sail.

July 1st, at four A.M., it began to blow in squalls very hard; took in one reef in each top-sail, and continued so until eight A.M., the weather being still thick and hazy.—No observation.

The next day she made still more water, but as every watch pumped it out, this was little regarded. At four P.M. took a second reef out of each top-sail, close reefed both, and down top-gallant yard; the gale still increasing.

At four A.M. the wind got round to north, and there was no likelihood of its abating. At eight, the captain, well satisfied that she was very crank and ought to have had more ballast, agreed to make for Bacon Island road, in North Carolina; and in the very act of wearing her, a sudden gust of wind laid her down on her beam ends, and she never rose again! At this time Mr. Purnell was lying in the cabin, with his clothes on, not having pulled them off since they left land. Having been rolled out of his bed, (on his chest,) with great difficulty he reached the round-house door. The first salutation he met with was from the step-ladder that went from the quarter-deck to the poop, which knocked him against the companion; (a lucky circumstance for those below, as, by laying the ladder against the companion, it served both him and the rest of the people who were in the steerage as a conveyance to windward;) having transported the two after guns forward to bring her more by the head, in order to make her hold a better wind: thus they got through the aftermost gun-port on the quarter-deck, and being all on her broadside, every movable rolled to leeward; and as the vessel overset, so did the boat, and turned bottom upwards. Her lashings being cast loose by order of the captain, and having no other prospect of saving their lives but by the boat, Purnell, with two others, and the cabin boy, who were excellent swimmers, plunged into the water, and with great difficulty righted her, when she was brimful, and washing with the water's edge. They then made fast the end of the main-sheet to the ring in her stern-post, and those who were in the fore-chains sent down the end of the boom-tackle, to which they made fast the boat's painter, and by which they lifted her a little out of the water, so that she swam about two or three inches free, but almost full. They then put the cabin boy into her, and gave him a bucket that happened to float by, and he bailed away as quick as he could, and soon after another person got in with another bucket, and in a short time got all the water out of her. They then put two long oars that were stowed in the larboard quarter of the Tyrrel into the boat, and pulled or rowed right to windward; for, as the wreck drifted, she made a dreadful appearance in the water; and Mr. Purnell and two of the people put off from the wreck, in search of the oars, rudder and tiller. After a long time they succeeded in picking them all up, one after another. They then returned to their wretched companions, who were all overjoyed to see them, having given them up for lost.

By this time night drew on very fast. While they were rowing in the boat, some small quantity of white biscuit (Mr. Purnell supposed about half a peck) floated in a small cask out of the round-house; but before it came to hand, it was so soaked with salt water that it was almost in a fluid state; and about double the quantity of common ship-biscuit likewise floated, which was in like manner soaked. This was all the provisions that they had; not a drop of fresh water could they get; neither could the carpenter get at any of the tools to scuttle her sides, for, could this have been accomplished, they might have saved plenty of provisions and water.

By this time it was almost dark. Having got one compass, it was determined to quit the wreck, and take their chance in the boat, which was nineteen feet six inches long, and six feet four inches broad: Mr. Purnell supposes it was now about nine o'clock: it was very dark. They had run three hundred and sixty miles by their dead reckoning, on a S.E. by E. course. The number in the boat was seventeen in all; the boat was very deep, and little hopes were entertained of either seeing land or surviving long. The wind got round to westward, which was the course they wanted to steer; but it began to blow and rain so very hard, that they were obliged to keep the boat before the wind and sea in order to preserve her above water. Soon after they had put off from the wreck the boat shipped two heavy seas, one after another, so that they were obliged to keep her before the wind and sea; for had she shipped another sea, she certainly would have swamped with them.

By sunrise the next morning, July 3d, they judged that they had been running E.S.E., which was contrary to their wishes. The wind dying away, the weather became very moderate. The compass which they had saved proved of no utility, one of the people having trod upon and broken it; it was accordingly thrown overboard. They now proposed to make a sail of frocks and trousers, but they had got neither needles nor sewing-twine: one of the people however had a needle in his knife, and another several fishing lines in his pockets, which were unlaid by some, and others were employed in ripping their frocks and trousers. By sunset they had provided a tolerable lugsail: having split one of the boat's thwarts, (which was of yellow deal,) with a very large knife which one of the crew had in his pocket, they made a yard and lashed it together by the strands of the fore-top-gallant halliards, that were thrown into the boat promiscuously. They also made a mast of one of the long oars, and set their sails with sheets and tacks made out of the strands of the top-gallant halliards. Their only guide was the north star. They had a tolerably good breeze all night; and the whole of the next day, July 4th, the weather continued very moderate, and the people were in as good spirits as their dreadful situation would permit.

July 5th, the wind and weather continued much the same, and they knew by the north star that they were standing in for land. The next day Mr. Purnell observed some of the men drinking salt water, and seeming rather fatigued. At this time they imagined the wind had got round to the southward, and they steered, as they thought, by the north star, to the north-west quarter; but on the 7th, the wind had got back to the northward and blew very fresh. They got their oars out the greatest part of the night; and the next day, the wind still dying away, the people labored alternately at the oars, without distinction. About noon the wind sprung up so that they lay on their oars, and, as they thought, steered about N.N.W., and continued so until about eight or nine o'clock in the morning of July 9th, when they all thought they were upon soundings, by the coldness of the water. They were in general in very good spirits. The weather continued still thick and hazy, and by the north star they found that they had been steering about north by west.

July 10.—The people had drank so much salt water, that it came from them as clear as it was before they drank it; and Mr. Purnell perceived that the second mate had lost a considerable share of his strength and spirits; and also, at noon, that the carpenter was delirious, his malady increasing every hour; about dusk he had almost overset the boat, by attempting to throw himself overboard, and otherwise behaving quite violently. As his strength, however, failed him, he became more manageable, and they got him to lie down in the middle of the boat, among some of the people. Mr. Purnell drank once a little salt water, but could not relish it; he preferred his own urine, which he drank occasionally as he made it. Soon after sunset the second mate lost his speech. Mr. Purnell desired him to lean his head on him: he died, without a groan or struggle, on the 11th of July, being the ninth day they were in the boat. In a few minutes after, the carpenter expired, almost in a similar manner. These melancholy scenes rendered the situation of the survivors more dreadful; it is impossible to describe their feelings. Despair became general; every man imagined his own dissolution was near. They all now went to prayers; some in the Welch language, some in Irish, and others in English; then, after a little deliberation, they stripped the two dead men and hove them overboard.

The weather being now very mild, and almost calm, they turned to, cleaned the boat, and resolved to make their sail larger out of the frocks and trousers of the two deceased men. Purnell got the captain to lie down with the rest of the people, the boatswain and one man excepted, who assisted him in making the sail larger, which they had completed by six or seven o'clock in the afternoon, having made a shroud out of the boat's painter, which served as a shifting back-stay. Purnell also fixed his red flannel waistcoat at the mast head, as a signal the most likely to be seen.

Soon after this some of them observed a sloop at a great distance, coming, as they thought, from the land. This roused every man's spirits: they got out their oars, at which they labored alternately, exerting all their remaining strength to come up with her; but night coming on, and the sloop getting a fresh breeze of wind, they lost sight of her, which occasioned a general consternation; however, the appearance of the north star, which they kept on their starboard bow, gave them hopes that they stood in for land. This night one William Wathing died; he was sixty-four years of age, and had been to sea fifty years: quite worn out with fatigue and hunger, he earnestly prayed, to the last moment, for a drop of water to cool his tongue. Early the next morning Hugh Williams also died, and in the course of the day, another of the crew; entirely exhausted, they both expired without a groan.

Early in the morning of July 13th, it began to blow very fresh, and increased so much that they were obliged to furl their sail, and keep their boat before the wind and sea, which drove them off soundings. In the evening their gunner died. The weather now becoming moderate, and the wind in the south-west quarter, they made sail, not one of them being able to row or pull an oar at any rate; they ran all this night with a fine breeze.

The next morning, July 14th, two more of the crew died, and in the evening they also lost the same number. They found they were on soundings again, and concluded the wind had got round to the north-west quarter. They stood in for the land all this night, and early on July 15th, two others died: the deceased were thrown overboard as soon as their breath had departed. The weather was now thick and hazy, and they were still certain that they were on soundings.

The cabin boy was seldom required to do any thing, and as his intellects at this time were very good, and his understanding clear, it was the opinion of Mr. Purnell that he would survive them all, but he prudently kept his thoughts to himself. The captain seemed likewise tolerably well, and to have kept up his spirits. On account of the haziness of the weather, they could not so well know how they steered in the day-time, as at night; for, whenever the north star appeared, they endeavored to keep it on their starboard bow, by which means they were certain of making the land some time or other. In the evening two more of the crew died; also, before sunrise, one Thomas Philpot, an old, experienced seaman, and very strong; he departed rather convulsed: having latterly lost the power of articulation, his meaning could not be comprehended. He was a native of Belfast, Ireland, and had no family. The survivors found it very difficult to heave his body overboard, as he was a very corpulent man.

About six or seven the next morning, July 16th, they stood in for land, according to the best of their judgement; the weather, still thick and hazy. Purnell now prevailed upon the captain and boatswain of the boat to lie down in the fore part of the boat, to bring her more by the head, in order to make her hold a better wind. In the evening the cabin boy, who lately appeared so well, breathed his last, leaving behind the captain, the boatswain, and Mr. Purnell.

The next morning, July 17th, Purnell asked his two companions if they thought they could eat any of the boy's flesh; and having expressed an inclination to try, and the boy being quite cold, he cut the inside of his thigh, a little above his knee, and gave a piece to the captain and boatswain, reserving a small piece for himself; but so weak were their stomachs that none of them could swallow a morsel of it; the body was therefore thrown overboard.

Early in the morning of the 18th, Mr. Purnell found both of his companions dead and cold! Thus destitute, he began to think of his own dissolution; though feeble, his understanding was still clear, and his spirits as good as his forlorn situation would possibly admit. By the color and coldness of the water, he knew he was not far from land, and still maintained hopes of making it. The weather continued very foggy. He lay to all this night, which was very dark, with the boat's head to the northward.

In the morning of the 19th it begain to rain; it cleared up in the afternoon, and the wind died away; still Purnell was convinced he was on soundings.

On the 20th, in the afternoon, he thought he saw land, and stood in for it; but night coming on, and it being now very dark, he lay to, fearing he might get on some rocks or shoals.

July 21st, the weather was very fine all the morning, but in the afternoon it became thick and hazy. Purnell's spirits still remained good, but his strength was almost exhausted: he still drank his own water occasionally.

On the 22d, he saw some barnacles on the boat's rudder, very similar to the spawn of an oyster, which filled him with great hopes of being near to land. He unshipped the rudder, and scraping them off with his knife, found they were of a salt fishy substance, and eat them; he was now so weak, and the boat having a great motion, that he found it a difficult task to ship the rudder.

At sunrise, July 23d, he became so sure that he saw land, that his spirits were considerably raised. In the middle of this day he got up, leaned his back against the mast, and received succor from the sun, having previously contrived to steer the boat in this position. The next day he saw, at a very great distance, some kind of a sail, which he judged was coming from the land, which he soon lost sight of. In the middle of the day he got up, and received warmth from the sun as before. He stood on all night for the land.

Very early in the morning of the 25th, after drinking his morning draught, to his inexpressible joy, he saw, while the sun was rising, a sail, and when the sun was up, found she was a two-mast vessel. He was, however, considerably perplexed, not knowing what to do, as she was a great distance astern and to the leeward. In order to watch her motion better, he tacked about. Soon after this he perceived she was standing on her starboard tack, which was the same he had been standing on for many hours. He saw she approached him very fast, and he lay to, for some time, till he believed she was within two miles of the boat, but still to leeward; therefore he thought it best to steer larger, when he found she was a topsail schooner, nearing him very fast. He continued to edge down towards her, until he had brought her about two points under his lee-bow, having it in his power to spring his luff, or bear away. By this time she was within half a mile, and he saw some of the people standing forward on her deck, and waving for him to come under their lee-bow. At the distance of about two hundred yards, they hove the schooner up in the wind, and kept her so until Purnell got alongside, when they threw him a rope, still keeping the schooner in the wind. They now interrogated him very closely; by the manner the boat and oars were painted, they imagined she belonged to a man-of-war, and that they had run away with her from some of his majesty's ships at Halifax, consequently that they would be liable to some punishment if they took him up; they also thought, as the captain and boatswain were lying dead in the boat, they might expose themselves to some contagious disorder. Thus they kept Purnell in suspense for some time. They told him they had made the land that morning from the mast-head, and that they were running along shore for Marblehead, to which place they belonged, and where they expected to be the next morning. At last they told him he might come on board; which, as he said, he could not do without assistance;

when the captain ordered two of his men to help him. They conducted him aft on the quarter-deck, where they left him resting against the companion. They were now for casting the boat adrift, when Purnell told them she was not above a month old, built at New York, and if they would hoist her in, it would pay them well for their trouble. To this they agreed, and having thrown the two corpses overboard, and taken out the clothes that were left by the deceased, they hoisted her and made sail.

Being now on board, Purnell asked for a little water; captain Castleman (for that was his name) ordered one of his sons (having two on board) to fetch him some; when he came in with the water, his father looked to see how much he was bringing him, and thinking it too much, threw a part of it away, and desired him to give the remainder, which he drank, being the first fresh water he had tasted for twenty-three days. As he leaned all this time against the companion, he became very cold, and begged to go below: the captain ordered two men to help him down to the cabin, where they left him sitting on the cabin deck, leaning upon the lockers, all hands being now engaged in hoisting in and securing the boat. This done, all hands went down to breakfast, except the man at the helm. They made some soup for Purnell, which he thought very good, but at that time could eat but very little, and in consequence of his late draughts, he had broke out in many parts of his body, so that he was in great pain whenever he stirred. They made a bed for him out of an old sail, and behaved very attentive. While they were at breakfast a squall of wind came on, which called them all upon deck; during their absence, Purnell took up a stone bottle, and without smelling or tasting it, but thinking it was rum, took a hearty draught of it, and found it to be sweet oil; having placed it where he found it, he lay down.

They still ran along shore with the land in sight, and were in great hopes of getting into port that night, but the wind dying away, they did not get in till nine o'clock the next night. All this time Purnell remained like a child; some one or other was always with him, to give whatever he wished to eat or drink.

As soon as they came to anchor, captain Castleman went on shore, and returned on board the next morning, with the owner, John Pickett, Esq. Soon after, they got Purnell into a boat and carried him on shore; but he was still so very feeble, that he was obliged to be supported by two men. Mr. Pickett took a very genteel lodging for him, and hired a nurse to attend him; he was immediately put to bed, and afterwards provided with a change of clothes. In the course of the day he was visited by every doctor in the town, who all gave him hopes of recovering; but told him it would be some time; for the stronger the constitution, (said they,) the longer it takes to recover its lost strength. Though treated with the utmost tenderness and humanity, it was three weeks before he was able to come down stairs. He stayed in Marblehead two months, during which he lived very comfortably, and gradually recovered his strength. The brig's boat and oars were sold for ninety-five dollars, which paid all his expenses, and procured him a passage to Boston. The nails of his fingers and toes withered away almost to nothing, and did not begin to grow for many months after.

[6]

A Famine in the American Ship *Peggy*

WHEN POE had his characters in *The Narrative of Arthur Gordon Pym* draw lots to determine who should be sacrificed that the others might live, he drew directly upon this narrative of the *Peggy*, using the same order of events and the same words. Poe's whole novel was based on this genre, as the title indicates, and the modern psychological interpretations of *Pym* ignore the factual background from which Poe worked. One complication was that Poe knew almost nothing of the sea; consequently *Pym* is a farrago of nautical absurdities combined with suspenseful action.

The *Peggy* was making the short voyage from the Azores to New York, but her provisioning was certainly scanty and her luck bad. This account is taken from the same Thomas anthology that Poe used.

AN EXTRAORDINARY FAMINE IN THE

AMERICAN SHIP PEGGY,

On her return from the Azores to New York,

in 1765.

F AMINE frequently leads men to the commission of the most horrible excesses: insensible, on such occasions, to the appeals of nature and reason, man assumes the character of a beast of prey; he is deaf to every representation, and coolly mediates the death of his fellow-creature.

One of these scenes, so afflicting to humanity, was, in the year 1765, exhibited in the brigantine the Peggy, David Harrison, commander, freighted by certain merchants of New York, and bound to the Azores. She arrived without accident at Fayal, one of those islands, and having disposed of her cargo, took on board a lading of wine and spirits. On the 24th of October, of the same year, she set sail on her return to New York.

On the 29th, the wind, which had till then been favorable, suddenly shifted. Violent storms, which succeeded each other, almost without interruption, during the month of November, did much damage to the vessel. In spite of all the exertions of the crew, and the experience of the captain, the masts went by the board, and all the sails, excepting one, were torn to rags: and, to add to their distress, several leaks were discovered in the hold.

At the beginning of December, the wind abated a little, but the vessel was driven out of her course; and, destitute of masts, sails, and rigging, she was perfectly unmanageable, and drifted to and fro, at the mercy of the waves. This, however, was the smallest evil; another of a much more alarming nature soon manifested itself. Upon examining the state of the provisions, they were found to be almost totally exhausted. In this deplorable situation, the crew had no hope of relief, but from chance.

A few days after this unpleasant discovery, two vessels were descried early one morning, and a transient ray of hope cheered the unfortunate crew of the Peggy. The sea ran so high as to prevent captain Harrison from approaching the ships, which were soon out of sight. The disappointed seamen, who were in want of every thing, then fell upon the wine and brandy, with which the ship was laden. They allotted to the captain two small jars of water, each containing about a gallon, being the remainder of their stock. Some days elapsed, during which the men, in some measure, appeased the painful cravings of hunger, by incessant intoxication.

On the fourth day, a ship was observed bearing towards them, in full sail: no time was lost in making signals of distress, and the crew had the inexpressible satisfaction to perceive that they were answered. The sea was sufficiently calm to permit the two vessels to approach each other. The strangers seemed much affected by the account of their sufferings and misfortunes, and promised them a certain quantity of biscuit; but it was not immediately sent on board, the captain alleging, as an excuse for the delay, that he had just begun a nautical observation, which he was desirous to finish. However unreasonable such a pretext appeared, under the present circumstances, the famished crew of the Peggy was obliged to submit. The time mentioned by the captain had nearly expired, when, to their extreme mortification, the latter regardless of his promise, crowded all his sails and bore away. No language is adequate to describe the despair and consternation which then overwhelmed the crew. Enraged, and destitute of hope they fell upon whatever they had spared till then. The only animals that remained on board were a couple of pigeons and a cat, which were devoured in an instant. The only favor they showed the captain was, to reserve for him the head of the cat. He afterwards declared, that however disgusting it would have been on any other occasion, he thought it, at that moment, a treat exquisitely delicious. The unfortunate men then supported their existence by living on oil, candles, and leather, and these were entirely consumed by the 28th of December.

From that day until the 13th of January, it is impossible to tell, in what manner they subsisted. Captain Harrison had been for some time unable to leave his cabin, being confined to his bed by a severe fit of the gout. On the last mentioned day, the sailors went to him in a body, with the mate at their head; the latter acted as spokesman, and after an affecting representation of the deplorable state to which they were reduced, declared that it was necessary to sacrifice one, in order to save the rest; adding, that their resolution was irrevocably fixed, and that they intended to cast lots for the victim.

The captain, a tender and humane man, could not hear such a proposition without shuddering; he represented to them that they were men, and ought to regard each other as brethren; that by such an assassination, they would forever consign themselves to universal execration, and commanded them, with all his authority, to relinquish the idea of committing such an atrocious crime. The captain was silent; but he had spoken to deaf men. They all with one voice replied, that it was indifferent to them, whether he approved of their resolution or not; that they had only acquainted him with it, out of respect, and because he would run the same risk as themselves; adding that, in the general misfortune, all command and distinction were at an end. With these words, they left him, and went upon deck, where the lots were drawn.

A negro, who was on board and belonged to captain Harrison, was the victim. It is more than probable, that the lot had been consulted only for the sake of form, and that the wretched black was proscribed, the moment the sailors first formed their resolution. They instantly sacrified him. One of the crew tore out his liver and devoured it, without having the patience to dress it by broiling, or in any other manner. He was soon afterwards taken ill, and died the following day in convulsions, and with all the symptoms of madness. Some of his comrades proposed to keep his body to live upon, after the negro was consumed; but this advice was rejected by the majority, doubtless on account of the malady which had carried him off. He was, therefore, thrown overboard, and consigned to the deep.

The captain, in the intervals, when he was least tormented by the gout, was not more exempt from the attacks of hunger, than the rest of the crew, but he resisted all the persuasions of his men to partake of their horrid repast. He contented himself with the water which had been assigned to him, mixing it with a small quantity of spirits, and this was the only sustenance he took during the whole period of his distress.

The body of the negro, equally divided, and eaten with the greatest economy, lasted till the 26th of January. On the 29th, the famished crew deliberated upon selecting a second victim. They again came to inform the captain of their intention, and he appeared to give his consent, fearing lest the enraged sailors might have recourse to the lot without him. They left it with him to fix upon any method that he should think proper. The captain, summoning all his strength, wrote upon small pieces of paper, the name of each man who was then on board the brigantine, folded them up, put them into a hat, and shook them well together. The crew, meanwhile, preserved an awful silence; each eye was fixed, and each mouth was open, while terror was strongly impressed upon every countenance. With a trembling hand, one of them drew, from the hat, the fatal billet, which he delivered to the captain, who opened it and read aloud the name of DAVID FLATT. The unfortunate man, on whom the lot had fallen, appeared perfectly resigned to his fate:—"My friends, (said he to his companions,) the only favor I request of you, is, not to keep me long in pain; dispatch me as speedily as you did the negro." Then turning to the man who had performed the first execution, he added:—"It is you, I choose to give me the mortal blow." He requested an hour to prepare himself for death, to which his comrades could only reply with tears. Meanwhile, compassion, and the remonstrances of the captain, prevailed over the hunger of the most hard-hearted. They unanimously resolved to defer the sacrifice till eleven o'clock the following morning. Such a short reprieve afforded very little consolation to FLATT.

The certainty of dying the next day made such a deep impression upon the mind, that his body, which, for above a month, had withstood the almost total privation of nourishment, sank beneath it. He was seized with a violent fever, and his state was so much aggravated by a delirium, with which it was accompanied, that some of the sailors proposed to kill him immediately, in order to terminate his sufferings. The majority, however, adhered to the resolution which had been taken, of waiting till the following morning.

At ten o'clock in the morning of the 30th of January, a large fire was already made to dress the limbs of the unfortunate victim, when a sail was descried, at a distance. A favorable wind drove her towards the Peggy, and she proved to be the Susan, returning from Virginia, and bound to London.

The captain could not refrain from tears at the affecting account of the sufferings endured by the famished crew. He lost no time in affording them relief, supplying them immediately with provisions and rigging, and offered to convoy the Peggy to London. The distance from New York, their proximity to the English coast, together with the miserable state of the brigantine, induced the two captains to proceed to England. The voyage was prosperous; only two men died; all the others gradually recovered their strength. Flatt himself was restored to perfect health, after having been so near the gates of death.

[7]

Loss of His Majesty's Ship *Phoenix*

This narrative of the loss of the *Phoenix*—apparently a strong, well-officered, and well-manned ship—gives a very good picture of the plight of even the best ships in the hurricanes of the Jamaica Station. Ten other ships were lost in the same storm. Lieutenant Archer's letter has considerable interest of its own, with its staccato dialogue, its family boastfulness, and its references to Sir Hyde Parker's "condescension." Parker later was Nelson's superior at the Battle of Copenhagen; his willingness to allow Archer to take responsibility close to rocks and seeking help at Port Royal may explain his lack of cooperation when Nelson was attacking the batteries of Denmark.

The very first part of the letter is largely concerned with Archer's hope of capturing Spanish or American ships. Any ships or cargoes taken were sold, and the money was divided among the crewmen of the successful ships. Archer's first lieutenant's share might have been large if a convoy had been captured.

One comment of Archer's probably would not have surprised any person of his own time but is a little startling in the twentieth century. Few people now would make the quick shift from detailing catastrophe to praise of God: "Out of the four men-of-war that were there, not one was in being at the end of that time, and not a soul alive but those left of our crew. Many of the houses where we had been so merry, were so completely destroyed, that scarcely a vestige remained to mark where they stood. Thy works are wonderful, O God! praised be thy holy name!"

This account is from Thomas, who gives no source for Archer's letter. Probably it first appeared in some newspaper.

HIS MAJESTY'S SHIP PHOENIX,

Off the Island of Cuba,

in the year 1780.

T HE Phoenix, of forty-four guns, captain Sir Hyde Parker, was lost in a hurricane, off Cuba, in the year 1780. The same hurricane destroyed the Thunderer, seventy-four; Stirling Castle, sixty-four; La Blanche, forty-two; Laurel, twenty-eight; Andromeda, twenty-eight; Deal Castle, twenty-four; Scarborough, twenty; Beaver's Prize, sixteen; Barbadoes, fourteen; and Victor, ten guns. Lieutenant Archer was first lieutenant of the Phoenix at the time she was lost. His narrative in a letter to his mother contains a most correct and animated account of one of the most awful events in the service. It is so simple and natural as to make the reader feel himself on board the Phoenix. Every circumstance is detailed with feeling, and powerful appeals are continually made to the heart. It must likewise afford considerable pleasure to observe the devout spirit of a seaman frequently bursting forth, and imparting sublimity to the relation.

At sea, June 30, 1780.

My Dearest Madam,

I am now going to give you an account of our last cruise in the Phoenix; and must premise, that should any one see it beside yourself, they must put this construction on it—that it was originally intended for the eyes of a mother, and a mother only, as, upon that supposition, my feelings may be tolerated. You will also meet with a number of sea terms, which, if you don't understand, why, I cannot help you, as I am unable to give a sea description in any other words.

To begin then:—On the 2d of August, 1780, we weighed and sailed for [from] Port Royal, bound from [for?] Pensacola, having two store-ships under convoy, and to see safe in; then cruise off the Havannah, and in the gulf of Mexico, for six weeks. In a few days

53

we made the two sandy islands, that look as if they had just risen out of the sea, or fallen from the sky; inhabited nevertheless, by upwards of three hundred English, who get their bread by catching turtles and parrots, and raising vegetables, which they exchange with ships that pass, for clothing and a few of the luxuries of life, as rum, &c.

About the 12th we arrived at Pensacola, without any thing remarkable happening, except our catching a vast quantity of fish, sharks, dolphins, and bonettos. On the 13th sailed singly, and on the 14th had a very gale of wind at north, right off the land, so that we soon left the sweet place, Pensacola, a distance astern. We then looked into the Havannah, saw a number of ships there, and knowing that some of them were bound round the bay, we cruised in the track: a fortnight, however, passed, and not a single ship hove in sight to cheer our spirits. We then took a turn or two round the gulf, but not near enough to be seen from the shore. Vera Cruz we expected would have made us happy, but the same luck still continued; day followed day, and no sail. The dollar bag began to grow a little bulky, for every one had lost two or three times, and no one had won: (this was a small gambling party entered into by Sir Hyde and ourselves; every one put a dollar into a bag, and fixed on a day when we should see a sail, but no two persons were to name the same day, and whoever guessed right first was to have the bag.)

Being now tired of our situation, and glad the cruise was almost out, for we found the navigation very dangerous, owing to unaccountable currents; so shaped our course for cape Antonio. The next day the man at the mast-head, at about one o'clock in the afternoon, called out: "A sail upon the weather bow! Ha! Ha! Mr. Spaniard, I think we have you at last. Turn out all hands! Make sail. All hands! give chase!" There was scarcely any occasion for this order, for the sound of a sail being in sight flew like wildfire through the ship, and every sail was set, in an instant, almost before the orders were given. A lieutenant at the mast-head, with a spy glass, "What is she?" "A large ship studding athwart before the wind. P-o-r-t! Keep her away! set the studding sails ready!" Up comes the little doctor, rubbing his hands; "Ha! Ha! I have won the bag." "The devil take you and the bag; look, what's ahead will fill all our bags." Mast-head again; "Two more sail on the larboard beam!" "Archer, go up and see what you can make of them." "Upon deck there; I see a whole fleet of twenty sail coming right before the wind." "Confound the luck of it; this is some convoy or other, but we must try if we can pick some of them out." "Haul down the studding sails! Luff! bring her to the wind! Let us see what we can make of them."

About five we got pretty near them, and found them to be twenty-six sail of Spanish merchantmen, under convoy of three line-of-battle ships, one of which chased us; but when she found we were playing with her (for the old Phoenix had heels) she left chase, and joined the convoy; which they drew up into a lump, and placed themselves at the outside; but we kept smelling about till after dark. O, for the Hector, the Albion, and a frigate, and we should take the whole fleet and convoy, worth some millions! About eight o'clock perceived three sail at some distance from the fleet; dashed in between them and gave chase, and were happy to find they steered from the fleet. About twelve, came up with a large ship of twenty-six guns. "Archer, every man to his quarters! run the lower deck guns out, and light the ship up: show this fellow our force; it may prevent his firing into us and killing a man or two." No sooner said than done. "Hoa, the ship ahoy! lower your sails, and bring to instantly, or I'll sink you." Clatter, clatter, went the blocks, and away flew all the sails in proper confusion. "What ship is that?" "The Polly." "Whence came you!" "From Jamaica." "Where are you bound?" "To New York." "What ship is that?" "The Phoenix." Huzza, three times by the whole ship's company. An old grum fellow of a sailor standing close by me: "O, d -- n your three cheers, we took you to be something else." Upon examination we found it to be as he reported, and that they had fallen in with the Spanish fleet that morning, and were chased the whole day, and that nothing saved them but our stepping in between; for the Spaniards took us for three consorts, and the Polly took the Phoenix for a Spanish frigate, till we hailed them. The other vessels in company were likewise bound to New York. Thus was I, from being worth thousands in idea, reduced to the old four shillings six-pence again; for the little doctor made the most prize money of us all that day, by winning the bag, which contained between thirty and forty dollars; but this is nothing to what we sailors sometimes undergo.

After parting company, we steered S.S.E. to go round Antonio, and so to Jamaica, (our cruise being out,) with our fingers in our mouths, and all of us as green as you please. It happened to be my middle watch, and about three o'clock, when the man upon the forecastle bawls out "Breakers ahead, and land upon the lee bow;" I looked out, and it was so, sure enough. "Ready about, put the helm down! Helm a lee!" Sir Hyde hearing me put the ship about, jumped upon deck. "Archer, what's the matter? You are putting the ship about without my orders!" Sir 'tis time to go about; the ship is almost ashore, there is the land. "Good God, so it is! Will the ship stay?" Yes, sir, I believe she will, if we don't make any confusion; she is all aback—forward now? "Well, (says he,) work the ship, I will not speak a single word." The ship stayed very well. Then heave the lead! see what water we have! "Three fathom." Keep the ship away, W.N.W. "By the mark three." "This won't do, Archer." No, sir, we had better haul more to the northward; we came S.S.E. and had better steer N.N.W. "Steady, and a quarter three." This may do, we deepen a little. "By the deep four." Very well, my lad, heave quick. "Five fathom." That's a fine fellow! another cast nimbly. "Quarter less eight." That will do, come, we shall get clear bye and bye. "Mark under water five." What's that? "Only five fathom, sir." Turn all hands up, bring the ship to an anchor, boy. Are the anchors clear? "In a moment, sir,—All clear." What water have you in the chains now? "Eight, half nine." Keep fast the anchors till I call you. "Aye, aye sir, all fast." "I have no ground with this line." How many fathoms have you out? pass along the deep sea-line! "Aye, aye, sir." Heave away, watch! watch! bear away, veer away. "No ground, sir, with a hundred fathom." That's clever, come Madame Phoenix, there is another squeak in you yet—all down but the watch; secure the anchors again; heave the main-top-sail to the mast; luff, and bring her to the wind!

I told you, Madam, you should have a little sea-jargon: if you can understand half of what is already said, I wonder at it, though it is nothing to what is to come yet, when the old hurricane begins. As soon as the ship was a little to rights, and all quiet again, Sir Hyde came to me in the most friendly manner, the tears almost starting from his eyes—"Archer, we ought all to be much obliged to you for the safety of the ship, and perhaps of ourselves. I am particularly so; nothing but that instantaneous presence of mind and calmness saved her; another ship's length and we should have been fast on shore; had you been the least diffident, or made the least confusion, so as to make the ship baulk in her stays, she must have been inevitably lost." Sir, you are very good, but I have done nothing that I suppose any body else would not have done, in the same situation. I did not turn all the hands up, knowing the watch able to work the ship; besides, had it spread immediately about the ship that she was almost ashore, it might have created a confusion that was better avoided. "Well," says he, " 'tis well indeed."

At daylight we found that the current had set us between the Colladora rocks and cape Antonio, and that we could not have got out any other way than we did; there was a chance, but Providence is the best pilot. We had sunset that day twenty leagues to the S.E. of our reckoning by the current.

After getting clear of this scrape, we thought ourselves fortunate, and made sail for Jamaica, but misfortune seemed to follow misfortune. The next night, my watch upon deck too, we were overtaken by a squall, like a hurricane while it lasted; for though I saw it coming, and prepared for it, yet, when it took the ship, it roared, and laid her down so, that I thought she would never get up again. However, by keeping her away, and clueing up every thing, she righted. The remainder of the night we had very heavy squalls, and in the morning found the main-mast sprung half the way through:

one hundred and twenty-three leagues to the leeward of Jamaica, the hurricane months coming on, the head of the main-mast almost off, and at a short allowance; well, we must make the best of it. The main-mast was well fished, but we were obliged to be very tender of carrying the sail.

Nothing remarkable happened for ten days afterwards, when we chased a Yankee man-of-war for six hours, but could not get near enough to her before it was dark, to keep sight of her; so that we lost her because unable to carry any sail on the main-mast. In about twelve days more made the island of Jamaica, having weathered all the squalls, and put into Montego bay for water; so that we had a strong party for kicking up a dust on shore, having found three men-of-war lying there. Dancing, &c. &c., till two o'clock every morning; little thinking what was to happen in four days' time: for out of the four men-of-war that were there, not one was in being at the end of that time, and not a soul alive but those left of our crew. Many of the houses where we had been so merry, were so completely destroyed, that scarcely a vestige remained to mark where they stood. Thy works are wonderful, O God! praised be thy holy name!

September the 30th, weighed; bound for Port Royal, round the eastward of the island; the Barbadoes and Victor had sailed the day before, and the Scarborough was to sail the next. Moderate weather until October the 2d. Spoke the Barbadoes off Port Antonio in the evening. At eleven at night it began to snuffle, with a monstrous heavy bill from the eastward. Close reefed the top-sails. Sir Hyde sent for me: "What sort of weather have we, Archer?" It blows a little, and has a very ugly look; if in any other quarter but this, I would say we were going to have a gale of wind. "Aye, it looks so very often here when there is no wind at all; however, don't hoist the top-sails till it clears a little, there is no trusting any country." At twelve I was relieved; the weather had the same rough look: however, they made sail upon her, but had a very dirty night. At eight in the morning I came up again, found it blowing hard from the E.N.E. with close reefed top-sails upon the ship, and heavy squalls at times. Sir Hyde came upon deck: "Well, Archer, what do you think of it?" O, sir, 'tis only a touch of the times, we shall have an observation at twelve o'clock; the clouds are beginning to break; it will clear up at noon, or else blow very hard afterwards. "I wish it would clear up, but I doubt it much. I was once in a hurricane in the East Indies, and the beginning of it had much the same appearance as this. So take in the top-sails, we have plenty of sea-room."

At twelve, the gale still increasing, wore ship, to keep as near mid-channel, between Jamaica and Cuba, as possible; at one the gale increasing still; at two harder! Reefed the courses, and furled them; brought to under a foul mizzen stay-sail, head to the northward. In

the evening no sign of the weather taking off, but every appearance
of the storm increasing, prepared for a proper gale of wind; secured
all the sails with spare gaskets; good rolling tackles upon the yards;
squared the booms; saw the boats all made fast; new lashed the guns;
double breeched the lower deckers; saw that the carpenters had the
tarpaulins and battens all ready for the hatchways; got the top-gallant-
mast down upon the deck; jib-boom and sprit-sail-yard fore and aft;
in fact, did every thing we could think of to make a snug ship.

The poor devils of birds now began to find the uproar in the
elements, for numbers, both of sea and land kinds, came on board of
us. I took notice of some, which happening to be to leeward, turned
to windward, like a ship, tack and tack; for they could not fly against
it. When they came over the ship they dashed themselves down upon
the deck, without attempting to stir till picked up, and when let go
again, they would not leave the ship, but endeavored to hide themselves from the wind.

At eight o'clock a hurricane; the sea roaring, but the wind still
steady to a point; did not ship a spoonful of water. However, got the
hatchways all secured, expecting what would be the consequence,
should the wind shift; placed the carpenters by the main-mast, with
broad axes, knowing, from experience, that at the moment you may
want to cut it away to save the ship, an axe may not be found. Went
to supper; bread, cheese, and porter. The purser frightened out of
his wits about his bread bags; the two marine officers as white as
sheets, not understanding the ship's working so much, and the noise
of the lower deck guns; which, by this time, made a pretty screeching
to the people not used to it; it seemed as if the whole ship's side was
going at each roll. Wooden, our carpenter, was all this time smoking
his pipe and laughing at the doctor; the second lieutenant upon deck,
and the third in his hammock.

At ten o'clock I thought to get a little sleep; came to look into my
cot; it was full of water; for every seam, by the straining of the ship,
had begun to leak. Stretched myself, therefore, upon deck, between
two chests, and left orders to be called, should the least thing happen.
At twelve a midshipman came to me: "Mr. Archer, we are just going
to wear ship, sir!" O, very well, I'll be up directly; what sort of
weather have you got? "It blows a hurricane." Went upon deck,
found Sir Hyde there. "It blows damn'd hard, Archer." It does indeed, sir. "I don't know that I ever remember its blowing so hard
before; but the ship makes a very good weather of it upon this tack
as she bows the sea; but we must wear her, as the wind has shifted to
the S.E. and we are drawing right upon Cuba; so do you go forward,
and have some hands stand by; loose the lee yard-arm of the fore-sail,
and when she is right before the wind, ship the clue garnet close up,
and roll up the sail." Sir! there is no canvas can stand against this

a moment; if we attempt to loose him, he will fly into ribands in an instant, and we may lose three or four of our people; she'll wear by manning the fore shrouds. "O, I don't think she will." I'll answer for it, sir; I have seen it tried several times on the coast of America with success. "Well, try it; if she does not wear, we can only loose the fore-sail afterwards." This was a great condescension from such a man as Sir Hyde. However, by sending about two hundred people into the fore-rigging, after a hard struggle, she wore; found she did not make so good weather on this tack as on the other; for as the sea began to run across, she had not time to rise from one sea, before another dashed against her. Began to think we should lose our masts, as the ship lay very much along, by the pressure of the wind constantly upon the yards and masts alone: for the poor mizzen-stay-sail had gone in shreds long before, and the sails began to fly from the yards through the gaskets into coach whips. My God! to think that the wind could have such force.

Sir Hyde now sent me to see what was the matter between decks, as there was a good deal of noise. As soon as I was below, one of the Marine officers calls out: "Good God! Mr. Archer, we are sinking, the water is up to the bottom of my cot." Pooh, pooh! As long as it is not over your mouth, you are well off; what the devil do you make this noise for? I found there was some water between decks, but nothing to be alarmed at: scuttled the deck, and it ran into the well; found she made a good deal of water through the sides and decks; turned the watch below to the pumps, though only two feet of water in the well; but expected to be kept constantly at work now, as the ship labored much, with scarcely a part of her above water but the quarter-deck, and that but seldom. "Come, pump away, my boys. Carpenters, get the weather chain-pump rigged." "All ready, sir." "Then man it, and keep both pumps going."

At two o'clock the chain pump was choked; set the carpenters at work to clear it; the two head pumps at work upon deck: the ship gained upon us while our chain-pumps were idle; in a quarter of an hour they were at work again, and we began to gain upon her. While I was standing at the pumps, cheering the people, the carpenter's mate came running to me with a face as long as my arm: "O, Sir! the ship has sprung a leak in the gunner's room." Go, then, and tell the carpenter to come to me, but do not speak a word to any one else. Mr. Goodinoh, I am told there is a leak in the gunner's room; go and see what is the matter, but do not alarm any body, and come and make your report privately to me. In a short time he returned; "Sir, there is nothing there, it is only the water washing up between the timbers, that this booby has taken for a leak." O, very well; go upon deck and see if you can keep any of the water from washing down below. "Sir, I have had four people constantly keeping the

hatchways secure, but there is such a weight of water upon the deck
that nobody can stand it when the ship rolls." The gunner soon afterwards came to me, saying, "Mr. Archer, I should be glad if you would
step this way into the magazine for a moment." I thought some
damned thing was the matter, and ran directly. Well, what is the
matter here? He answered, "The ground tier of powder is spoiled,
and I want to show you that it is not out of carelessness in me in
stowing it, for no powder in the world could be better stowed. Now,
sir, what am I to do? If you do not speak to Sir Hyde, he will be
angry with me." I could not forbear smiling to see how easy he took
the danger of the ship, and said to him, let us shake off this gale of
wind first, and talk of the damaged powder afterwards.

At four, we had gained upon the ship a little, and I went upon
deck, it being my watch. The second lieutenant relieved me at the
pumps. Who can attempt to describe the appearance of things upon
deck? If I was to write forever, I could not give you an idea of it—a
total darkness all above; the sea on fire, running as it were in Alps, or
Peaks of Teneriffe; (mountains are too common an idea;) the wind
roaring louder than thunder (absolutely no flight of imagination,) the
whole made more terrible, if possible, by a very uncommon kind of
blue lightning; the poor ship was very much pressed, yet doing what
she could, shaking her sides, and groaning at every stroke. Sir Hyde
upon deck, lashed to windward! I soon lashed myself alongside of
him, and told him the situation of things below, saying the ship did
not make more water than might be expected in such weather, and
that I was only afraid of a gun breaking loose. "I am not in the least
afraid of that; I have commanded her six years, and have had many a
gale of wind in her; so that her iron work, which always gives way
first, is pretty well tried. Hold fast! that was an ugly sea; we must
lower the yards, I believe, Archer; the ship is much pressed." If we
attempt it sir, we shall lose them, for a man aloft can do nothing; besides, their being down would ease the ship very little; the main-mast
is a sprung mast; I wish it was overboard without carrying any thing
else along with it; but that can soon be done, the gale cannot last forever; it will soon be daylight now. Found by the master's watch that
it was five o'clock, though but a little after four by ours: glad it was
so near daylight, and looked for it with much anxiety. Cuba, thou
art much in our way! Another ugly sea; sent a midshipman to bring
news from the pumps; the ship was gaining on them very much, for
they had broken one of their chains, but it was almost mended again.
News from the pump again. "She still gains! A heavy lee!" Back
water from the leeward, half way up the quarter deck; filled one of the
cutters upon the booms, and tore her all to pieces; the ship lying
almost on her beam-ends, and not attempting to right again. Word

from below that the ship still gained on them, as they could not stand
to the pumps, she lay so much along. I said to Sir Hyde:—This is no
time, sir, to think of saving the masts; shall we cut the main-mast
away? "Aye! as fast as you can." I accordingly went into the weather
chains with a pole ax, to cut away the lanyards; the boatswain went
to leeward, and the carpenters stood by the mast. We were all ready,
and a very violent sea broke right on board of us, carried every thing
upon deck away, filled the ship with water, the main and mizzen-
masts went, the ship righted, but was in the last struggle of sinking
under us.

As soon as we could shake our heads above water, Sir Hyde ex-
claimed, "We are gone, at last, Archer! foundered at sea!" Yes sir,
farewell, and the Lord have mercy upon us! I then turned about to
look at the ship; and though she was struggling to get rid of some of
the water; but all in vain, she was almost full below. "Almighty God!
I thank thee, that now I am leaving this world, which I have always
considered as only a passage to a better, I die with a full hope of thy
mercies through the merits of Jesus Christ, thy Son, our Savior!"

I then felt sorry that I could swim, as by that means I might be a
quarter of an hour longer dying than a man who could not, and it is
impossible to divest ourselves of a wish to preserve life. At the end of
these reflections I thought I heard the ship thump and grinding
under our feet; it was so. Sir, the ship is ashore! "What do you say?"
The ship is ashore, and we may save ourselves yet! By this time the
quarter-deck was full of men who had come up from below; and the
Lord have mercy upon us, flying about from all quarters. The ship
now made every body sensible that she was ashore, for every stroke
threatened a total dissolution of her whole frame; found she was
stern ashore, and the bow broke the sea a good deal, though it was
washing clean over at every stroke. Sir Hyde cried out: "Keep to the
quarter-deck, my lads, when she goes to pieces, it is your best chance!"
Providentially got the fore-mast cut away, that she might not pay
round broadside. Lost five men cutting away the foremast, by the
breaking of a sea on board just as the mast went. That was nothing;
every one expected it would be his own fate next; looked for daybreak
with the greatest impatience. At last it came; but what a scene did it
show us! The ship upon a bed of rocks, mountains of them on one
side, and Cordilleras of water on the other; our poor ship grinding
and crying out at every stroke between them; going away by piece-
meal. However, to show the unaccountable workings of Providence,
that which often appears to be the greatest evil, proves to be the
greatest good! That unmerciful sea lifted and beat us up so high
among the rocks, that at last the ship scarcely moved. She was very
strong, and did not go to pieces at the first thumping, though her

decks tumbled in. We found afterwards that she had beat over a ledge of rocks, almost a quarter of a mile in extent beyond us, where if she had struck, every soul of us must have perished.

I now began to think of getting on shore, so stripped off my coat and shoes for a swim, and looked for a line to carry the end with me. Luckily could not find one, which gave me time for recollection: "This won't do for me, to be the first man out of the ship, and first lieutenant; we may get to England again, and people will think I paid a great deal of attention to myself, and did not care for any body else. No, that won't do; instead of being first, I'll see every man, sick and well, out of her before me."

I now thought there was no probability of the ship's soon going to pieces, therefore had not a thought of instant death; took a look round with a kind of philosophic eye, to see how the same situation affected my companions, and was surprised to find the most swaggering, swearing bullies in fine weather, now the most pitiful wretches on earth, when death appeared before them. However, two got safe; by which means, with a line, we got a hawser on shore, and made fast to the rocks, upon which many ventured and arrived safely. There were some sick and wounded on board, who could not avail themselves of this method; we therefore got a spare top-sail-yard from the chains and placed one end ashore and the other on the cabin window, so that most of the sick got ashore this way.

As I had determined, so I was the last man out of the ship; this was about ten o'clock. The gale now began to break. Sir Hyde came to me, and taking me by the hand was so affected that he was scarcely able to speak. "Archer, I am happy beyond expression to see you on the shore; but look at our poor Phoenix." I turned about, but could not say a single word, being too full: my mind had been too intensely occupied before; but every thing now rushed upon me at once, so that I could not contain myself, and I indulged for a full quarter of an hour.

By twelve it was pretty moderate; got some sails on shore and made tents; found great quantities of fish driven up by the sea into holes of the rocks, knocked up a fire, and had a most comfortable dinner. In the afternoon made a stage from the cabin windows to the rocks, and got out some provisions and water, lest the ship should go to pieces, in which case we must all have perished of hunger and thirst; for we were upon a desolate part of the coast, and under a rocky mountain, that could not supply us with a single drop of water.

Slept comfortably this night, and the next day; the idea of death vanishing by degrees, the prospect of being prisoners, during the war, at the Havannah, and walking three hundred miles to it through the woods, was rather unpleasant. However, to save life for the present, we employed this day in getting more provisions and water on shore, which was not an easy matter, on account of decks, guns, and rubbish, and ten feet water that lay over them. In the evening I proposed to Sir Hyde to repair the remains of the only boat left, and to venture in her to Jamaica myself; and in case I arrived safe, to bring vessels to take them all off; a proposal worthy of consideration. It was next day agreed to; therefore, got the cutter on shore, and set the carpenters to work on her; in two days she was ready, and at four o'clock in the afternoon, I embarked with four volunteers and a fortnight's provision; hoisted English colors as we put off from shore, and received three cheers from the lads left behind, and set sail with a light heart; having not the least doubt, that, with God's assisstance, we should come and bring them all off. Had a very squally night, and a very leaky boat, so as to keep two buckets constantly baling. Steered her, myself, the whole night by the stars, and in the morning saw the coast of Jamaica, distant twelve leagues. At eight in the evening, arrived at Montego bay.

I must now begin to leave off, particularly as I have but half an hour to conclude; else my pretty little short letter will lose its passage, which I should not like, after being ten days, at different times, writing it; beating up with the convoy to the northward, which is a reason that this epistle will never read well; for I never sat down with a proper disposition to go on with it; but as I knew something of the kind would please you, I was resolved to finished it: yet it will not bear an overhaul; so do not expose your son's nonsense.

But to proceed—I instantly sent off an express to the Admiral, another to the Porcupine man-of-war, and went myself to Martha Bray to get vessels; for all their vessels here, as well as many of their horses, were gone to *Moco*. Got three small vessels, and set out back again to Cuba, where I arrived the fourth day after leaving my companions. I thought the ship's crew would have devoured me on my landing; they presently whisked me up on their shoulders, and carried me to the tent; where Sir Hyde was.

I must omit many little occurrences that happened on shore, for want of time; but I shall have a number of stories to tell, when I get alongside of you; and the next time I visit you, I shall not be in such a hurry to quit you as I was the last; for then I hoped my nest would have been pretty well feathered:—But my tale is forgotten.

I found the Porcupine had arrived that day, and the lads had built a boat almost ready for launching, that would hold fifty of them, which was intended for another trial, in case I had foundered. Next day, embarked all our people that were left, amounting to two hundred and fifty; for some had died of the wounds they received in getting on shore; others of drinking rum, and others had straggled into the country. All our vessels were so full of people, that we could not take away the few clothes that were saved from the wreck; but that was a trifle since we had preserved our lives and liberty. To make short of my story, we all arrived safe at Montego Bay, and shortly after at Port Royal, in the Janus, which was sent on purpose for us, and were all honorably acquitted for the loss of the ship. I was made admiral's aid de camp, and a little time afterwards sent down to St. Juan as a captain of the Resource, to bring what were left of the poor devils to Blue Fields, on the Musquito shore, and then to Jamaica, where they arrived after three months absence, and without a prize, though I looked out hard off Porto Bello and Carthagena. Found, in my absence, that I had been appointed captain of the Tobago, where I remain his majesty's most true and faithful person, and my dear mother's most dutiful son.

———ARCHER.

[8]

Loss of His Majesty's Ship *Centaur*

THE STORY of the loss of the *Centaur* apparently first appeared as a pamphlet published in London by Captain Inglefield in 1783, *Narrative Concerning the Loss of His Majesty's Ship the Centaur, of 74 Guns.* Perhaps the author felt that he had to justify himself for leaving his ship, which sank with all left on board, but there is little evidence in the narrative that he felt that a captain should go down with his ship. His conduct can be compared with that of Lieutenant Archer of the *Phoenix* in the preceding narrative, who wrote, "This won't do for me, to be the first man out of the ship, and first lieutenant . . . instead of being the first, I'll see every man, sick and well, out of her before me." It is interesting to note that when J. G. Lockhart reprinted the story of the loss of the *Centaur* in his *Strange Adventures of the Sea* (London, 1925), he slightly changed the wording of Captain Inglefield's account to make the leaving of the ship almost involuntary.

As noted in the Introduction, the storm which sank the *Centaur* was one of the worst on record and one of the most expensive in lives and ships. This account is from *Remarkable Shipwrecks*.

HIS MAJESTY'S SHIP CENTAUR,

Of Seventy-four Guns,

September 23, 1782.

AFTER the decisive engagement in the West Indies, on the glorious 12th of April, 1782, when the French fleet under count de Grasse was defeated by admiral Sir George Rodney, several of the captured ships, besides many others, were either lost or disabled, on their homeward-bound passage, with a large convoy. Among those lost was the Centaur, of seventy-four guns, whose commander, captain Inglefield, with the master and ten of the crew, experienced a most providential escape from the general fate.

The captain's narrative affords the best explanation of the manner and means by which this signal deliverance was effected. Those only who are personally involved in such a calamity can describe their sensations with full energy, and furnish, in such detail, those traits of the heart which never fail to interest.

The Centaur (says captain Inglefield) left Jamaica in rather a leaky condition, keeping two hand-pumps going, and when it blew fresh, sometimes a spell with a chain-pump when necessary. But I had no apprehension that the ship was not able to encounter a common gale of wind.

In the evening of the 16th of September, when the fatal gale came on, the ship was prepared for the worst weather usually met in those latitudes, the main-sail was reefed and set, the top-gallant masts struck, and the mizzen-yard lowered down, though at that time it did not blow very strong. Towards midnight it blew a gale of wind, and the ship made so much water that I was obliged to turn all hands up to spell the pumps. The leak still increasing, I had thoughts to try the ship before the sea. Happy I should have been, perhaps, had I in this been determined. The impropriety of leaving the convoy, except in the last extremity, and the hopes of the weather growing moderate, weighed against the opinion that it was right.

About two in the morning the wind lulled, and we flattered ourselves the gale was breaking. Soon after we had much thunder and lightning from the south-east, with rain, when it began to blow strong in gusts of wind, which obliged me to haul the main-sail up, the ship being then under bare poles. This was scarcely done, when a gust of wind, exceeding in violence any thing of the kind I had ever seen or had any conception of, laid the ship upon her beam ends. The water forsook the hold and appeared between decks, so as to fill the men's hammocks to leeward: the ship lay motionless, and to all appearance irrecoverably overset. The water increasing fast, forced through the cells of the ports, and scuttled in the ports from the pressure of the ship. I gave immediate directions to cut away the main and mizzen masts, hoping that when the ship righted to wear her. The mizzen-mast went first, upon cutting one or two of the lanyards, without the smallest effect on the ship; the main-mast followed, upon cutting the lanyard of one shroud; and I had the disappointment to see the foremast and bowsprit follow. The ship upon this immediately righted, but with great violence; and the motion was so quick, that it was difficult for the people to work the pumps. Three guns broke loose upon the main-deck, and it was some time before they were se-cured. Several men being maimed in this attempt, every movable was destroyed, either from the shot thrown loose from the lockers, or the wreck of the deck. The officers, who had left their beds naked when the ship overset in the morning, had not an article of clothes to put on, nor could their friends supply them.

The masts had not been over the sides ten minutes before I was informed the tiller had broken short in the rudder-head; and before the chocks could be placed, the rudder itself was gone. Thus we were as much disastered as it was possible, lying at the mercy of the wind and sea; yet I had one comfort, that the pumps, if any thing reduced the water in the hold; and as the morning came on (the 17th) the weather grew more moderate, the wind having shifted, in the gale, to north-west.

At daylight I saw two line-of-battle ships to leeward; one had lost her fore-mast and bowsprit, the other her main-mast. It was the gen-eral opinion on board the Centaur, that the former was the Canada, the other the Glorieux. The Ramil[l]ies was not in sight, nor more than fifteen sail of merchant ships.

About seven in the morning I saw another line-of-battle ship ahead of us, which I soon distinguished to be the Ville de Paris, with all her masts standing. I immediately gave orders to make the signal of distress, hoisting the ensign on the stump of the mizzen-mast, union downwards, and firing one of the forecastle guns. The ensign blew away soon after it was hoisted, and it was the only one we had re-maining; but I had the satisfaction to see the Ville de Paris wear and stand towards us. Several of the merchant ships also approached us, and those that could hailed, and offered their assistance; but depend-ing upon the king's ship, I only thanked them, desiring, if they joined admiral Graves, to acquaint him of our condition. I had not the smallest doubt but the Ville de Paris was coming to us, as she ap-peared to us not to have suffered in the least by the storm, and having seen her wear, we knew she was under government of her helm; at this time, also, it was so moderate that the merchantmen set their top-sails: but, approaching within two miles she passed us to windward; this being observed by one of the merchant ships, she wore and came under our stern, offering to carry any message to her. I desired the master would acquaint captain Wilkinson that the Centaur had lost her rudder, as well as her masts; that she made a great deal of water, and that I desired he would remain with her until the weather grew moderate. I saw the merchantman approach afterwards near enough to speak to the Ville de Paris, but I am afraid that her condition was much worse than it appeared to be, as she continued upon that tack. In the mean time all the quarter-deck guns were thrown overboard, and all but six, which had overset, off the maindeck. The ship, lying in the trough of the sea, labored prodigiously. I got over one of the small anchors, with a boom and several gun carriages, veering out from the head-door by a large hawser, to keep the ship's bow to the sea; but this, with a top-gallant sail upon the stump of the mizzen-mast, had not the desired effect.

As the evening came on it grew hazy, and blew strong in squalls. We lost sight of the Ville de Paris, but I thought it a certainty that we should see her the next morning. The night was passed in constant labor at the pump. Sometimes the wind lulled, and the water diminished; when it blew strong again, the sea rising, the water again increased.

Towards the morning of the 18th I was informed there was seven feet of water upon the kelson; that one of the winches was broken; that the two spare ones would not fit, and that the hand-pumps were choked. These circumstances were sufficiently alarming; but upon opening the after-hold to get some rum up for the people, we found our condition much more so.

It will be necessary to mention, that the Centaur's after-hold was inclosed by a bulk-head at the after part of the well; here all the dry provisions and the ship's rum were stowed upon twenty chaldrons of coal, which unfortunately had been started on this part of the ship, and by them the pumps were continually choked. The chain-pumps were so much worn as to be of little use; and the leathers, which, had the well been clear, would have lasted twenty days, or more, were all consumed in eight. At this time it was observed that the water had not a passage to the well, for there was so much that it washed against the orlop-deck. All the rum, twenty-six puncheons, and all the provisions, of which there was sufficient for two months, in casks, were staved, having floated with violence from side to side until there was not a whole cask remaining: even the staves that were found upon clearing the hold were most of them broken in two pieces. In the fore-hold, we had a prospect of perishing: should the ship swim, we had no water but what remained in the ground tier; and over this all the wet provisions, and butts filled with salt-water, were floating, and with so much motion that no man could with safety go into the hold. There was nothing left for us to try but bailing with buckets at the fore-hatchway and fish-room; and twelve large canvas buckets were immediately employed at each. On opening the fish-room we were so fortunate as to discover that two puncheons of rum, which belonged to me, had escaped. They were immediately got up, and served out at times in drams; and had it not been for this relief, and some lime-juice, the people would have dropped.

We soon found our account in bailing; the spare pump had been put down the fore-hatchway, and a pump shifted to the fish-room; but the motion of the ship had washed the coals so small, that they had reached every part of the ship, and the pumps were soon choked. However, the water by noon had considerably diminished by working the buckets; but there appeared no prospect of saving the ship, if the gale continued. The labor was too great to hold out without water; yet the people worked without a murmur, and indeed with cheerfulness.

At this time the weather was more moderate, and a couple of spars were got ready for shears to set up a jury fore-mast; but as the evening came on, the gale again increased. We had seen nothing this day but the ship that had lost her main-mast, and she appeared to be as much in want of assistance as ourselves, having fired guns of distress; and before night I was told her fore-mast was gone.

The Centaur labored so much, that I had scarcely a hope she could swim till morning. However, by great exertion of the chain-pumps and bailing, we held our own, but our sufferings for want of water were very great, and many of the people could not be restrained from drinking salt-water.

At daylight (the 19th) there was no vessel in sight; and flashes from guns having been seen in the night, we feared the ship that we had seen the preceding day had foundered. Towards ten o'clock in the forenoon the weather grew more moderate, the water diminished in the hold, and the people were encouraged to redouble their efforts to get the water low enough to break a cask of fresh water out of the ground tier; and some of the most resolute of the seamen were employed in the attempt. At noon we succeeded with one cask, which, though little, was a seasonable relief. All the officers, passengers, and boys, who were not of the profession of seamen, had been employed thrumming a sail, which was passed under the ship's bottom, and I thought it had some effect. The shears were raised for the fore-mast; the weather looked promising, the sea fell, and at night we were able to relieve at the pumps and bailing every two hours. By the morning of the 20th the forehold was cleared of the water, and we had the comfortable promise of a fine day. It proved so, and I was determined to make use of it with every possible exertion. I divided the ship's company, with the officers attending them, into parties, to raise the jury fore-mast; to heave over the lower-deck guns; to clear the wrecks of the fore and after holds; to prepare the machine for steering the ship, and to work the pumps. By night the after-hold was as clear as when the ship was launched; for, to our astonishment, there was not a shovel of coals remaining, twenty chaldrons having been pumped out since the commencement of the gale. What I have called the wreck of the hold, was the bulk-heads of the after-hold, fish-room, and spirit-rooms. The standards of the cockpit, an immense quantity of staves and wood, and part of the lining of the ship, were thrown overboard, that if the water should again appear in the hold, we might have no impediment in bailing. All the guns were overboard, the fore-mast secured, and the machine, which was to be similar to that with which the Ipswich was steered, was in great forwardness; so that I was in hopes, the moderate weather continuing, that I should be able to steer the ship by noon the following day and at least save the people on some of the Western Islands. Had we had any other ship in company with us, I should have thought it my duty to have quitted the Centaur this day.

This night the people got some rest by relieving the watches; but in the morning of the 21st we had the mortification to find that the weather again threatened, and by noon it blew a gale. The ship labored greatly, and the water appeared in the fore and after-hold, and increased. The carpenter also informed me that the leathers were nearly consumed; and likewise that the chains of the pumps, by constant exertion and the friction of the coals, were considered as nearly useless.

As we had now no other resource but bailing, I gave orders that scuttles should be cut through the decks to introduce more buckets into the hold; and all the sail-makers were employed, night and day, in making canvas buckets; and the orlop-deck having fallen in on the larboard side, I ordered the sheet cable to be roused overboard. The wind at this time was at west, and being on the larboard tack, many schemes had been practised to wear the ship, that we might drive into a less boisterous latitude, as well as approach the Western Islands; but none succeeded: and having a weak carpenter's crew, they were hardly sufficient to attend the pumps; so that we could not make any progress with the steering machine. Another sail had been thrummed and got over, but we did not find its use; indeed there was no prospect but in a change of weather. A large leak had been discovered and stopped in the fore-hold and another in the lady's hole, but the ship appeared so weak from her laboring, that it was clear she could not last long. The after cock-pit had fallen in, the fore cock-pit the same, with all the store rooms down; the stern post was so loose, that as the ship rolled, the water rushed in on either side in great streams, which we could not stop.

Night came on, with the same dreary prospect as on the preceding, and was passed in continual efforts of labor. Morning came, (the 22d,) without our seeing any thing, or any change of weather, and the day was spent with the same struggles to keep the ship above water, pumping and bailing at the hatchways and scuttles. Towards night another of the chain pumps was rendered quite useless, by one of the rollers being displaced at the bottom of the pump, and this was without remedy, there being too much water in the well to get to it: we also had but six leathers remaining, so that the fate of the ship was not far off. Still the labor went on without any apparent despair, every officer taking his share of it, and the people were always cheerful and obedient.

During the night the water increased; but about seven in the morning of the 23d I was told that an unusual quantity of water appeared, all at once, in the fore-hold, which, upon my going forward to be convinced, I found but too true; the stowage of the hold ground-tier was all in motion, so that in a short time there was not a whole cask to be seen. We were convinced the ship had sprung a fresh leak. Another sail had been thrumming all night, and I was giving directions to place it over the bows, when I perceived the ship settling by the head, the lower deck bow-ports being even with the water.

At this period the carpenter acquainted me the well was staved in, destroyed by the wreck of the hold, and the chain pumps displaced and totally useless. There was nothing left but to redouble our efforts in bailing, but it became difficult to fill the buckets, from the quantity of staves, planks, anchor-stock, and yard-arm pieces, which were now washed from the wings, and floating from side to side with the motion of the ship. The people, till this period, had labored, as if determined to conquer their difficulties, without a murmur or without a tear; but now seeing their efforts useless, many of them burst into tears and wept like children.

I gave orders for the anchors, of which we had two remaining, to be thrown overboard, one of which (the spare anchor) had been most surprisingly hove in upon the forecastle and midships, when the ship had been upon her beam ends, and gone through the deck.

Every time that I visited the hatchway I observed the water increased, and at noon washed even with the orlop-deck: the carpenter assured me the ship could not swim long, and proposed making rafts to float the ship's company, whom it was not in my power to encourage any longer with a prospect of their safety. Some appeared perfectly resigned, went to their hammocks and desired their messmates to lash them in; others were lashing themselves to gratings and small rafts; but the most predominant idea was that of putting on their best and cleanest clothes.

The weather, about noon, had been something moderate, and as rafts had been mentioned by the carpenter, I thought it right to make the attempt, though I knew our booms could not float half the ship's company in fine weather; but we were in a situation to catch at a straw. I therefore called the ship's company together, told them my intention, recommending to them to remain regular and obedient to their officers. Preparations were immediately made to this purpose; the booms were cleared; the boats, of which we had three, viz. cutter, pinnace, and five-oared yawl, were got over the side; a bag of bread was ordered to be put in each, and any liquors that could be got at, for the purpose of supplying the rafts. I had intended myself to go in the five-oared yawl, and the coxswain was desired to get any thing from my steward that might be useful. Two men, captains of the tops, of the forecastle, or quartermasters, were placed in each of them, to prevent any person from forcing the boats, or getting into them until an arrangement was made. While these preparations were making, the ship was gradually sinking, the orlop-decks having been blown up by the water in the hold, and the cables floated to the gun-deck. The men had some time quitted their employment of bailing, and the ship was left to her fate.

In the afternoon the weather again threatened, and blew strongly in squalls; the sea ran high, and one of the boats (the yawl) was staved alongside and sunk. As the evening approached, the ship appeared little more than suspended in water. There was no certainty that she would swim from one minute to another; and the love of life, which I believe never showed itself later in the approach to death, began now to level all distinctions. It was impossible, indeed for any man to deceive himself with a hope of being saved upon a raft in such a sea; besides that, the ship in sinking, it was probable, would carry every thing down with her in a vortex, to a certain distance.

It was near five o'clock, when, coming from my cabin, I observed a number of people looking very anxiously over the side; and looking over myself, I saw that several men had forced the pinnace, and that more were attempting to get in. I had immediate thoughts of securing this boat before she might be sunk by numbers. There appeared not more than a moment for consideration; to remain and perish with the ship's company, to whom I could not be of use any longer, or seize the opportunity, which seemed the only way of escaping, and leave the people, with whom I had been so well satisfied on a variety of occasions that I thought I could give my life to preserve them. This, indeed, was a painful conflict, such as, I believe, no man can describe, nor have any just idea of who has not been in a similar situation.

The love of life prevailed. I called to Mr. Rainy, the master, the only officer upon deck, desired him to follow me, and immediately descended into the boat at the after part of the chains, but not with-

out great difficulty got the boat clear of the ship, twice the number
that the boat would carry pushing to get in, and many jumping into
the water. Mr. Baylis, a young gentleman fifteen years of age, leaped
from the chains, after the boat had got off, and was taken in. The
boat falling astern, became exposed to the sea, and we endeavored
to pull her bow round to keep her to the break of the sea, and to pass
to windward of the ship; but in the attempt she was nearly filled, the
sea ran too high, and the only probability of living was keeping her
before the wind.

It was then that I became sensible how little, if any, better our
condition was than that of those who remained in the ship; at best, it
appeared to be only a prolongation of a miserable existence. We were,
all together, twelve in number, in a leaky boat, with one of the gunwales staved, in nearly the middle of the Western ocean, without a
compass, without quadrant, without sail, without great coat or cloak,
all very thinly clothed, in a gale of wind, with a great sea running! It
was now five o'clock in the evening, and in half an hour we lost sight
of the ship. Before it was dark a blanket was discovered in the boat.
This was immediately bent to one of the stretches, and under it, as a
sail, we scudded all night, in expectation of being swallowed up by
every wave, it being with great difficulty that we could sometimes clear
the boat of the water before the return of the next great sea; all of us
half drowned, and sitting, except those who bailed, at the bottom of
the boat; and, without having really perished, I am sure no people
ever endured more. In the morning the weather grew moderate, the
wind having shifted to the southward, as we discovered by the sun.
Having survived the night, we began to recollect ourselves, and to
think of our future preservation.

When we quitted the ship the wind was at N.W. or N.N.W. Fayal
had borne E.S.E. two hundred and fifty or two hundred and sixty
leagues. Had the wind continued for five or six days, there was a
probability that running before the sea we might have fallen in with
some one of the Western Islands. The change of wind was death to
these hopes; for, should it come to blow, we knew there would be no
preserving life but by running before the sea, which would carry us
again to the northward, where we must soon afterwards perish.

Upon examining what we had to subsist on, I found a bag of
bread, a small ham, a single piece of pork, two quart bottles of water,
and a few of French cordials. The wind continued to the southward
for eight or nine days, and providentially never blew so strong but
that we could keep the side of the boat to the sea; but we were always
most miserably wet and cold. We kept a sort of reckoning, but the
sun and stars being somewhat hidden from us, for twenty-four hours,
we had no very correct idea of our navigation. We judged, that we

had nearly an E.N.E. course since the first night's run, which had carried us to the S.E. and expected to see the island of Corvo. In this, however, we were disappointed, and we feared that the southerly wind had driven us far to the northward. Our prayers were now for a northerly wind. Our condition began to be truly miserable, both from hunger and cold: for on the fifth day we had discovered that our bread was nearly all spoiled by salt-water, and it was necessary to go on an allowance. One biscuit divided into twelve morsels for breakfast, and the same for dinner; the neck of a bottle broken off, with the cork in, served for a glass, and this, filled with water, was the allowance for twenty-four hours for each man. This was done without any partiality or distinction; but we must have perished ere this, had we not caught six quarts of rain water; and this we could not have been blessed with, had we not found in the boat a pair of sheets, which by accident had been put there. These were spread when it rained, and when thoroughly wet, wrung into the kidd, with which we had bailed the boat. With this short allowance, which was rather tantalizing in our comfortless condition, we began to grow very feeble, and our clothes being continually wet, our bodies were, in many places, chafed into sores.

On the 15th day it fell calm, and soon after a breeze of wind sprung up from the N.N.W. and blew to a gale, so that we ran before the sea at the rate of five or six miles an hour under our blanket, till we judged we were to the southward of Fayal, and to the westward sixty leagues: but the wind blowing strong we could not attempt to steer for it. Our wishes were now for the wind to shift to the westward. This was the fifteenth day we had been in the boat, and we had only one day's bread, and one bottle of water remaining of a second supply of rain. Our sufferings were now as great as human strength could bear, but we were convinced that good spirits were a better support than great bodily strength; for on this day Thomas Matthews, quartermaster, the stoutest man in the boat, perished from hunger and cold: on the day before he had complained of want of strength in his throat, as he expressed it, to swallow his morsel, and in the night drank salt-water, grew delirious, and died without a groan. As it became next to a certainty that we should all perish in the same manner in a day or two, it was somewhat comfortable to reflect, that dying of hunger was not so dreadful as our imaginations had represented. Others had complained of these symptoms in their throats; some had drank their own urine; and all but myself had drank salt-water.

As yet despair and gloom had been successfully prohibited; and, as the evenings closed in, the men had been encouraged by turns to sing a song, or relate a story, instead of supper; but this evening I found it impossible to raise either. As the night came on it fell calm, and about midnight a breeze of wind sprang up, we guessed from the westward by the swell, but there not being a star to be seen, we were afraid of running out of our way, and waited impatiently for the rising sun to be our compass.

As soon as the dawn appeared, we found the wind to be exactly as we had wished, at W.S.W. and immediately spread our sail, running before the sea at the rate of four miles an hour. Our last breakfast had been served with the bread and water remaining, when John Gregory, quartermaster, declared with much confidence that he saw land in the S.E. We had so often seen fog-banks, which had the appearance of land, that I did not trust myself to believe it, and cautioned the people, (who were extravagantly elated) that they might not feel the effects of disappointment; till at length one of them broke out into a most immoderate swearing fit of joy, which I could not restrain, and declared he had never seen land in his life if what he now saw was not land.

We immediately shaped our course for it, though on my part with very little faith. The wind freshened; the boat went through the water at the rate of five or six miles an hour, and in two hours' time the land was plainly seen by every man in the boat, but at a very great distance, so that we did not reach it till ten at night. It must have been at least twenty leagues from us when first discovered; and I cannot help remarking, with much thankfulness, the providential favor shown to us in this instance.

In every part of the horizon, except where the land was discovered, there was so thick a haze that we could not have seen any thing for more than three or four leagues. Fayal, by our reckoning, bore E. by N. which course we were steering, and in a few hours, had not the sky opened for our preservation, we should have increased our distance from the land, got to the eastward, and of course missed all the island. As we approached the land our belief had strengthened that it was Fayal. The island of Pico, which might have revealed it to us, had the weather been perfectly clear, was at this time capped with clouds, and it was some time before we were quite satisfied, having traversed for two hours a great part of the island, where the steep and rocky shore refused us a landing. This circumstance was borne with much impatience, for we had flattered ourselves that we should meet with fresh water at the first part of the land we might approach; and being disappointed, the thirst of some had increased anxiety almost to a state of madness; so that we were near making the attempt to land in some places where the boat must have been dashed to pieces by the surf. At length we discovered a fishing canoe, which conducted us into the road of Fayal about midnight; but where the regulation of the port did not permit us to land till examined by the health officers; however, I did not think much of sleeping this night in the boat, our pilot having brought us some refreshments of bread, wine, and water. In the morning we were visited by Mr. Graham, the English consul, whose humane attention made very ample amends for the formality of the Portuguese. Indeed I can never sufficiently express the sense I have of his kindness and humanity, both to myself and people; for, I believe, it was the whole of his employment for several days to contrive the best means of restoring us to health and strength. It is true, I believe there never were more pitiable objects. Some of the stoutest men belonging to the Centaur were obliged to be supported through the streets of Fayal. Mr. Rainy, the master, and myself, were, I think, in better health than the rest; but I could not walk without being supported; and for several days, with the best and most comfortable provisions of diet and lodging, we grew rather worse than better.

[9]

LOSS OF THE *Grosvenor* INDIAMAN

THE NARRATIVE of the loss of the *Grosvenor* is quite a substantial account—
one of the longest found in the anthologies of wrecks and disasters; in many
anthologies it was placed first, apparently because the editors felt it would
interest most readers. The circumstances of the wreck were neither unusual
nor especially harrowing. The captain of the *Grosvenor*, in bad weather,
trusted too much to dead reckoning and feared unknown currents too little;
when the ship was about to pile up on the African coast, he thought he had
three hundred miles of sea room.

Certainly a major part of the interest in the story lay in speculation
about the fates of the white women—whether they had been adopted into
Caffre villages and had settled down as wives of Caffre warriors. This account states, ". . . the public mind was long harassed with the belief that
a few had been doomed to worse than death among the natives." The accuracy of this statement is proved by another popular narrative, "The Loss of
the Ship *Hercules*," which describes a wreck that occurred within sight of
where the *Grosvenor* struck. The captain of the *Hercules*, speaking to the
Caffres through an interpreter, asked about the survivors of the *Grosvenor*
and ended, ". . . but the fate of the two unfortunate ladies gave me so
much uneasiness that I most earnestly requested of them to tell me all they
knew of their situation. . . . They replied, and with apparent concern, that
one of the ladies had died a short time after her arrival at the kraal; but
they understood the other was living, and had several children by the chief."

The charitable Dutch searchers found three elderly white women, survivors of some earlier wreck who, cast ashore as children, could not tell whether they were Portuguese or English or Dutch or remember at all the life from which they had come. Katherine Gerould's "Vain Oblations" is based on a somewhat similar situation.

The major source for this account was undoubtedly George Carter's *Narrative of the Loss of the Grosvenor, East Indiaman,* London, 1791. Apparently most of the information about the journey to the settlements came from John Hynes, who first saw breakers on the night of the wreck, and who lived to tell the tale. All the anthologies I have seen print the account as it appeared in Duncan's *Mariner's Chronicle;* Thomas's verbatim copy is my source.

This narrative should not be confused with W. Clark Russell's *The Wreck of the Grosvenor,* which is a novel with an entirely different plot.

GROSVENOR INDIAMAN

On the Coast of Caffraria,

August 4, 1782.

In the melancholy catalogue of human woes, few things appear more eminently disastrous than the general fate of the Grosvenor's crew. Shipwreck is always, even in its mildest form, a calamity which fills the mind with horror; but, what is instant death, compared to the situation of those who had hunger, thirst, and nakedness to contend with; who only escaped the fury of the waves to enter into conflicts with the savages of the forest, or the greater savages of the human race; who were cut off from all civilized society, and felt the prolongation of life to be only the lengthened pains of death?

The Grosvenor sailed from Trinicomale, June 13th, 1782, on her homeward bound voyage, and met with no memorable occurrence till the 4th of August, the fatal day on which she went on shore.

During the two preceding days it had blown very hard, the sky was overcast, so that they were unable to take an observation; and it is likewise probable, that from their vicinity to the shore, they had been carried out of their course by currents. The combination of these circumstances may account for the error in their reckoning, which occasioned the loss of the ship. It appears that captain Coxson had declared, a few hours before the disaster took place, that he computed the ship to be at least one hundred leagues from the nearest land, and this opinion lulled them into a false security.

John Hynes, one of the survivors, being aloft with some others, in the night-watch, saw breakers ahead, and asked his companions if they did not think land was near. In this opinion they all coincided, and hastened to inform the third mate, who was the officer of the watch. The infatuated young man only laughed at their apprehensions; upon which one of them ran to the cabin to acquaint the captain, who instantly ordered to wear ship. But before this could be accomplished, her keel struck with great force; in an instant every person on board hastened on the deck, and apprehension and horror were impressed on every countenance.

The captain endeavored to dispel the fears of the passengers, and begged them to be composed. The pumps were sounded, but no water found in the hold, as the ship's stern lay high on the rocks. In a few minutes the wind blew off the shore, which filled them with apprehensions lest they should be driven out to sea, and thus lose the only chance they had of escaping. The powder room was by this time full of water, the masts were cut away, without any effect, and the ship being driven within a cable's length of shore, all hopes of saving her vanished.

This dismal prospect produced distraction and despair, and it is impossible to describe the scene that ensued. Those who were most composed set about forming a raft, hoping by means of it to convey the women, the children, and the sick, to land. Meanwhile three men attempted to swim to the shore with the deep-sea line; one perished in the attempt, but the other two succeeded. By these a hawser was, at length, carried to the shore and fastened round the rocks, in which operation they were assisted by great numbers of the natives, who had come down to the water's edge to witness the uncommon sight.

The raft being by this time completed, was launched overboard, and four men got upon it to assist the ladies; but they had scarcely taken their station before the hawser, which was fastened around it, snapped in two, by which accident it was upset, and three of the men drowned. In this dilemma, every one began to think of the best means of saving himself. The yawl and jolly-boat had already been dashed to pieces by the violence of the surf; so that the only means of preservation now left was by the hawser made fast to the rocks, hand over hand. Several got safe on shore in this manner, while others, to the number of fifteen, perished in the difficult attempt.

The ship soon separated just before the main-mast. The wind, at the same time, providentially shifted to the old quarter, and blew directly to the land; a circumstance which contributed greatly to the preservation of those on board, who all got on the poop, as being nearest to the shore. The wind and surges now impelling them, that part of the wreck on which the people were rent asunder fore and aft, the deck splitting in two. In this distress they crowded upon the starboard quarter, which soon floated into shoal water, the other parts of the wreck breaking off those heavy seas which would otherwise have ingulphed or dashed them to pieces. Through this fortunate incident, all on board, even the ladies and children, got safe on shore, except the cook's mate, a black, who, being drunk, could not be prevailed upon to leave the wreck.

Before this arduous business was well effected night came on, and the natives having retired, several fires were lighted with fuel from the wreck, and the whole company supped on such provisions as they picked up on the shore. Two tents were formed of sails that had drifted to the shore, and in these the ladies were left to repose, while the men wandered about in search of such articles as might be of service.

On the morning of the 5th, the natives returned, and, without ceremony, carried off whatever suited their fancy. This conduct excited a thousand apprehensions, particularly in the minds of the females, for their personal safety; but observing that the savages contended themselves with plunder, their fears were somewhat allayed.

The next day was employed in collecting together all the articles that might be useful in the journey to the Cape, to which they imprudently resolved to direct their course; a resolution which involved them in complicated misery, and which can be justified by no wise principle. From the wreck they might easily have built a vessel capable of containing them all, and by coasting along, they might have reached the nearest of the Dutch settlements with half the danger or risk to which they were then exposing themselves. Distress, however, sometimes deprives men of all presence of mind; so the crew of the Grosvenor, having just escaped the dangers of the sea, appear to have considered land as the most desirable alternative, without reflecting on the almost insuperable obstacles that lay in their way.

On examining their stores, they found themselves in possession of two casks of flour and a tub of pork, that had been washed on the beach, and some arrack, which the captain prudently ordered to be staved lest the natives should get at it, and by intoxication increase their natural ferocity.

Captain Coxson now called together the survivors, and having divided the provisions among them, asked if they consented to his continuing in the command, to which they unanimously agreed. He then informed them, that from the best calculation he could make, he was in hopes of being able to reach some of the Dutch settlements in fifteen or sixteen days. In this calculation the captain was probably not much mistaken. Subsequent observations prove that the Grosvenor must have been wrecked between the twenty-seventh and

twenty-eighth degrees of south latitude; and as the Dutch colonies
extend beyond the thirty-first degree, they might have accomplished
the journey within the time specified, had not rivers intervened and
retarded their progress.

As the English advanced they were stopped by
Every thing being arranged, they set out on their journey on the
seventh, leaving behind only an old East-India soldier, who, being
lame, preferred trusting himself to the natives till some more favorable
opportunity of getting away should present itself; adding, that he
might as well die with them as end his life on the way with pain and
hunger.

As they moved forward they were followed by some of the natives,
while others remained at the wreck. Those who accompanied them
plundered them, from time to time, of whatever they liked, and sometimes threw stones at them. After proceeding a few miles they were
met by a party of about thirty of the natives, whose hair was fastened
up in a comical form, and their faces painted red. Among these was
a man who spoke Dutch, who, it afterwards appeared, was a runaway
slave from the Cape, on account of some crimes, and was named
Trout. When this man came up to the English he inquired who they
were, and whither they were going. Finding by their answers that
they had been cast away, he informed them, that their intended journey to the Cape would be attended with unspeakable difficulties from
the natives, the wild beasts, and the nature of the country through
which they would have to pass.

Though this did not contribute to raise their spirits they tried
to engage him as a guide, but no arguments could prevail upon him
to comply with their wishes. Finding all their solicitations fruitless,
they pursued their journey for four or five days, during which they
were constantly surrounded by the natives, who took from them whatever they pleased, but invariably retired on the approach of night.

As they proceeded they saw many villages, which they carefully
avoided, that they might be less exposed to the insults of the natives.
At length they came to a deep gully, where they were met by three
Caffres, armed with lances, which they held several times to the captain's throat. Irritated beyond all patience by their conduct, he
wrenched one of the lances from their hands and broke it. Of this
the natives seemed to take no notice, and went away; but the next
day, on coming to a large village, they there found the three men,
with three or four hundred of their countrymen, all armed with
lances and targets. As the English advanced they were stopped by
these people, who began to pilfer and insult them, and at last fell
upon and beat them.

Conceiving that it was the intention of the natives to kill them,
they formed a resolution to defend themselves to the last extremity.
Accordingly, placing the women, the children, and the sick at some

distance, the remainder, to the number of eighty or ninety, engaged their opponants in a kind of running fight for upwards of two hours, when our countrymen, gaining an eminence, where they could not be surrounded, a kind of parley took place. In this unfortunate encounter many were wounded on both sides, but none killed. After a pacification had taken place, the English cut the buttons from their coats, and presented them to the natives, upon which they went away and returned no more.

The following night they were terrified with the noise of wild beasts, so that the men were obliged to keep watch to prevent their too near approach. What a dreadful situation, especially for females of delicate habits, and so lately possessing all the luxuries that eastern refinement could afford!

When morning arrived they were again joined by Trout, who had been on board the wreck, and had loaded himself with various articles of iron and copper, which he was carrying to his habitation. He cautioned them against making any resistance in future, for as they were not furnished with any weapons of defence, opposition would only tend to irritate the natives and increase obstructions. With this advice he left them.

Having made some progress during the day, they agreed to pass the night near a deep gully, but were so disturbed by the howlings of wild beasts that they could get but little sleep. Though a large fire was kept up to intimidate these unwelcome visiters, they came so near as to occasion a general alarm.

The next day, as they were advancing, a party of natives came down upon them, and plundered them, among other things, of their tinder-box, flint, and steel, which proved an irreparable loss. They were now obliged to carry with them a firebrand by turns, the natives following them until it was almost dark. At length they came to a small river, where they determined to stop during the night. Before the natives retired they became more insolent than ever, robbing the gentlemen of their watches, and the ladies of the diamonds which they had secreted in their hair. Opposition was in vain; the attempt to resist these outrages being productive of fresh insults, and even blows.

The following day they crossed the river. Here their provisions being nearly expended, and the delay and fatigue occasioned by travelling with the women and children being very great, the sailors began to murmur, and each seemed resolved to shift for himself. Accordingly the captain, with Mr. Logie, the first mate, and his wife, the third mate, colonel James and lady, Mr. and Mrs. Hosea, Mr. Newman, a passenger, the purser, the surgeon, and five of the children, agreed to keep together, and travel as before; many of the sailors were also prevailed upon to attend them, by the liberal promises of the passengers.

On the other hand, Mr. Shaw, the second mate, Mr. Trotter, the fourth, Mr. Harris, the fifth, captain Talbot, Messrs. Williams and Taylor, M. D'Espinette, several other gentlemen, and their servants, together with a number of the seamen, in all forty-three persons, among whom was Hynes, from whom much information was afterwards obtained, resolved to hasten forward. A young gentleman of the name of Law, seven or eight years of age, crying after one of the passengers, they agreed to take him with them, and to carry him by turns when tired.

This separation was equally fatal, cruel, and impolitic; however, the second mate's party having been stopped by a river, they once more joined with great satisfaction, and travelled in company the whole of that day and part of the next.

They now arrived at a large village, where they found Trout, who introduced his wife and child to them, and begged a piece of pork. He informed them that this was his residence, and repeated his former declaration, that the natives would not suffer him to depart, even of he were inclined to return to his own country. He, however, communicated various articles of information relative to their journey, for which they made due acknowledgements; but it is to be lamented that he could not be induced to extend his services, or rather that his crimes and character rendered him dangerous to be trusted, and fearful of trusting himself among Christians.

During their conversation with Trout, the natives surrounded them in numbers, and continued to follow them till dusk. The two companies passed the night together, but that distress, which ought to have been the bond of unity, was unfortunately perverted into an occasion for dissaffection and complaint.

Their provisions running very short, a party went down to the sea-side to seek for shell-fish on the rocks, and found a considerable quantity of oysters, muscles, and limpets. These were divided among the women, the children, and the sick; for the tide happening to come in before they had collected a sufficient stock, some of the wretched troop were obliged to put up with a very scanty allowance. After a repast which rather excited than gratified their appetites, they continued their march, and about noon reached a small village, where an old man approached them, armed with a lance, which he levelled, making at the same time a noise somewhat resembling the report of a musket. From this circumstance, it is probable, he was acquainted with the use of fire-arms, and apprehended they would kill his cattle, for he immediately drove his herd into the kraall; an inclosure, where they are always secured upon the appearance of danger, and during the night. The old man took no farther notice of the English, but they were followed by some of the other inhabitants of the village, who behaved extremely ill.

The final separation now took place; they parted to meet no more. In adopting this resolution they appear to have been influenced by motives which had, at least, the specious appearance of reason. They conceived, that by pursuing different routes, and travelling in small parties, they should be less the object of jealousy to the natives, and could the more easily procure subsistence. To counterbalance these advantages, however, they lost that unity of action, that systematic direction, which a prudent superior can communicate to those under his care; and by rejecting established authority, they soon split into parties, guided only by caprice, and swayed by temporary views. After all, they did not part without evincing those emotions so honorable to human nature: their misfortunes had, in some measure, levelled distinctions, and the services of the lowest were regarded as tokens of friendship, not expressions of duty.

From this period the fate of the captain, and his associates, is almost wholly unknown. But imagination cannot form a scene of deeper distress than what the delicate and tender sex, and the innocent children, must have experienced. From the accounts of some of the party who survived their distresses, and subsequent inquiries, it is probable, that the hand of death soon released them from their accumulated ills; though the public mind was long harassed with the belief that a few had been doomed to worse than death among the natives.

The separation being decided upon, the party which had attached itself to the second mate travelled till it was quite dark, when, arriving at a convenient spot, they kindled a fire and reposed for the night.

Next day they proceeded, as they conjectured, thirty miles; and though they saw great numbers of the natives they received from them not the least molestation. Towards the close of the day they reached an extensive wood, and being fearful of entering it, lest they might lose their way, they spent a restless night on its verge, being terribly alarmed by the howlings of wild beasts.

They continued their route the following day till noon, without any other food than wild sorrel and such berries as they observed the birds to peck at. None of the natives made their appearance. The wanderers, having reached a point of the rocks, found some shell-fish, and after refreshing themselves they advanced till they came to the banks of a large river, where they reposed.

Next morning, finding the river very broad and deep, and several of the company being unable to swim, they resolved to follow its windings, and seek some place where it was fordable. In their way they passed many villages, the inhabitants of which were too much alarmed to yield them any assistance. Pursuing the course of the river a considerable way, and not finding it become narrower, they determined to construct catamarans, a kind of raft, in order to cross it. This being effected, with such materials as they found on the banks, those who could not swim were placed upon the float, which being impelled by the others, they all crossed it in safety, though the river was computed to be not less than two miles over.

It was now three days since they had left the sea, and during that period they had scarcely taken any nourishment but water and a little wild sorrel. They therefore again directed their course to the shore, where they were fortunate to find abundance of shell-fish, which afforded them a very seasonable refreshment.

After following the trendings of the coast for three or four days, during which the natives suffered them to pass without molestation, penetrating a pathless wood, where, perhaps, no human being ever trod, uncertain which way to proceed, incommoded by the heat, and exhausted by the fatigues of their march, they were almost ready to sink, when they reached the summit of a hill. Here they rested, and had the satisfaction to see a spacious plain before them, through which a fine stream meandered. As the wild beasts, however, were accustomed, in their nocturnal prowlings, to resort to this place for water, the situation of the travellers was perilous, and subject to continual alarms.

In the morning one of the party ascended a lofty tree to observe the trendings of the coast, after which they resumed their course, and entered another wood just as the night set in. Having passed it by paths which the wild beasts alone had made, they again reached the seacoast. Here they made fires, which, after the fatigues they had undergone, was a toilsome business, and threw into them the oysters they had collected, to make them open, as they had not a single knife remaining among them. On this spot they reposed, but found no water.

Next day, the wanderers, in the course of their journey, had the good fortune to discover a dead whale, which sight in their present situation afforded them no little satisfaction. The want of a knife to cut it up prevented them from taking full advantage of this accidental supply; some of them, though in the extremity of hunger, nauseated this food; while others, making a fire on the carcass, dug out the part thus roasted, with oyster-shells, and made a hearty meal.

A fine, level country now presented itself, the sight of which caused them to believe that their fatigues were near a termination, and that they had reached the northernmost part of the Dutch colonies. Here new dissensions arose, some advising that they should penetrate inland, while others persevered in the original plan of keeping in the vicinity of the sea-coast.

After many disputes another division of the party took place. Mr. Shaw, the fourth mate, Mr. Harris, the fifth, Messrs. Williams and Taylor, captain Talbot, and seamen, to the number of twenty-two persons, among whom was Hynes, the reporter, resolved to proceed inland. The carpenter, the ship's steward, M. D'Espinette, M. Olivier, with about twenty-four seamen, continued to follow the shore.

The party which took the interior proceeded for three days through a very pleasant country, where they saw a great number of deserted kraals. During this time they had nothing to subsist on but a few oysters, which they carried with them, and some berries and wild sorrel gathered on the way. The effects of hunger soon compelled them to return to the coast, where, as usual, they found a supply of shell-fish. As they were proceeding up a steep hill, soon after their separation, captain Talbot complained of great lassitude, and repeatedly sat down to rest himself. The company several times indulged him by doing the same; but perceiving that he was quite exhausted, they went on, leaving him and his faithful servant, Blair, sitting beside each other, and neither of them was heard of any more.

Having reposed near the shore, the next day, about noon, they arrived at a small river, where they found two of the carpenter's party, who, being unable to swim, had been left behind. The joy of these poor creatures, at the sight of their comrades, was excessive. They were preserved since they had been in this place almost by a miracle, for while they were gathering shell-fish on the beach their fire went out, so that it was wonderful how they escaped being devoured by the wild beasts.

They were with difficulty got over the river, and travelling on for four days more the party came to another river, of such breadth that none of them would attempt to pass it. Having no alternative, they marched along its banks in hopes of finding a practicable passage, and arrived at a village, where the natives showed them the inside of a watch, which some of the carpenter's party had given for a little milk. Mr. Shaw conceiving that such a traffic would not be unacceptable, offered them the inside of his watch for a calf. To these terms they assented, but no sooner had they obtained possession of the price than they withheld the calf, which was immediately driven out of the village.

They continued their march along the river for several days, and passed through several villages without molestation from the inhabitants, till they came to a part where they conceived they should be able to cross. Having constructed a catamaran, as before, they all passed the river in safety, excepting the two who had been left behind by the carpenter's party, and who were afraid to venture. These unfortunate men were never seen afterwards.

Having gained the opposite bank, the company now proceeded, in an oblique direction, towards the shore, which they reached about noon on the third day. The next morning, at the ebbing of the tide,

they procured some shell-fish, and having refreshed themselves, they
pursued their journey.

In the course of that day's march they fell in with a party of the
natives, belonging, as they imagined, to a new nation, by whom they
were beaten, and extremely ill treated. To avoid their persecutions
they concealed themselves in the woods till the savages had retired,
when they assembled again and resumed their march. They had not
proceeded far before they perceived the prints of human feet in the
sand, from which they concluded that their late companions were
before them. In the hope of rejoining them they traced their supposed
footsteps for a while, but soon lost them among the rocks and grass.

After some time they came to another river, not very broad, but
of considerable depth, which they passed in safety on a catamaran,
as before. Nothing remarkable occurred during the three following
days; but at the expiration of that period they overtook the carpenter's
party, whose sufferings they found had been even more severe than
their own. The carpenter himself had been poisoned by eating some
kind of fruit, with the nature of which he was unacquainted: M.
D'Espinette and M. Olivier, worn out with famine and fatigue, had
been left to their fate. The unfortunate little traveller, Law, was still
with them, and had hitherto supported every hardship in an astonishing manner.

Thus once more united they proceeded together till they came
to a sandy beach, where they found a couple of planks with a spike
nail in each. This convinced them that some European ships had
been near the coast, or that they were in the vicinity of some settlement. The nails were prizes of the first consequence; these, being
flattened between two stones, were shaped into something like knives,
and, to men in their situation, were considered a most valuable ac-
quisition.

In a short time they came to another river, on whose banks they
accidentally found fresh water, which induced them to rest there for
the night. In the morning they crossed the river, and on examining
the sea-shore they found another dead whale, which diffused a general joy, till a large party of the natives, armed with lances, came
down upon them. These people, however, perceiving the deplorable
condition of the travellers, conducted themselves in such a pacific
manner as to dispel their apprehensions. One of them even lent
those who were employed upon the whale his lance, by means of
which, and their two knives, they cut it into chunks, and carried off
a considerable quantity, till they could find wood and water to dress it.

On coming to a river the following day, another of the party
drooped, and they were under the cruel necessity of leaving him behind. Having plenty of provisions, they now proceeded four days

without intermission, and procuring a stick, they sat about making a kind of calendar, by cutting a notch for every day; but, in crossing a river, this register of time was lost, and the care they had taken to compute their melancholy days was of no avail.

They soon reached a new river, where they halted for the night. The frequent impediments of rivers much retarded their progress. Few of these, however, are of very great magnitude at any distance from the sea; but as the travellers derived all their subsistence from the watery element, they were obliged to submit to the inconvenience of passing them in general where the tide flowed. This will account for difficulties, from which, had it been practicable, a more inland course would have exempted them.

As the weather was very unfavorable next morning, some of the company were afraid to cross the river, upon which Hynes, and about ten more, being impatient to proceed, swam across, leaving the rest, among whom was master Law, behind them. Having gained the opposite shore, they proceeded till they came to a place where they met with shell-fish, wood, and water. Here they halted two days, in expectation of the arrival of the others; but as it still blew fresh, they concluded that their more timorous companions had not ventured to cross the river; therefore thinking it in vain to wait any longer, they went forward.

They had not travelled many hours before they had the good fortune to discover a dead seal on the beach. One of their knives being in possession of this party, they cut up their prey, dressed part of the flesh on the spot, and carried the rest with them.

The next morning the party left behind overtook them. It was not conducted by the ship's steward, and in the interval from the recent separation it appeared that they had suffered extremely from the natives, from hunger, and fatigue, and that five of them were no more. Thus these unfortunate men were rapidly losing some of their body; yet the reflection of their forlorn condition did not rouse them to the good effects of unanimity, which alone, had it been either a permanent principle, or enforced by an authority to which they ought to have submitted, might have saved them many distresses, and would have tended to the preservation of numbers. Concord is always strength; the contrary, even in the happiest circumstances, is weakness and ruin.

Having shared the remainder of the seal among them, and taken some repose, they again proceeded in one body, and after some time came to a lofty mountain, which it was necessary to cross, or go round the bluff point of a rock on which the surf beat with great violence. The latter appearing to be much the shortest passage, they chose it, but had much reason to repent their determination, as they had a miraculous escape with their lives. Some of them not only lost their provisions, but their firebrands, which they had hitherto carefully carried with them, were extinguished by the waves.

Dispirited by this essential loss, which was their chief protection from the wild beasts, they felt the misery of their situation with aggravated force, and an additional gloom clouded their further prospects. Marching along in this disconsolate mood, they fell in with some female natives, who immediately fled. When the travellers came up to the spot where these women had been first descried, they had the satisfaction to find that the fire on which they had been dressing muscles was not extinguished. With joy they lighted their brands, and after a few hours repose they pursued their course.

Next day they arrived at a village, where the natives offered to barter a young bullock with them. The inside of a watch, some buttons, and other trifles, were offered and readily accepted in exchange; the beast being delivered up, was despatched by the lance of one of the natives. The Caffres were pleased to receive back the entrails, and the carcass being divided up in the most impartial manner, our people took up their abode for the night near the village, and the next morning passed another river on a catamaran.

The bullock was the only sustenance they had hitherto received from the natives, by barter or favor, excepting that the women sometimes gave the poor child who accompanied them some milk. Among the most barbarous nations, the females, to the honor of their sex, are always found to be comparatively humane, and never was there a more just object of commiseration than master Law. Hitherto he had got on tolerably well, through the benevolent attention of his companions. He walked when able, and when tired they carried him in turn without a murmur. None ever obtained any food without allowing him a share. When the rest were collecting shell-fish he was left to watch the fire, and on their return he participated in the spoils.

They now entered a sandy desert, which they were ten days in passing. In this desolate tract they had many rivers to pass; and had it not been for the supply of food they carried with them, they must all have perished. However, they had wood in abundance, seldom failed to find water by digging in the sand, and being safe from the apprehensions of the natives, this appears to have been the most pleasant part of their journey.

Having crossed the desert, they entered the territories of a new nation, by whom they were sometimes maltreated, and at others were suffered to pass without molestation. Being now on the borders of the ocean, they fell in with a party of the natives, who, by signs, advised them to go inland; and complying with their directions, they soon arrived at a village, where they found only women and children. The women brought out a little milk, which they gave to master Law.

It was contained in a small basket, curiously formed of rushes, and so compact as to hold any kind of liquid. Here they had the opportunity of examining several huts, and observed the mode in which the natives churn their butter. The milk is put into a leather bag, which is suspended in the middle of the tent, and pushed backward and forward by two persons, till the butter arrives at a proper consistence. When thus prepared, they mix it with soot, and anoint themselves with the composition, which proves a defense against the intense heat of the climate, and renders their limbs uncommonly pliant and active.

While the travellers were resting themselves, the men belonging to the village returned from hunting, each bearing upon the point of his spear a piece of deer's flesh. They formed a ring around the strangers, and seemed to gaze on them with admiration. After having satisfied their curiosity, they produced two bowls of milk, which they appeared willing to barter; but as our wretched countrymen had nothing to give in exchange, they drank it up themselves.

Scarcely had they finished their meal, when they all rose up, and in an instant went off into the woods, leaving the Englishmen under some apprehensions as to the cause of this sudden motion. In a short time, however, they returned with a deer, and though our people earnestly entreated to be permitted to partake of the spoil, the natives not only disregarded their solicitations, but likewise insisted on their quitting the kraal. This they were obliged to comply with, and after walking a few miles they lay down to rest.

For several days they pursued their journey without any remarkable occurrence. They frequently fell in with the natives, who had great numbers of oxen, but they would part with nothing without a return, which was not in the power of the travellers to make. They had, however, the negative satisfaction of not being annoyed in their progress. They now came to another river, where they saw three or four huts, containing only women and children. The flesh of sea-cows and sea-lions was hanging up to dry, of which the women gave the travellers a part. They slept that night at a small distance from these huts.

Next morning, Hynes and nine others swam across the river, but the rest were too timorous to make the attempt. Those who had crossed the river soon afterwards had the good fortune to observe a seal asleep, just at high-water mark, and having cut off his retreat, they found means to kill him. Having divided the flesh, they travelled four or five days, occasionally falling in with the natives, who, upon the whole, behaved with tolerable forbearance.

They now arrived at another river, which they were obliged to cross, and proceeding on their route, the next day found a whale; and thus being well supplied with provisions they resolved to halt for their companions; but after waiting in vain two days they proceeded without them. They afterwards found that their companions had taken a more inland route, and had got before them. Having, therefore, cut up as much of the whale as they could carry, and being much refreshed, they proceeded with alacrity, having now no necessity to loiter in quest of food.

Thus they travelled for more than a week, and in their way discovered some pieces of rags, which satisfied them that their late associates had got the start of them. They now entered an extensive sandy desert, and finding, towards the close of the first day, but little prospect of obtaining either wood or water, they were much disheartened. To their joy, however, at the entrance of a deep gully they saw the following words traced on the sand: *Turn in here and you will find plenty of wood and water.* This cheered them like a revelation from heaven, and on entering the gully they found the notification verified, and the remains of several fires, which assured them that their late companions had reposed in the same place.

They proceeded several days, proportionably exhausted with fatigue as they advanced, but without any memorable occurrence. They now came to a bluff point of a rock, which projected so far into the sea as to obstruct their progress, so that they were obliged to direct their course more inland. To add to their distress, their provisions were again exhausted, when, arriving at a large pond, they luckily found a number of land-crabs, snails, and some sorrel in the vicinity, and on these they made a satisfactory meal.

As soon as it dawned they resumed their journey, and entering a wood, they observed many of the trees torn up by the roots. While they were lost in amazement at this phenomenon, to their terror and astonishment thirty or forty large elephants started up out of the long grass, with which the ground was covered. The travellers stood some moments in suspense, whether they would retreat or advance; but, by taking a circuitous course, they passed these enormous creatures without any injury. The grass in which they lay was not less than eight or nine feet high. This may appear strange to those who are not acquainted with the luxuriant vegetation of tropical climates, but other travellers, of unquestionable veracity, have made the same remarks on Africa.

Having reached the sea-shore that night, our travellers were miserably disappointed by the state of the tide, which deprived them of their usual supplies of shell-fish. To such extremities were they, in consequence, reduced, that some of them, who had made shoes of the hide of the bullock obtained in barter from the natives, singed off the hair, broiled and eat them. This unsavory dish they rendered as palatable as possible by means of some wild celery they found on the spot, and the whole party partook of it.

At low water they went as usual to the rocks to procure shell-fish;

and as they proceeded they often perceived evident traces of that division of their party which had got the start of them. In two days' time they fell in with a hunting party of the natives, who offered no molestation to our people as they passed, and for several days they everywhere behaved with the same forbearance.

After passing two rivers, and finding no fresh water near them, they entered a sterile country, where the natives appeared to have nothing to subsist on but what they derived from hunting and fishing. What then must have been the situation of our travellers! They had not a drop of water for several days; and a few berries which they occasionally picked up were the only alleviation of their burning thirst. However, they soon reached Caffraria, properly so called, which they found to be a fine and prosperous country.

During their march through this territory our travellers were absolutely starving in the midst of plenty. They saw abundance of cattle, but so tenacious were the natives of their property, that they would not part with any thing gratuitously, and our people had nothing to give in barter. So apprehensive were the Caffres, lest these poor vagrants might commit depredations, that they constantly secured their cattle as they approached, and even used violence to keep them at a distance. So true is it that in all countries poverty is considered rather as a crime than a misfortune, and that he who has nothing to bestow is immediately suspected of an intention to take away.

But the Caffres have been characterized as a humane and inoffensive people. How are we then to reconcile this description with the conduct they displayed to our countrymen? May not the idea, that they were Dutchmen, solve the difficulty? Between the Caffres and the Dutch colonists an inveterate enmity existed at that period. The Caffres had been treated with unparalleled cruelty and oppression by the white people with whom they were conversant; all white people were, therefore, probably regarded as enemies. Among uncivilized nations, wherever any intercourse has been established with Europeans, the character of the latter, in general, have been determined from the conduct of a worthless few. Thus, as on other important occasions, many suffer for the vices of individuals.

Our travellers, everywhere repelled, or regarded with apprehension, at length came to a river, and having crossed it, were met by a party of the natives, one of whom had adorned his hair with a piece of a silver buckle, which was known to have belonged to the ship's cook. It seems the cook, who set a particular value upon his buckles, had covered them with bits of cloth, to conceal them from the natives; but at length hunger had compelled him to break them up, in order to barter them for food; but no sooner was the price deposited than the natives broke their engagement, as had been their general practice, except in one solitary instance, and drove the claimants away.

Hynes and his party were roughly handled by the natives they had fallen in with. To avoid their persecution, they travelled till late at night, and after reposing for a few hours, they recommenced their journey before it was light, that they might escape a repetition of their ill treatment.

Next, day, about noon, they reached a spot where there was good water, and a probability of finding an abundance of shell-fish; here, being much fatigued, they determined to spend the night. While in this situation they were overtaken by a tremendous storm of thunder and lightning, and the rain poured down in such torrents that they were obliged to hold up their canvass frocks over the fire to save it from being extinguished. Next day, at low water, they found shell-fish, as usual, staid some time to dry their clothes, and then resumed their journey. Coming to a large village the inhabitants fell upon them with such fury, that several of them were wounded, in consequence of which, one man died soon afterwards. Hynes received a wound in his leg from a lance, and being knocked down, was left senseless on the spot by his companions, who supposed him to be dead. However, in a few hours, to their great joy, he rejoined his countrymen, who had despaired of ever seeing him again.

From this time they lost sight of the habitations of the natives, and entered a sandy desert, where it was with the utmost difficulty they could procure any sustenance. At intervals, indeed, they experienced the usual bounty of the sea, and having collected as many shell-fish as possible, they opened them in the fire, and taking out the animal, left the shell, which greatly diminished the labor of carriage.

Having passed the desert, they arrived at a large river, which, as they afterwards learned from the Dutch, is called Bosjesman's river. Here they found Thomas Lewis, one of the party which had gone before them, who, having been taken ill, was abandoned to his fate. He informed them that he had travelled inland and seen many huts, at one of which he obtained a little milk, and at another was beaten away. He added, that having reached the place where he now was, he found himself too weak to cross the river, and was, therefore, determined to return to the nearest kraal, indifferent as to his reception or his life. In vain his companions strove to overcome this determination. They flattered him with the hope of yet being able to reach the Cape, but their encouragement was ineffectual. Both his body and mind were broken down; he had drained the cup of affliction to the dregs; despair had laid her iron hand upon him, and sealed him for her own. In spite of all their entreaties he went back to the natives, and once more had the good fortune to receive assistance, when he could least of all expect it, and in such a shape as proved effectual to his preservation. But we are anticipating events.

On exploring the sea-coast, our people, to their great joy, discovered another whale, and having cut the flesh into junks, took with them as much of it as they were able to carry. Again losing sight of the natives and their huts, they were kept in perpetual alarm by the wild beasts, which were here more numerous than in any part of the country through which they had hitherto passed.

On the fourth day, after passing the river, they overtook the ship's steward and master Law, who still survived inexpressible hardships. From them they learned that the cooper had been buried the preceding evening in the sand; but when Hynes and the steward went to take a farewell view of the spot, they found, to their surprise and horror, that the body had been carried off by some carnivorous animal, which had evidently dragged it to a considerable distance.

Hynes' party presented the steward and child with some of the flesh of the whale, by which they were much refreshed; and for eight or ten days more they all proceeded in company. At length, they came to a point of rocks, and as the whale was by this time wholly consumed, they went round the edge in search of such sustenance as the sea might afford. This took up so much time that they were obliged to sleep on the rock, where they could procure no water but what was very brackish. In the morning the steward and the child were both taken ill, and being unable to proceed, the party agreed to halt till the next day. The extreme coldness of the rock on which they had slept produced a sensible effect on them all; the steward and child still continued very ill. Their companions, therefore, agreed to wait another day, when, if no favorable turn took place, they would be under the painful necessity of abandoning them to their fate. But their humanity was not put to this severe test, for in the course of the following night this poor child resigned his breath, and ceased any longer to share their fatigues and sorrows. They had left him, as they supposed, asleep, near the fire round which they had all rested during the night; but when they had made their arrangements for breakfast, and wished to call him to participate, they found that his soul had taken its flight to another world.

Forgetting their own misery they sensibly felt for the loss of this tender youth, and the affliction of the steward in particular was inexpressible. This child had been the object of his fondest care, during a long and perilous journey, and it was with the utmost difficulty that his companions could tear him from the spot.

They had not proceeded far before one of the party asked for a shell of water, which being given him, he solicited a second, and as soon as he had drunk it, lay down and instantly expired. So much were they habituated to scenes of distress, that, by this time, death had ceased to be regarded as shocking; it was even considered by them as a consummation rather to be wished for than dreaded. They left the poor man where he dropped, and had not advanced far, when another complained of extreme weakness, and sat down upon the sand by the sea-side. Him too they left, compelled by severe necessity, in order to seek for wood and water, promising, if they were successful, to return and assist him.

Having sought in vain for a comfortable resting-place for the night, they were all obliged to respose on the sands. Recollecting the situation of their comrade, one of the party went back to the spot where he had been left, but the unhappy man was not to be found; and as he had nothing to shelter or protect him, it is more than probable that he was carried off by wild beasts.

With the first approach of day they resumed their journey, but their situation was now more deplorable than ever. Having had no water since the middle of the preceding day, they suffered exceedingly from thirst, the glands of their throats and their mouths were much swollen; and in the extremity of thirst they were induced to swallow their own urine.

This was the crisis of calamity. The misery they now underwent was too shocking to relate. Having existed for two days without food or water, they were reduced to such an extremity that when any of them could not furnish himself with a draught of urine, he would borrow a shell full of his more fortunate companion till he was able to repay it. The steward, whose benevolence ought to immortalize his memory, now followed his little favorite to another world. In short, to such a state of wretchedness were they now reduced, that death was stripped of all its terrors.

Next morning two more of the party were reduced to a very languid state; one of them, unable to proceed a step farther, lay down, and his companions, incapable of affording him any assistance, took an affectionate farewell, and left him to expire.

Towards evening they reached a deep gully, which they entered, in the hope of meeting with fresh water. Here they found another of the Grosvenor's crew lying dead, with his right hand cut off at the wrist. A circumstance so singular could not fail to attract the notice of his companions, especially as they recollected that it had been the common asseveration of the deceased,—*May the devil cut my right arm off if it not be true!* It had a sensible effect upon his comrades for a time, as they superstitiously imagined that Providence had interfered, by a miracle, to show its indignation against his profaneness. One of the company, who had lost his own clothes in crossing a river, took the opportunity of supplying himself by stripping the dead man, and then they proceeded till night, without any other sustenance than what their own water afforded them.

Next day brought no alleviation of their miseries. Necessity impelled them to proceed, though hope scarcely darted a ray through the gloom of their prospects. The whole party was, at last, reduced to three persons, Hynes, Evans, and Wormington, and these could hope to survive their companions only a very few days. Their faculties rapidly declined, they could scarcely hear or see, and a vertical sun darted its beams so intensely that it was with the utmost difficulty they could proceed.

Their misery, from thirst, now became so intolerable, that Wormington earnestly importuned his companions to determine by lot which of them should die, in order that the others might be preserved by drinking his blood. Hynes, though almost childish, was shocked at the proposal; his tears flowed abundantly, and he declared, that as long as he was able to walk he could not think of casting lots; but that, if he should be obliged to drop, they might then use him as they pleased. Upon this, Wormington, shaking hands with Hynes and Evans, suffered them to proceed without him.

Every hour now seemed to throw a deeper gloom over their fate; nature could support them no more. Hynes and Evans, however, made another effort to advance, without even indulging a hope of the possibility of relief. They this day saw something before them which had the appearance of large birds, but their surprise may be conceived when, upon a nearer approach they discovered them to be men. Nearly blind and idiots, they did not at first recollect their newly found companions, but after some time they recognised in them four of the steward's party from which they had been separated. One of them, a boy, named Price, advanced to meet them, and gave them the pleasing information, that his associates had fresh water in their possession. This inspired them with new life, and reciprocal inquiries were made relative to the fate of their lost companions. The three men whom Hynes and his companion had overtaken were named Berney, Leary, and De Lasso, who hearing that Wormington was left behind, the two latter went in search of him, charging those who remained not to suffer Hynes and Evans to drink too freely of the water, as several had expired from the eagerness with which they swallowed that fluid after long abstinence.

Wormington was recovered by the humanity of those who went in search of him, and a painful detail of suffering succeeded. It appeared that the captain's steward had been buried in the sand of the last desert over which they passed, and that the surivivors were reduced to such extremity, that after his interment two of the party were sent back to cut off his flesh for their immediate support; but while proceeding upon this horrid errand, they had the good fortune to discover a young seal, newly driven on shore, and fresh bleeding, which proved a most seasonable relief. They farther stated, that they had obtained shell-fish in the sand, when none were to be seen upon it, by observing the manner in which the birds scratched for them. Without this discovery they must inevitably have perished.

Hynes and Evans, recounting their adventures to the party they had joined, among other circumstances mentioned that the ship's steward, whom they had left to expire on the road, had on very decent clothes. This tempted one of them to propose to Evans, who was by this time pretty well recovered, to go back to the spot and strip the body, but the steward could not be found, and concluded that the wild beasts had anticipated their design. In the evening Evans returned, but without his companion, who had been so indolent and advanced with such a slow pace, that the former was obliged to leave him behind. As he was never seen afterwards, no doubt can be entertained but that he likewise fell a victim to the ravenous beasts. These were so numerous as to be seen in troops of twenty or more; and it was the common and effectual practice of the travellers to shout as loud as possible to drive away those formidable animals.

Having now arrived at a favorable spot for water and shell-fish, they employed two days in collecting provisions for their future march, and in refreshing themselves. Rest and food had an astonishing effect in restoring not only the powers of the body, but of the mind; and in a short time they thought themselves qualified to encounter new fatigues.

With extreme difficulty and danger they passed a large river, supposed to be the Sontag, on a catamaran, and having reached the opposite shore, they looked back with terror and amazement on their fortunate escape from being driven out to sea by the rapidity of the stream. Here they likewise found a kind of shell-fish which buries itself in the sand, and which increased their supplies.

The united party, consisting of six persons, pursued their route over a desert country, where neither hut nor native was to be seen, and in six days reached the Schwartz river, as they afterwards learned, on the banks of which they took up their abode for the night.

The country, at length, began to assume a fertile and cultivated appearance, and some huts appeared at a distance from the shore. While contemplating with pleasure this change of prospect, the grass near them took fire, and spread with great rapidity. They all used every effort to extinguish it, lest this involuntary mischief should provoke the resentment of the natives, or the blaze call them to the spot.

Next morning they swam over the river in safety, and soon discovered another dead whale lying on the sea-shore. Thus supplied with food they purposed resting here a few days, if they could have found fresh water, but that necessary article being wanting, they cut up as much of the whale as they could carry, and proceeded on their route. In two hours they came to a thicket, where they met with water, and halted to rest.

Next morning four of the party went back to the whale for a larger supply, De Lasso and Price being left in charge of the fire. As

Price was collecting fuel he perceived at a little distance two men with guns, and being intimidated at the sight, he returned hastily to the fire, whither the welcome intruders pursued him. These men belonged to a Dutch settlement in the neighborhood, and were in search of some strayed cattle. One of them, named John Battores, supposed to be a Portuquese, was able to converse with De Lasso, the Italian, so as to be understood; a circumstance as fortunate as it was little to be expected. Battores having learned the outline of their melancholy story, accompanied them to the whale, where their companions were employed in cutting away the flesh. Affected at the sight of these miserable objects, he desired them to throw away what they had been collecting, promising them better fare when they reached the habitation to which he belonged.

In vain shall we attempt to describe the sensations of the shipwrecked wanderers on receiving this intelligence, and that they were within four hundred miles of the Cape. The joy that instantly filled every bosom produced effects as various as extraordinary; one man laughed, another wept, and the third danced with transport.

On reaching the house of Mynheer Christopher Roostooff, to whom Battores was bailiff, they were treated with the kindest attention. The master, on being acquainted with their distress, immediately ordered bread and milk to be set before them; but acting rather on principles of humanity than prudence, he furnished them such a quantity that their weak stomachs were overloaded. After their meal, sacks were spread upon the ground for them to repose on.

It had been so long since they had known any thing of the calculation of time, that they were unacquainted even with the name of the month; and they were given to understand, that the day of their deliverance was the twenty-ninth of November; so that one hundred and seventeen days had revolved their melancholy hours since they were shipwrecked; a period of suffering almost unparalleled, and during which they had often been miraculously preserved.

Next morning Mynheer Roostooff killed a sheep for the entertainment of his guests, and another Dutchman, of the name of Quin, came with a cart and six horses to convey them towards the Cape. The boy, Price, being lame, from the hardships he had undergone, was detained at Roostooff's house, who kindly undertook his cure, and promised to send him after the others when he had recovered. The rest of the party proceeded to Quin's house, where they were hospitably entertained four days.

From that time they were forwarded in carts, from one settlement to another, till they arrived at Swellendam, about one hundred miles from the Cape. Wherever they passed they experienced the humanity of the farmers, and their wants were relieved with a liberal hand.

At Swellendam they were detained till orders should be received from the governor at the Cape, in regard to their future destiny, Holland and Great Britain being at that time at war. At length two of the party were ordered to be forwarded to the Cape in order to be examined, while the rest were to remain at Swellendam. Accordingly Wormington, and Leary proceeded to the Cape, where, after being strictly interrogated, they were sent on board a Dutch man-of-war lying in the bay, with orders that they should be sent to work. While in this situation, Wormington having discovered that the boatswain was engaged in some fraudulent practices, imprudently threatened to give information, on which the boatswain, desiring him and his companion to step into a boat, conveyed them on board a Dutch East Indiaman, just getting under way, and by this fortunate incident they first reached their native land.

But to return to the fate of the rest. Though the flames of war were raging between the two nations, the Dutch government, at the Cape, being informed of the particulars of the loss of the Grosvenor, with a humanity which does them infinite honor, despatched a large party in quest of the unhappy wanderers. This detachment consisted of one hundred Europeans, and three hundred Hottentots, attended by a great number of wagons, each drawn by eight bullocks. The command was given to captain Muller, with orders to proceed, if possible, to the wreck, and to endeavor to discover such of the sufferers as were still wandering about the country, or in the hands of the natives.

De Lasso and Evans accompanied this expedition as guides; but Hynes, being still very weak, was left at Swellendam. The party was well provided with such articles as were most likely to insure them a favorable reception from the natives, and procure them the liberty of the unfortunate persons they might find in their way. They proceeded with spirit and alacrity, till the Caffres, in consequence of their antipathy to the colonists, interrupted the expedition. In their progress they found Thomas Lewis, who had been abandoned by his companions, as before mentioned, and William Hatterly, who was servant to the second mate, and had continued with that party till he alone survived. Thus the fate of one division was ascertained.

At other places on the road they met with seven lascars, and two black women, one of whom was servant to Mrs. Logie, and the other to Mrs. Hosea. From these women they learned, that soon after Hynes' party had left the captain and the ladies, they also took separate routes; the latter intending to join the lascars, but what became of them after this separation was unknown. They, indeed, saw the captain's coat on one of the natives, but whether he died or was killed could never be discovered.

After the enmity of the natives prevented the progress of the wagons, some of the party travelled forward fifteen days on horseback, in the prosecution of their plan, but the Caffres still continuing to harass them, they were obliged to return, after an absence of about three months.

Captain Muller returned to Swellendam, with the three Englishmen, the seven lascars, and the two black women, the boy, Price, and the two guides, De Lasso and Evans. The people of color were detained at Swellendam; but the English were forwarded to the Cape, where, after being examined by the governor, they were permitted to take their passage to Europe in a Danish ship, the captain of which promised to land them in England; but, excepting Price, who was set on shore at Weymouth, they were all carried to Copenhagen, from whence they at last found their way to England.

Such was the termination of the adventures of these unfortunate people; but the inquiry concerning the fate of the captain and his party was not dropped. Though it is probable that before the first Dutch expedition could have reached them they all paid the debt of nature; rumors had been spread that several of the English were still in captivity among the natives, and these obtained such general belief, that M. Vailant, whose philanthropy equalled his genius and resolution, made another attempt to discover the reputed captives; but he could learn nothing decisive as to their situation or final fate.

The public mind, however, continued still to be agitated, and the interest which all nations took in the fate of the unhappy persons, particularly the women, some of whom it was reported had been seen, induced a second party of Dutch colonists, with the sanction of government, to make another effort to explore the country, and to reach the wreck.

These men, amply provided, set out on the twenty-fourth of August, [1783], from Kaffer Keyl's river, towards cape Natal, on the coast of which the Grosvenor was supposed to have been wrecked. Of this expedition we have a journal kept by Van Reenen, one of the party, and published by captain Riou. It would not be generally interesting to the reader to give the meagre details of distance travelled, and elephants killed; of danger encountered, and rivers crossed; we shall therefore confine ourselves to such incidents as appear to deserve notice, or are connected with the melancholy subject of our narrative.

After proceeding an immense way, on the third of November they arrived among the Hambonaas, a nation quite different from the Caffres. They have a yellow complexion, and their long, coarse hair is frizzled up in the form of a turban. Some of these people informed our adventurers, that, subject to them, there was a village of bastard Christians, descended from people shipwrecked on the coast, of whom three old women were still alive and married to a Hambonaa chief.

This intelligence roused their curiosity, and they were fortunate enough to obtain an interview with the old women in question, who said they were sisters, but having been shipwrecked when children, they could not say to what nation they originally belonged. The Dutch adventurers offered to take them and their children back on their return, at which they seemed much pleased. It appears probable, that the reports which had been spread, in regard to some European women being among the natives, originated from this circumstance, and as the existence of any other white people in this quarter was neither known nor suspected, it was naturally concluded that they must have belonged to the Grosvenor.

The Dutch afterwards fell in with Trout, whose name has been mentioned in the preceding narrative. He at first engaged to conduct them to the spot where the Grosvenor was wrecked, and informed them that nothing was then to be seen, excepting some cannon, iron, ballast, and lead: adding, that all the unfortunate crew of the ship had perished, some by the hands of the natives and the rest of hunger.

Trout, who, it is to be feared, was guilty of much duplicity from the first, pretended that he was a freeman, and had sailed in an English ship from Malacca; but finding himself likely to be detected, and probably much apprehensive of being carried back to the Cape, he cautiously avoided the Dutch in the sequel, and left them to find their way to the wreck in the best manner they were able.

As they were proceeding to the spot, one of the party, named Houltshausen, unfortunately fell into a pit of burnt stakes, by which he was terribly wounded in the palm of one of his hands, which eventually produced a locked jaw, and terminated in his death. These pits are dug by the natives, and being covered over with branches of trees and grass, serve as snares for the elephants, which frequently fall into them, and are thus taken.

Several of the party, however, proceeded on horseback to the wreck, and found nothing more than what Trout had described remaining. It was plainly perceived that fires had been made in the vicinity, and on a rising ground, between two woods, was a pit, where things had been buried and dug out again. This likewise was tallied with the information of Trout, who told them that all the articles collected from the wreck had been dispersed over the country, and that most of them had been carried to Rio de la Goa, to be sold. That place was represented to be about four days' journey from the scene of the catastrophe.

The natives in the neighborhood expressed great astonishment that the Dutch had been at such infinite pains to come in search of the unfortunate crew, and they all promised, that in case of any similar disaster they would protect such people as might be thrown upon the coast, if they could be assured of obtaining beads, copper, and iron, for their trouble, which was liberally promised by the Dutch.

These intrepid adventurers, who were now four hundred and thirty-seven leagues distant from the Cape, and two hundred twenty-six beyond any Christian habitation, finding that nothing farther was to be discovered relative to the wreck, or the fate of the persons who had reached the shore, determined to return, particularly as Houltshausen's illness increased.

On their way back they called at the bastard Christian village, and would have taken under their protection the three old women, who seemed desirous of living among Christians, but they wished first to gather in their crops; adding, when that business was accomplished, their whole race, to the number of four hundred, would be happy to depart from their present settlement. Every indulgence was promised them in case they should be disposed to emigrate to the Cape. On seeing people of the same complexion as themselves they appeared to be exceedingly agitated.

On their homeward journey the Dutch shot many elephants and sea-cows; but on the first of December they met with a terrible accident, while employed in cutting up the sea-cows killed the preceding day. "As we were thus engaged (says the journalist), a large elephant made up to the wagons; we instantly pursued and attacked him, when, having received several shot, by which he twice fell, he crept into a very thick underwood. Thinking we had killed him, Tjaart Vander Valdt, Lodewyk Prins, and Ignatus Mulder, advanced to the spot, when he rushed out furiously from the thicket, and catching hold of Prins with his trunk, trod him to death, driving one of his tusks through the body, and throwing it up into the air to the height of thirty feet.

"The others, perceiving that there was no possibility of escaping on horseback, dismounted, and crept into the thicket to hide themselves. The elephant seeing nothing in view but one of the horses, followed him for some time, but then turning about came back to the spot where the dead man was left. At this instant our whole party renewed the attack, and after he had received several more wounds, again escaped into the thickest part of the wood.

"We now supposed ourselves safe, but while we were digging a grave for our unfortunate companion, the elephant rushed out again, and drove us all from the place. Tjaart Vander Valdt got another shot at him: a joint attack being commenced, he began to stagger, and falling, the Hottentots despatched him as he lay on the ground."

The rest of their journey afforded little worth notice. In January, 1791, they reached their respective homes, after surmounting incredible difficulties, in an expedition to which they were prompted solely by a principle of humanity, and the desire of relieving, if any remained alive, such of our countrymen as might be among the natives. No intelligence of this kind could, however, after the most diligent inquiries, be obtained. They were, indeed, informed that the ship's cook had been alive about two years before the period of their journey, but that he then caught the small-pox and died.

We cannot conclude this mournful narrative better than with the sensible reflections of captain Riou.

"Had the party (says he) that set out in search of these shipwrecked people, in 1783, prosecuted their journey with the same degree of zeal and resolution that Van Reenen's party manifested, it is possible they might have discovered and relieved some who have since perished. Yet, as they could not have arrived at the place of the wreck in less than six months after the disaster happened, there is no great probability for supposing that after such a length of time had elapsed, any great number of the unfortunate sufferers could be remaining alive.

"But what we have most to regret is, that, perhaps, the failure of the endeavors of the unfortunate crew to save their lives was owing to their own misconduct. It is too often the case, that disorder and confusion are the consequences of extreme distress, and that despair, seizing on the unprincipled mind, hurries it on to a subversion of all good order and discipline: so that at the moment when the joint efforts of the whole are most necessary for the common good, each desponding, thoughtless member acts from the impulse of the moment, in whatever manner his tumultuous feelings may direct; and from an erroneous idea of self-interest, or wonderful as it may appear, from a desire of gratifying a rebellious and turbulent spirit, at a time when it can be done with impunity, is always ready to overturn every plan that may be proposed by his superiors, and the considerate few that happen to be of the party.

"Such must have been, and such we are indeed told was, the situation of the crew of Grosvenor subsequent to their shipwreck.

"Though it may be said to be very easy to see errors when their consequences are apparent, it will not surely be too much to assert, that when this ship's crew was once safely on shore, with the advantage of such articles as they could procure from the wreck, their situation, however deplorable, could not be considered as hopeless. For had a chosen body of ten or twenty men marched a few days to the northward, they must have fallen in with Rio de la Goa, where it seldom happens that there is not a French or Portuguese slave ship. But allowing Captain Coxson was much out of his reckoning, and that he supposed himself much nearer to the Cape than he really was, they might then have existed on the sea-coast, in that climate, sheltered by huts, till ready to set out, and by preserving order and discipline, and conducting themselves properly in regard to the natives, they might gradually have proceeded in safety to the territories of the Dutch.

"Had the crew continued under the orders of their officers, either of those objects might have been accomplished, by men whose minds were not wholly resigned to despair; or they might have subsisted on what provision they could pick up from the wreck, together with what they could purchase from the natives, till a boat could have been constructed and sent to solicit assistance from the Cape.

"These reflections have been extended by considering the circumstances in which the shipwrecked people were placed; from all which it may fairly be concluded, that the greater part might have effected a return to their native land, had they been guided by any idea of the advantages of discipline and subordination.

"It is to be hoped, then, that the fatal consequence attending disorderly conduct on these calamitous occasions, will impress on the minds of seamen this incontrovertible truth, that their only hope of safety must depend upon obedience."

[10]

Loss of the *Halsewell* East Indiaman

THE LOSS of the *Halsewell*, like that of the *Earl of Abergavenny*, illustrates the relative helplessness of even well-found sailing ships in familiar waters. The English Channel was not called the Narrow Seas for nothing, and the combination of bad weather and a lee shore was lethal. This narrative gives one of the few instances of well-organized and effective help offered to the victims of shipwreck two hundred years ago; doubtless the quarrymen were accustomed to taking orders, and they were certainly less fearful of heights and working with rope support than most people would have been. The benevolence of the master of the Crown Inn of Blanford is noted in the last paragraph of the narrative. In 1786 the Red Cross was one generous inn-keeper with a comfortable dinner and a few half-crowns.

Henry Meriton and John Rogers, officers of the *Halsewell* and survivors of the wreck, published *A Circumstantial Narrative of the Loss of the Halsewell* in London in 1786. That account was probably the basis for Thomas's narrative given here.

HALSEWELL EAST INDIAMAN.

THE Halsewell East Indiaman, of seven hundred and fifty-eight tons burthen, Richard Pierce, Esq. commander, having been taken up by the Directors to make her third voyage to coast and bay, fell down to Gravesend the 16th of November, 1785, and there completed her lading. Having taken the ladies and other passengers on board at the Hope, she sailed through the Downs on Sunday, January the 1st, 1786, and the next morning, being abreast of Dunnose, it fell calm.

The ship was one of the finest in the service, and supposed to be in the most perfect condition for her voyage; and the commander a man of distinguished ability and exemplary character. His officers possessed unquestionable knowledge in their profession; the crew, composed of the best seamen that could be collected, was as numerous as the establishment admits. The vessel likewise contained a considerable body of soldiers, destined to recruit the forces of the company in Asia.

The passengers were Miss Eliza Pierce, and Miss Mary Anne Pierce, daughters of the commander; Miss Amy Paul, and Miss Mary Paul, daughters of Mr. Paul, of Somersetshire, and relations of captain Pierce; Miss Elizabeth Blackburne, daughter of captain B. likewise in the service of the East India company: Miss Mary Haggard, sister to an officer on the Madras establishment; Miss Ann Mansell, a native of Madras, but of European parents, who had received her education in England; and John George Schutz, Esq. returning to Asia, where he had long resided, to collect a part of his fortune which he had left behind.

On Monday, the 2d of January, at three P.M. a breeze springing up from the south, they ran in shore to land the pilot. The weather coming on very thick in the evening, and the wind baffling, at nine they were obliged to anchor in eighteen fathoms water. They furled their top-sails, but were unable to furl their courses, the snow falling thick and freezing as it fell.

Tuesday, the 3d, at four o'clock A.M. a violent gale came on from E.N.E. and the ship driving, they were obliged to cut their cables and run out to sea. At noon, they spoke with a brig to Dublin, and having put their pilot on board of her, bore down channel immediately. At eight in the evening, the wind freshening, and coming to the southward, they reefed such sails as were judged necessary. At ten, it blew a violent gale at south, and they were obliged to carry a press of sail to keep the ship off the shore. In this situation, the hause-plugs, which, according to a recent improvement, were put inside, were washed in, and the hause-bags washed away, in consequence of which they shipped a great quantity of water on the gun-deck.

Upon sounding the well, they found that the vessel had sprung a leak, and had five feet of water in her hold; they clued up the main top-sail, hauled up the main-sail, and immediately attempted to furl both, but failed in the attempt. All the pumps were set to work, on the discovery of the leak.

Wednesday the 4th, at two A.M. they endeavored to wear the ship, but without success. The mizzen-mast was instantly cut away, and a second attempt made to wear, which succeeded no better than the former. The ship having now seven feet of water in her hold, and the leak gaining fast on the pumps, it was thought expedient for the preservation of the ship, which appeared to be in immediate danger of foundering, to cut away the main-mast. In its fall, Jonathan More-ton, coxswain, and four men, were carried overboard by the wreck and drowned. By eight o'clock, the wreck was cleared, and the ship got before the wind. In this position she was kept about two hours, during which the pumps reduced the water in the hold two feet.

At ten in the morning the wind abated considerably, and the ship labored extremely, rolled the fore top-mast over on the larboard side, which, in the fall, tore the fore-sail to pieces. At eleven, the wind came to the westward, and the weather clearing up, the Berry-Head was distinguished, at the distance of four or five leagues. Having erected a jury main-mast, and set a top-gallant-sail for a main-sail, they bore up for Portsmouth, and employed the remainder of the day in getting up a jury mizzen-mast.

On Thursday the 5th, at two in the morning, the wind came to the southward, blew fresh, and the weather was very thick. At noon, Portland was seen bearing north by east, distant about two or three leagues. At eight at night, it blew a strong gale at south; the Portland lights were seen bearing north-west, distant four or five leagues, when they wore ship and got her head to the westward. Finding they lost ground on that tack, they wore her again, and kept stretching to the eastward, in the hope of weathering Peverel Point, in which case they intended to have anchored in Studland bay. At eleven, they saw St. Alban's Head, a mile and a half to the leeward, upon which they took in sail immediately, and let go the small bower anchor, which brought up the ship at a whole cable, and she rode for about an hour, and then drove. They now let go the sheet anchor, and wore away a whole cable; the ship rode about two hours longer when she drove again.

In this situation the captain sent for Mr. Meriton, the chief officer, and asked his opinion concerning the probability of saving their lives. He replied with equal candor and calmness, that he apprehended there was very little hope, as they were then driving fast on shore, and might expect every moment to strike. It was agreed that the boats could not then be of any use, but it was proposed that the officers should be confidentially requested, in case an opportunity presented itself, of making it serviceable, to reserve the long boat for the ladies and themselves, and this precaution was accordingly taken.

About two, in the morning of Friday the 6th, the ship still driving, approaching the shore very fast, the same officer again went into the cuddy where the captain then was. Captain Pierce expressed extreme anxiety for the preservation of his beloved daughters, and earnestly asked Mr. Meriton, if he could devise any means of saving them. The latter expressed his fears that it would be impossible, adding, that their only chance would be to wait for the morning upon which the captain lifted up his hands in silent distress.

At this moment the ship struck with such violence, as to dash the heads of those who were standing in the cuddy against the deck above them, and the fatal blow was accompanied by a shriek of horror, which burst at the same instant from every quarter of the ship.

The seamen, many of whom had been remarkably inattentive and remiss in their duty during a great part of the storm, and had actually skulked into their hammocks, leaving the working of the pump, and the other labors required by their situation, to the officers, roused to a sense of their danger, now poured upon the deck, to which the utmost endeavors of their officers could not keep them while their assistance might have been useful. But it was now too late; the ship continued to beat upon the rocks, and soon bilged, falling with her broadside towards the shore. When the ship struck, several of the men caught hold of the ensign staff, under the apprehension of her going to pieces immediately.

At this critical juncture, Mr. Meriton offered his unhappy companions the best advice that could possibly be given. He recommended that they should all repair to that side of the ship which lay lowest on the rocks, and take the opportunities that might then present themselves of escaping singly to the shore. He then returned to the round-house, where all the passengers and most of the officers were assembled. The latter were employed in affording consolation to the unfortunate ladies, and with unparalleled magnanimity, suffering their compassion for the amiable companions of their own danger, and the dread of almost inevitable destruction. At this moment what must have been the feelings of a father—of such a father as captain Pierce?

The ship had struck on the rocks near Seacombe, on the island of Purbeck, between Peverel-point and St. Alban's Head. On this part of the shore the cliff is of immense height, and rises almost perpendicularly. In this particular spot the cliff is excavated at the base, presenting a cavern ten or twelve yards in depth, and equal in breadth to the length of a large ship. The sides of the cavern are so nearly upright as to be extremely difficult of access, and the bottom of it is strewed with sharp and uneven rocks which appear to have been rent from above by some convulsion of nature. It was at the mouth of this cavern that the unfortunate vessel lay stretched almost from side to side, and presented her broadside to the horrid chasm. But, at the time the ship struck it was too dark to discover the extent of their danger, and the extreme horror of their situation.

The number in the round-house was now increased to nearly fifty, by the admission of three black women and two soldier's wives, with the husband of one of the latter, though the sailors, who had demanded entrance to get a light, had been opposed and kept out by the officers. Captain Pierce was seated on a chair, or some other movable, between his two daughters, whom he pressed alternately to his affectionate bosom. The rest of the melancholy assembly were seated on the deck, which was strewed with musical instruments, and the wreck of furniture, boxes, and packages.

Here Mr. Meriton, after having lighted several wax candles, and all the glass lanthorns he could find, likewise took his seat, intending to wait till daylight, in the hope that it would afford him an opportunity of effecting his own escape, and also rendering assistance to the partners of his danger. But, observing that the ladies appeared parched and exhausted, he fetched a basket of oranges from some part of the round-house, with which he prevailed on some of them to refresh themselves.

On his return he perceived a considerable alteration in the appearance of the ship. The sides were visibly giving way, the deck seemed to heave, and he discovered other evident symptoms that she could not hold together much longer. Attempting to go forward to look out, he instantly perceived that the ship had separated in the middle and that the fore-part had changed its position, and lay rather farther out towards the sea. In this emergency he determined to seize the present moment, as the next might have been charged with his fate, and to follow the example of the crew and the soldiers, who were leaving the ship in numbers, and making their way to a shore, with the horrors of which they were yet unacquainted.

To favor their escape an attempt had been made to lay the ensign-staff from the ship's side to the rocks, but without success, for it snapped to pieces before it reached them. By the light of a lanthorn, however, Mr. Meriton discovered a spar, which appeared to be laid from the ship's side to the rocks, and upon which he determined to attempt his escape. He accordingly lay down upon it, and thrust himself forward, but soon found that the spar had no communication with the rock. He reached the end and then slipped off, receiving a violent contusion in his fall. Before he could recover his legs, he was washed off by the surge, in which he supported himself by swimming till the returning wave dashed him against the back of the cavern. Here he lay hold of a small projection of the rock, but was so benumbed that he was on the point of quitting it, when a seaman, who had already gained a footing, extended his hand and assisted him till he could secure himself on a little shelf of the rock, from which he clambered still higher till he was out of the reach of the surf.

Mr. Rogers, the third mate, remained with the captain and the ladies nearly twenty minutes after Mr. Meriton had left the ship. The latter had not long quitted the round house, before the captain inquired what was become of him, and Mr. Rogers replied, that he had gone upon deck to see what could be done. A heavy sea soon afterwards broke over the ship, upon which the ladies expressed great concern at the apprehension of his loss. Mr. Rogers proposed to go and call him, but this they opposed, fearful lest he might share the same fate.

The sea now broke in at the fore part of the ship, and reached as far as the main-mast. Captain Pierce and Mr. Rogers then went together, with a lamp, to the stern gallery, where, after viewing the rocks, the captain asked Mr. Rogers if he thought there was any possibility of saving the girls. He replied, he feared not; for they could discover nothing but the black surface of the perpendicular rock, and not the cavern which afforded shelter to those who had escaped. They then returned to the round house, where captain Pierce again seated himself between his two daughters, struggling to suppress the parental tear which then started into his eye.

The sea continuing to break in very fast, Mr. Rogers, Mr. Schutz, and Mr. M'Manus, a midshipman, with a view to attempt their escape, made their way to the poop. They had scarcely reached it, when a heavy sea breaking over the wreck, the round house gave way, and they heard the ladies shriek at intervals, as if the water had reached them; the noise of the sea at other times drowned their voices.

Mr. Brimer had followed Mr. Rogers to the poop, where, on the coming of the fatal sea, they jointly seized a hen-coop, and the same wave which whelmed those who remained below in destruction, carried him and his companion to the rock, on which they were dashed with great violence, and miserably bruised.

On this rock were twenty-seven men; but it was low water, and being convinced that, upon the flowing of the tide, they must all be washed off, many endeavored to get to the back or sides of the cavern beyond the reach of the returning sea. Excepting Mr. Rogers and Mr. Brimer, scarcely more than six succeeded in this attempt. Of the remainder, some experienced the fate they sought to avoid, others perished in endeavoring to get into the cavern.

Mr. Rogers and Mr. Brimer, however, having reached the cavern, climbed up the rock, on the narrow shelves of which they fixed themselves. The former got so near to his friend, Mr. Meriton, as to exchange congratulations with him; but between these gentlemen, there were about twenty men, none of whom could stir but at the most imminent hazard of his life. When Mr. Rogers reached this station, his strength was so nearly exhausted, that had the struggle continued a few minutes longer he must inevitably have perished.

They soon found that though many who had reached the rocks below, had perished in attempting to ascend, yet that a considerable number of the crew, seamen, soldiers, and some of the inferior officers, were in the same situation with themselves. What that situation was, they had still to learn. They had escaped immediate death; but they were yet to encounter a thousand hardships for the precarious chance of escape. Some part of the ship was still discernible, and they cheered themselves in this dreary situation, with the hope that it would hold together till day break. Amidst their own misfortunes, the sufferings of the females filled their minds with the acutest anguish; every returning sea increased their apprehensions for the safety of their amiable and helpless companions.

But, alas! too soon were these apprehensions realized. A few minutes after Mr. Rogers had gained the rock, a general shriek, in which the voice of female distress was lamentably distinguishable, announced the dreadful catastrophe! In a few moments, all was hushed, excepting the warring winds and the dashing waves. The wreck was whelmed in the bosom of the deep, and not an atom of it was ever discovered. Thus perished the Halsewell, and with her, worth, honor, skill, beauty, and accomplishments!

This stroke was a dreadful aggravation of woe to the trembling and scarcely half-saved wretches, who were clinging about the sides of the horrid cavern. They felt for themselves, but they wept for wives, parents, fathers, brothers, sisters,—perhaps lovers!—all cut off from their dearest, fondest hopes!

Their feelings were not less agonized by the subsequent events of that ill-fated night. Many who had gained the precarious stations on the rocks, exhausted with fatigue, weakened by bruises, and benumbed with cold, quitted their hold, and falling headlong, either upon the rocks below, or into the surf, perished beneath the feet of their wretched associates, and by their dying groans and loud acclamations, awakened terrific apprehensions of a similar fate in the survivors.

At length, after three hours of the keenest misery, the day broke on them, but far from bringing with it the expected relief, it served only to discover to them all the horrors of their situation. They were convinced, that had the country been alarmed by the guns of distress, which they continued to fire several hours before the ship struck, but, which, from the violence of the storm, were unheard, they could neither be observed by the people above, as they were completely ingulphed in the cavern, and overhung by the cliff; nor was any part of the wreck remaining to indicate their probable place of refuge. Below, no boat could live to search them out, and had it been possible to acquaint those who were willing to assist them, with their exact situation, they were at a loss to conceive how any ropes could be conveyed into the cavern to facilitate their escape.

The only method, that afforded any prospect of success, was to creep along the side to its outer extremity, to turn the corner on a ledge scarcely as broad as a man's hand, and to climb up the almost perpendicular precipices, nearly two hundred feet in height. In this desperate attempt, some succeeded, while others, trembling with terror, and exhausted with bodily and mental fatigue, lost their precarious footing, and perished.

The first men who gained the summit of the cliff were the cook, and James Thompson, a quarter-master. By their individual exertions they reached the top, and instantly hastened to the nearest house, to make known the situation of their fellow-sufferers. Eastington, the habitation of Mr. Garland, steward, or agent, to the proprietors to the Purbeck quarries, was the house at which they first arrived. That gentleman immediately assembled the workmen under his direction, and with the most zealous humanity exerted every effort for the preservation of the surviving part of the crew of the unfortunate ship.

Mr. Meriton had, by this time, almost reached the edge of the precipice. A soldier, who preceded him, stood upon a small projecting rock, or stone, and upon the same stone Mr. Meriton had fastened his hands to assist his progress. Just at this moment the quarrymen arrived, and seeing a man so nearly within their reach they dropped a rope, of which he immediately laid hold. By a vigorous effort to avail himself of the advantage, he loosened the stone, which giving way, Mr. Meriton must have been precipitated to the bottom, had not a rope been lowered to him at the instant, which he seized, while in the act of falling, and was safely drawn to the summit.

The fate of Mr. Brimer was peculiarly severe. He had been married only nine days before the ship sailed, to the daughter of Captain Norman, of the Royal Navy, came on shore, as it has been observed, with Mr. Rogers, and, like him, got up the side of the cavern. Here he remained till the morning, when he crawled out; a rope was thrown him, but he was either so benumbed with the cold as to fasten it about him improperly, or so agitated as to neglect to fasten it at all. Whatever was the cause, the effect proved fatal; at the moment of his supposed preservation he fell from his stand, and was unfortunately dashed to pieces, in sight of those who could only lament the deplorable fate of an amiable man and skilful officer.

The method of affording help was remarkable, and does honor to the humanity and intrepidity of the quarrymen. The distance from the top of the rock to the cavern, over which it projected, was at least one hundred feet: ten of these formed a declivity to the edge, and the remainder was perpendicular. On the very brink of this precipice stood two daring fellows, with a rope tied round them, and fastened above to a strong iron bar fixed into the ground. Behind these, in like manner, stood others, two and two. A strong rope, likewise properly secured, passed between them, by which they might hold, and support themselves from falling. Another rope, with a noose ready fixed, was then let down below the cavern, and the wind blowing hard, it was sometimes forced under the projecting rock, so that the sufferers could reach it without crawling to the edge. Whoever laid hold of it, put the noose around his waist, and was drawn up with the utmost care and caution by their intrepid deliverers.

In this attempt, however, many shared the fate of the unfortunate Mr. Brimer. Unable, through cold, perturbation of mind, weakness, or the inconvenience of the stations they occupied, to avail themselves of the succor that was offered them, they were precipitated from the stupendous cliff, and either dashed to pieces on the rocks, or falling into the surge, perished in the waves.

Among these unhappy sufferers, the death of a drummer was attended with circumstances of peculiar distress. Being either washed off the rocks by the sea, or falling into the surf, he was carried by the returning waves beyond the breakers. His utmost efforts to regain them were ineffectual, he was drawn further out to sea, and being a remarkably good swimmer, continued to struggle with the waves, in the view of his commiserating companions, till his strength was exhausted, and he sank,—to rise no more!

It was late in the day when all the survivors were carried to a place of safety, excepting William Trenton, a soldier, who remained on his perilous stand till the morning of Saturday, the 7th, exposed to the united horrors of extreme personal danger, and the most acute disquietude of mind.

The surviving officers, seamen, and soldiers, being assembled at the house of their benevolent deliverer, Mr. Garland, they were mustered, and found to amount to 74, out of more than 240, which was nearly the number of the crew and passengers when she sailed through the Downs. Of the rest, it is supposed that fifty or more sank with the Captain and the ladies in the round house, and that upwards of seventy reached the rocks, but were washed off, or perished in falling from the cliffs. All those who reached the summit survived, excepting two or three, who expired while being drawn up, and a black who died a few hours after he was brought to the house. Many, however, were so miserably bruised, that their lives were doubtful, and it was a considerable time before they perfectly recovered their strength.

The benevolence and generosity of the master of the Crown Inn, at Blanford, deserves the highest praise. When the distressed seamen arrived at that town he sent for them all to his house, and having given them the refreshment of a comfortable dinner, he presented each man with half a crown to help him on his journey.

Loss of His Majesty's Ship *Amphion*

THE LOSS of the *Amphion* is an example of still another maritime hazard, peculiar to ships of war. Fighting ships had to carry considerable quantities of gunpowder, and explosion was always a possibility. In this case the combination of high explosives and a drunken and possible larcenous gunner was fatal to over 200 people—though there is no certain knowledge of how the explosion came about.

Gilly's list of 417 ships lost from the Royal Navy between 1793 and 1849 includes the names of seven ships burned and four exploded, with one that might have been either. Explosion was not statistically a great danger, but when it occurred the loss of life was always very high.

Thomas is the source for this narrative.

LOSS OF

HIS B. MAJESTY'S SHIP AMPHION.

THE Amphion frigate, Captain Israel Pellow [Pellew], after having cruised some time in the North Seas, had at length received an order to join the squadron of frigates commanded by Sir Edward Pellow [Pellew]. She was on her passage, when a hard gale of wind occasioning some injury to the fore-mast, obliged her to put back into Plymouth, off which place she then was. She accordingly came into the Sound, anchored there on the 19th [September, 1796], then went up into harbor the next morning.

On the 22d, at about half past four P.M., a violent shock, as of an earthquake, was felt at Stone-house, and extended as far off as the Royal hospital and the town of Plymouth. The sky towards the Dock appeared red, like the effect of a fire; for near a quarter of an hour, the cause of this appearance could not be ascertained, though the streets were crowded with people running different ways in the utmost consternation.

When the alarm and confusion had somewhat subsided, it first began to be known that the shock had been occasioned by the explosion of the Amphion. Several bodies and mangled remains were picked up by the boats in Harmoaze; and their alacrity on this occasion was particularly remarked and highly commended. The few who remained alive of the crew were conveyed, in a mangled state, to the Royal Hospital. As the frigate was originally manned from Plymouth, the friends and relations of her unfortunate ship's company mostly lived in the neighborhood. It is dreadful to relate what a scene took place—arms, legs and lifeless trunks, mangled and disfigured by gunpowder, were collected and deposited at the hospital, having been brought in sacks to be owned. Bodies still living, some with the loss of limbs, others having expired as they were being conveyed thither; men, women and children, whose sons, husbands, and fathers were among the unhappy number, flocking round the gates, entreating admittance. During the first evening nothing was ascertained concerning the cause of this event, though numerous reports were instantly circulated. The few survivors, who, by the following day, had, in some degree, regained the use of their senses, could not give the least account. One man who was brought alive to the Royal Hospital, died before night, another before the following morning; the boatswain and one of the sailors appeared likely, with great care, to do well. Three or four men who were at work in the tops, were blown up with them, and falling into the water, were picked up with very little hurt. These, with the two before mentioned, and one of the sailor's wives, were supposed to be the only survivors, besides the captain and two of the lieutenants.

The following particulars were, however, collected from the examination of several persons before Sir Richard King, the port-admiral, and the information procured from those, who saw the explosion from the Dock.

The first person known to have observed any thing was a young midshipman in the Cambridge guard-ship, lying not far distant from the place where the Amphion blew up; who having a great desire to observe every thing relative to a profession into which he had just entered, was looking through a glass at the frigate, as she lay along side of the sheer-hulk, and was taking in her bowsprit. She was lashed to the hulk; and the Yarmouth, an old receiving ship, was lying on the opposite side, quite close to her, and both within a few yards of the Dock-yard jetty. The midshipman said, that the Amphion suddenly appeared to rise altogether upright from the surface of the water, until he nearly saw the keel; the explosion then succeeded; the masts seemed to be forced up into the air, and the hull instantly to sink. All this passed in the space of two minutes.

The man who stood at the Dock-yard stairs, said, that the first he heard of it was a kind of hissing noise, and then followed the explosion, when he beheld the masts blown up into the air. It was very strongly reported that several windows were broken in the Dock by the explosion, and that in the Dock-yard, much mischief was done by the Amphion's guns going off when she blew up; but though the shock was felt as far off as Plymouth, and at Stone-house, enough to shake the windows, yet it is a wonderful and miraculous fact, that surrounded as she was in the harbor, with ships close along-side of the jetty, and lashed to another vessel, no damage was done to any thing but herself. It is dreadful to reflect, that owing to their inten-tion of putting to sea the next day, there were nearly one hundred men, women and children, more than her complement on board, taking leave of their friends, besides the company who were at two dinners given in the ship, one of which was by the captain.

Captain Israel Pellow, and captain William Swaffield, of his Majesty's ship Overyssel, who was at dinner with him and his first lieutenant, were drinking their wine; when the first explosion threw them off their seats, and struck them against the carlings of the upper deck, so as to stun them. Captain Pellow, however, had sufficient presence of mind to fly to the cabin-windows, and seeing the two hausers, one slack in the bit and the other taut, threw himself with an amazing leap, which he afterwards said, nothing but his sense of danger could have enabled him to take, upon the latter, and by that means saved himself from the general destruction, though his face had been badly cut against the carlings, when he was thrown from his seat. The first lieutenant saved himself in the same manner, by jump-ing out of the window, and by being also a remarkably good swim-mer; but captain Swaffield, being, as it was supposed, more stunned, did not escape. His body was found on the twenty-second of October, with his skull fractured, appearing to have been crushed between the sides of the vessels.

The sentinel at the cabin door happened to be looking at his watch; how he escaped no one can tell, not even himself. He was, however, brought on shore, and but little hurt; the first thing he felt was, that his watch was dashed out of his hands, after which he was no longer sensible of what happened to him. The boatswain was standing on the cat-head; the bowsprit had been stepped for three hours; the gammoning and every thing on; and he was directing the men in rigging out the jib-boom, when suddenly he felt himself driven upwards and fell into the sea. He then perceived that he was entangled in the rigging, and had some trouble to get clear; when being taken up by a boat belonging to one of the men of war, they found that his arm was broken. One of the surviving seamen declared to an officer of rank, that he was preserved in the following truly astonishing manner:—He was below at the time the Amphion blew up, and went to the bottom of the ship; he recollected that he had a knife in his pocket, and taking it out, cut his way through the com-panion of the gun-room, which was already shattered with the explo-sion; then letting himself up to the surface of the water, he swam unhurt to the shore. He showed his knife to the officer, and declared he had been under water full five minutes.

It was likewise said, that one of the sailor's wives had a young child in her arms; the fright of the shock made her take such fast hold of it, that though the upper part of her body alone remained, the child was found alive, locked fast in her arms, and likely to do well.

Mr. Spry, an auctioneer who had long lived in great respectability at Dock, with his son and god-son, had gone on board to visit a friend, and were all lost.

About half an hour before the frigate blew up, one of her lieutenants, and lieutenant Campbell of the marines, and some of the men got into the boat at the dock-yard stairs, and went off to the ship. Lieutenant Campbell had some business to transact at the Marine barracks in the morning, and continuing there some time, was engaged by the officers to stay to dinner and spend the evening with them. Some persons, however, who had, in the interval, come from the Amphion, informed lieutenant Campbell there were some letters on board for him. As they were some which he was extremely anxious to receive, he left the barracks about half an hour before dinner to fetch them, intending to return immediately; but while he was on board, the ship blew up. He was a young man universally respected and lamented by the corps, as well as by all who knew him. One of the lieutenants who lost his life was the only support of an aged mother and sister, who, at his death, had neither friend nor relation left to comfort and protect them. The number of people who were afterwards daily seen at Dock, in deep mourning for their lost relatives, was truly melancholy.

Captain Pellow was taken up by the boats and carried to the Commissioner Fanshaw's house, in the dock-yard, very weak with the exertions he had made, and so shocked with the distressing cause of them, that he at first appeared scarcely to know where he was, or to be sensible of his situation. In the course of a day or two, when he was a little recovered, he was removed to the house of a friend, Dr. Hawker of Plymouth.

Sir Richard King had given a public dinner in honor of the coronation. Captain Charles Rowley, of the Unite frigate, calling in the morning, was engaged to stay, and excused himself from dining, as he had previously intended, on board the Amphion.

Captain Darby of the Bellerophon, was also to have dined with captain Pellow, and had come round in his boat from Cawsand Bay; but having to transact some business concerning the ship with Sir Richard King, it detained him half an hour longer at Stone-house than he expected. He had just gone down to the beach, and was stepping into the boat to proceed up to Harmoaze when he heard the fatal explosion. Captain Swaffield was to have sailed the next day, so that the difference of twenty-four hours would have saved that much lamented and truly valuable officer. His brother, Mr. J. Swaffield, of the Pay-Office, being asked to the same dinner, had set off with him from Stone-house, but before he had reached the Dock, a person came after him upon business, which obliged him to return, and thus saved him from sharing his brother's untimely fate.

Many conjectures were formed concerning the cause of this catastrophe. Some conceived it to be owing to neglect, as the men were employed in drawing the guns, and contrary to rule, had not extinguished all the fires, though the dinners were over. This, however, the first lieutenant declared to be impossible, as they could not be drawing the guns, the key of the magazine hanging, to his certain knowledge, in his cabin, at the time. Some of the men likewise declared that the guns were drawn in the Sound, before they came to Harmoaze. It was also insinuated, that it was done intentionally, as several of the bodies were afterwards found without clothes, as if they had prepared to jump overboard before the ship could have time to blow up. As no mutiny had ever appeared in the ship, it seems unlikely that such a desperate plot should have been formed, without any one who survived, having the least knowledge of it. It is, besides, a well-known fact, that in almost every case of shipwreck, where there is a chance of plunder, there are wretches so destitute of the common feelings of humanity as to hover round the scene of horror, in hopes, by stripping the bodies of the dead, and seizing whatever they can lay their hands on, to benefit themselves.

It was the fore-magazine which took fire; had it been the after one, much more damage must have ensued. The moment the explosion was heard, Sir Richard arose from dinner, and went in his boat on board the hulk, where the sight he beheld was dreadful; the deck covered with blood, mangled limbs and entrails blackened with gunpowder, the shreds of the Amphion's pendant and rigging hanging about her, and pieces of her shattered timbers strewed all around. Some people at dinner in the Yarmouth, though at a very small distance, declared that the report they heard did not appear to be louder than the firing of a cannon from the Cambridge, which they imagined it to be, and had never risen from dinner, till the confusion upon deck led them to think that some accident had happened.

At low water, the next day, about a foot and a half of one of the masts appeared above water; and for several days, the dock-yard men were employed in collecting the shattered masts and yards, and dragging out what they could procure from the wreck. On the twenty-ninth, part of the fore-chains was hauled, shattered and splintered, also the head and cut-water.

On the 3rd of October, an attempt was made to raise the Amphion, between the two frigates, the Castor and Iphigenia, which were accordingly moored on each side of her; but nothing could be got up, excepting a few pieces of the ship, one or two of her guns, some of the men's chests, chairs, and part of the furniture of the cabin. Some bodies floated out from between decks, and among the rest a midshipman's. These, and all that could be found, were towed round by boats through Stone-house bridge, up to the Royal Hospital stairs, to be interred in the burying ground. The sight for many weeks was truly dreadful; the change of tide washing out the putrid bodies, which were towed round by the boats when they would scarcely hold together.

Bodies continued to be found so late as the 30th of November, when the Amphion having been dragged round to another part of the dock-yard jetty, to be broken up, the body of a woman was washed out from between decks. A sack was also dragged up, containing gun-powder, covered over at the top with biscuit, and this in some measure confirmed an idea which had before gained ground, that the gunner had been stealing powder to sell, and had concealed what he could get out by degrees, in the above manner; and that, thinking himself safe on a day when every one was entertaining his friends, he had carelessly been among the gunpowder without taking the necessary precautions. As he was said to have been seen at Dock very much in liquor in the morning, it seems probable that this might have been the cause of a calamity as sudden as it was dreadful.

[12]

LOSS OF THE FRENCH SHIP *Droits de L'Homme*

THIS NARRATIVE by an English captive has a certain amount of interest in its comments on the lack of subordination in the French republican navy, in its quite normal experience of lack of cooperation and endeavor on the part of the people on shore, and in its presentation of the relatively good feeling of the French toward the English prisoners (as shown in their being sent home as soon as possible without exchanges being demanded). The major interest for some readers, however, lies in the fact that this narrative was almost certainly the source from which Herman Melville drew the name of his merchant ship in *Billy Budd, Foretopman,* his posthumous novel. Melville (as noted in the Introduction of this book) recorded in *Redburn* reading a book on shipwrecks and disasters, mentioned such reading in *Mardi,* and was given a copy of Duncan's *Mariner's Chronicle* by Hawthorne. A contemporary anonymous review of *Moby Dick,* "A Trio of American Sailor-Authors," *Dublin Review,* Jan., 1856 (cited in *Moby Dick as Doubloon,* New York, 1970, pp. 98–99) states, with complete accuracy," [Melville] has read prodigiously on all nautical subjects—naval history, narratives of voyages and shipwrecks, &c.—and he never scruples to deftly avail himself of these stores of information."

Rights-of-Man is a marvelously ironic name for the ship from which Billy Budd was kidnapped; he had no rights at all when the *Indomitable* hove in sight. Melville's ironic sense may have responded also to this narrative of the loss of the French ship. The *Droits de L'Homme,* so bravely named, grounded on the rocks of Audernie Bay, and the crew and passengers came into those most basic of all human rights—hunger, thirst, suffering, and death.

This narrative is from *Remarkable Shipwrecks.*

> ". . . the lieutenant pushed off from the *Rights-of-Man.* That was the merchant-ship's name; though by her master and crew abbreviated in sailor fashion into the *Rights.*"

> ". . . the new recruit . . . making a salutation as to the ship herself, 'And good-by to you too, old *Rights-of-Man!*' "

> HERMAN MELVILLE, *Billy Budd, Foretopman,*
> section 1.

DROITS DE L'HOMME.

On the 5th of January, 1797, returning home on leave of absence from the West Indies, in the Cumberland letter of marque, for the recovery of my health, saw a large man-of-war off the coast of Ireland, being then within four leagues of the mouth of the river Shannon. She hoisted English colors, and decoyed us within gun-shot, when she substituted the tri-colored flag, and took us. She proved to be les Droits de L'Homme, of 74 guns, commanded by the *ci devant* baron, now citizen La Crosse, and had separated from a fleet of men-of-war, on board of which were twenty thousand troops, intended to invade Ireland. On board of this ship was General Humbert, who afterwards effected a descent in Ireland (in 1799) with nine hundred troops and six hundred seamen.

On the 7th of January, went into Bantry Bay to see if any of the squadron were still there, and on finding none, the ship proceeded to the southward. Nothing extraordinary occurred until the evening of the 13th, when two men-of-war hove in sight, which afterwards proved to be the Indefatigable and Amazon frigates. It is rather remarkable that the captain of the ship should inform me, that the squadron which was going to engage him was Sir Edward Pellew's, and declared, as was afterwards proved by the issue, that "he would not yield to any two English frigates, but would sooner sink his ship with every soul on board." The ship was then cleared for action, and we English prisoners, consisting of three infantry officers, two captains of merchantmen, two women, and forty-eight seamen and soldiers, were conducted down to the cable tier at the foot of the fore-mast.

The action began with opening the lower deck ports, which, however, were soon shut again, on account of the great sea, which occasioned the water to rush in to such a degree that we felt it running on the cables. I must here observe, that the ship was built on a new construction, considerably longer than men-of-war of her rate, and her lower deck, on which she mounted thirty-two pounders French, equal to forty pounders English, was two feet and a half lower than usual. The situation of the ship, before she struck on the rocks, has been fully represented by Sir Edward Pellew, in his letter of the 17th of January, to Mr. Nepean: the awful task is left for me to relate what ensued.

At about four in the morning, a dreadful convulsion, at the foot of the foremast, roused us from a state of anxiety for our fate to the idea that the ship was sinking!—It was the fore-mast that fell over the side; in about a quarter of an hour an awful mandate from above was re-echoed from all parts of the ship: *Pauvres Anglais! pauvres Anglais! Montez bien vite, nous sommes tous perdus!*—"Poor Englishmen! poor Englishmen! Come on deck as fast as you can, we are all lost!" Every one rather flew than climbed. Though scarcely able to move before, from sickness, yet I now felt an energetic strength in all my frame, and soon gained the upper deck, but what a sight! dead, and wounded, and living, intermingled in a state terrible beyond description: not a mast standing, a dreadful loom of the land, and breakers all around us. The Indefatigable, on the starboard quarter, appeared standing off, in a most tremendous sea, from the Penmark Rocks, which threatened her with instant destruction. To the great humanity of her commander, those few persons who survived the shipwreck, are indebted for their lives, for had another broadside been fired, the commanding situation of the Indefatigable must have swept off, at least, a thousand men.—On the starboard side was seen the Amazon, within two miles, just struck on shore. Our own fate drew near. The ship struck and immediately sunk! Shrieks of horror and dismay were heard from all quarters, while the merciless waves tore from the wreck many early victims. Day-light appeared, and we beheld the shore lined with people, who could render us no assistance. At low water, rafts were constructed, and the boats were got in readiness to be hoisted out. The dusk arrived, and an awful night ensued. The dawn of the day brought with it still severer miseries than the first, for the wants of nature could scarcely be endured any longer, having been already near thirty hours without any means of subsistence, and no possibility of procuring them. At low water a small boat was hoisted out, and an English captain and eight sailors succeeded in getting to the shore. Elated at the success of these men, all thought their deliverance at hand, and many launched out on their rafts, but, alas! death soon ended their hopes.

Another night renewed our afflictions. The morning of the third, fraught with still greater evils, appeared; our continual sufferings made us exert the last effort, and we, English prisoners, tried every means to save as many of our fellow-creatures as lay in our power.— Larger rafts were constructed, and the largest boat was got over the side. The first consideration was to lay the surviving wounded, the women, and the helpless men, in the boat, but the idea of equality so fatally promulgated among the French, destroyed all subordination, and nearly one hundred and twenty having jumped into the boat, in defiance of their officers, they sank her.—The most dreadful sea that I ever saw, seemed at that fatal moment to aggravate the calamity; nothing of the boat was seen for a quarter of an hour, when the bodies floated in all directions; then appeared, in all their horrors, the wreck, the shores, the dying and the drowned! Indefatigable in acts of humanity, an adjutant-general, Renier, launched himself into the sea, to obtain succor from the shore, and perished in the attempt.

Nearly one half of the people had already perished, when the horrors of the fourth night renewed all our miseries. Weak, distracted, and destitute of every thing, we envied the fate of those whose lifeless corpses no longer wanted sustenance. The sense of hunger was already lost, but a parching thirst consumed our vitals. Recourse was had to urine and salt water, which only increased our want; half a hogshead of vinegar indeed floated up, of which each had half a wine glass; it afforded a momentary relief, yet soon left us again in the same state of dreadful thirst. Almost at the last gasp, every one was dying with misery, and the ship, now one third shattered away from the stern, scarcely afforded a grasp to hold by, to the exhausted and helpless survivors.

The fourth day brought with it a more serene sky, and the sea seemed to subside, but to behold, from fore to aft, the dying in all directions, was a sight too shocking for the feeling mind to endure. Almost lost to a sense of humanity, we no longer looked with pity on those whom we considered only as the forerunners of our own speedy fate, and a consultation took place, to sacrifice some one to be food for the remainder. The die was going to be cast, when the welcome sight of a man-of-war brig renewed our hopes. A cutter speedily followed, and both anchored at a short distance from the wreck. They then sent their boats to us, and by means of large rafts, about one hundred, out of four hundred, who attempted it, were saved by the brig that evening. Three hundred and eighty were left to endure another night's misery, when, dreadful to relate, above one half were found dead the next morning!

I was saved about ten o'clock, on the morning of the 18th, with my two brother officers, the Captain of the ship, and General Humbert. They treated us with great humanity on board the cutter, giving us a little weak brandy and water every five or six minutes, and after that, a basin of good soup. I fell on the locker in a kind of trance for nearly thirty hours, and swelled to such a degree as to require medical aid to restore my decayed faculties. Having lost all our baggage, we were taken to Brest almost naked, where they gave us a rough shift of clothes, and in consequence of our sufferings, and the help we afforded in saving many lives, a cartel was fitted out by order of the French government to send us home, without ransom or exchange. We arrived at Plymouth on the 7th of March following.

To that Providence, whose great workings I have experienced in this most awful trial of human afflictions, be ever offered the tribute of my praise and thanksgiving.

LOSS OF THE *Apollo* FRIGATE

THIS NARRATIVE, from *Remarkable Shipwrecks,* published in Hartford by Andrus and Starr in 1813, is another example of the kind of incompetence too often shown in these accounts. The Commodore was universally blamed for the loss of almost half his convoy; fifteen minutes more of darkness would have meant the loss of the whole fleet. The vessels were outside the narrow Channel waters, were following a familiar course in one of the best-known parts of the Atlantic, and still managed to pile up on the coast of Portugal. It would be interesting to know whether the commanding officer was ever entrusted with another responsibility.

LOSS OF THE

APOLLO FRIGATE,

AND TWENTY-NINE SAIL OF WEST-INDIAMEN, NEAR FIGUERA,

ON THE COAST OF PORTUGAL,

APRIL 2, 1804,

By an officer of the Apollo.

MONDAY, the 26th of March, sailed from the Cove of Cork, in company with his majesty's ship Carysfort, and Sixty-Nine sail of merchant ships, under convoy for the West-Indies; 27th, were out of sight of land, with a fair wind, blowing a strong gale, and steering W.S.W. The 28th, 29th, and 30th, weather and course nearly the same; 31st, the wind came more to the westward, but more moderate. Sunday, the 1st of April, at noon, observed in lat. 40 deg. 51 min. north; longitude, per account, 12 deg. 20 min. west; at eight o'clock on Sunday evening the wind shifted to the S.W. blowing very fresh; course S.S.E. At ten, up main-sail, and set the main stay-sail. At a quarter past ten the main-sail split by the sheeting giving way; called all hands upon deck. At half past ten strong breezes and squally; took in foretop sail, and set the fore-sail. At half past eleven the maintop-sail split; furled it and the main-sail. The ship was now under her fore-sail, main, and mizen storm stay-sail; the wind blowing hard, with a very heavy sea.

About half past three on Monday morning, the 2d, the ship struck the ground, to the astonishment of every one on board; and, by the above reckoning, we then conjectured upon an unknown shore. She continued striking the ground very heavily several times, by which her bottom was materially damaged, making much water; the chain-pumps were rigged with the utmost dispatch, and the men began to pump, but in about ten minutes she beat and drove over the shoal. On endeavoring to steer her, found her rudder carried away—she then got before the wind; the pumps were kept going, but from the quantity of water she shipped, there appeared every probability of her soon foundering, from her filling, and sinking very fast.

After running about five minutes, the ship struck the ground again, with such tremendous shocks, that all were fearful she would instantly go to pieces, and she kept stricking and driving farther on the sands, the sea making breaches completely over her. The lanyards of the main and mizen rigging being cut away, the masts fell, with a tremendous crash, over the larboard side; the fore-mast went immediately after. The ship then fell on her starboard side, with the gunwale under water. The violence with which she struck the ground, and the weight of the guns, those on the quarter-deck tearing away the bulwark, soon made the ship a perfect wreck abaft; only four or five guns could possibly be fired to alarm the convoy, and give notice of danger. On her stricking the second time, most pitiful cries were heard everywhere between decks, many of the men giving themselves up to inevitable death. I was told that I might as well stay below, as there was an equal likelihood of perishing if I got upon deck. I determined to go, but first attempted to enter my cabin, though in danger of having my legs broken by the chests floating about, and the bulk-heads giving way; I therefore desisted, and endeavored to get upon the deck, which I effected, after being several times washed down the hatchway, by the immense volume of water incessantly pouring down. The ship still beating the ground very violently, made it necessary to cling fast to some part of the wreck, to prevent being carried by the surges, or hurled by the dreadful concussions, overboard; the people holding fast by the larboard bulwark of the quarter-deck, and the main channels, while our Captain stood naked upon the cabin sky-light grating, holding fast by the stump of the mizen-mast, and making use of every soothing expression which could have been suggested to encourage men in such a perilous situation. Most of the officers and men were entirely naked, not having time to slip on a pair of trowsers. Our horrible situation every moment became more dreadful; until day light appearing, about half past four o'clock, discovered to us the land, at about two cables length distance, a long sandy beach, reaching to Cape Mondego, three leagues to the southward of us. On day-light clearing up, we could perceive between twenty and thirty sail of the convoy ashore, both to the northward and southward, and several of them perfect wrecks. Being now certain of being on the coast of Portugal, from seeing the above Cape, I am sorry to say, no person in the ship had the least idea of being so near that coast. It blowing hard, and a very great swell of the sea, (or what is generally termed, waves, running mountains high,) there was little prospect of being saved. About eight o'clock, there being every likelihood of the ship's going to pieces, and the after part laying lowest, Captain Dixon ordered every person forward, which it was very difficult to comply with, from the motion of the main-mast working on the larboard gunwale, there being no other way to get forward. Mr. Cook, the boatswain, had his thigh broken, in endeavoring to get about over the side; of six fine boats not one was saved, being all staved and carried over the booms, &c. Soon after the people got forward, the ship parted at the gangways. The crew were now obliged to stow themselves in the fore channels, and from thence to the bowsprit end, to the number of two hundred and twenty; for out of two hundred and forty persons on board when the ship struck, I suppose twenty to have previously perished between decks, and otherwise. Mr. Lawton, the gunner, the first person who attempted to swim on shore, was drowned; afterwards Lieutenant Wilson; Mr. Runcie, surgeon; Mr. M'Cabe, surgeon's mate; Mr. Stanley, master's mate; and several men, shared the same fate, by reason of the sea breaking in enormous surges over them, though excellent swimmers. About thirty persons had the good fortune to reach the shore, upon planks and spars, among whom were Lieutenant Harvey, and Mr. Callam, master's mate. Monday night our situation was truly horrid, the old men and boys dying through hunger and fatigue, with Mr. Proby, and Mr. Hayes, midshipmen. Captain Dixon remained all this night upon the bowsprit.

Tuesday morning presented us no better prospect of being relieved from the jaws of death; the wind blowing stronger, and the sea much more turbulent. About noon this day our drooping spirits were somewhat relieved by seeing Lieut. Harvey and Mr. Callam, hoisting out a boat from one of the merchant ships, to come to the assistance of their distressed shipmates. They several times attempted to launch her through the surf, but being a very heavy boat, and the sea on the beach acting so powerfully against them, that they could not possibly effect it, though assisted by nearly one hundred men, of the merchant sailors, and of the Portuguese peasants. Several men went upon rafts this day, made from pieces of the wreck, but not one soul reached the shore; the wind having shifted, and the current setting out, they were all driven to sea, among whom was our Captain, who, about three in the afternoon, went on the jib boom with three seamen; anxious to save the remainder of the ship's company, and too sanguine of getting safe on shore, he ventured upon the spar, saying, on jumping into the sea, "My lads, I'll save you all." In a few seconds he lost his hold of the spar, which he could not regain; he drifted to sea, and perished. Such was also the fate of the three brave volunteers who chose his fortune.

The loss of our Captain, who, until now, had animated the almost lifeless crew, as well as the noble exertions of Lieut. Harvey and Mr. Callam to launch the boat, not succeeding, every gleam of hope vanished, and we looked forward for certain death the ensuing night, not only from cold, hunger, and fatigue, but the expectation of the remaining part of the wreck going to pieces every moment. Had not the Apollo been a new and well-built ship, that small portion of her could not have so long resisted the waves, and stuck so well together, particularly as the after part from the chess-trees was gone, the starboard bow under water, the castle-deck nearly perpendicular, the weight of the guns hanging to the larboard bulwark, on the inside, and the bower and spare anchors on the outside, which it was not prudent to cut away, as they afforded resting places to a considerable number of men, there being only the fore channels, and cathead, where it was possible to live in, and about which were stowed upwards of one hundred and fifty men; it being impracticable to continue any longer in the head, or upon the bowsprit, by reason of the breakers washing completely over those places. The night drawing on, the wind increasing with frequent showers of rain, the sea washing over us, and looking every instant for the fore castle giving way, when we must all have perished together, afforded a spectacle truly deplorable; the bare recollection of which, even now, makes me shudder. The piercing cries of the people this dismal night, at every sea coming over them, which happened every two minutes, were pitiful in the extreme; the water running from the head down all over the body, keeping us continually wet. This shocking night, the remaining strength of every person was exerted for his individual safety. From the crowding so closely together, in such a narrow compass, and the want of something to moisten our mouths, several poor wretches were suffocated; which frequently reminded me of the Black Hole, with this difference only, that those poor sufferers were confined by strong walls, we by water; the least movement, without clinging fast, would have launched us into eternity. Some of the unfortunate crew drank salt water; several their own urine; some chewed leather; myself and many more chewed lead; from which we conceived we found considerable relief; by reason of its drawing the saliva, which we swallowed. In less than an hour after the ship struck the ground, all the provisions were under water, and the ship a wreck, so that it was impossible to procure any part. After the most painful night that is possible to conceive, on daylight appearing, we observed Lieut. Harvey and Mr. Callam, again endeavoring to launch the boat. Several attempts were made without success, a number of men belonging to the merchant ships being much bruised and hurt in assisting; alternate hopes and fears now pervaded our wretched minds; 15 men got safe on shore this morning on pieces of the wreck. About three in the afternoon of Wednesday the 4th, we had the inexpressible happiness of seeing the boat launched through the surf, by the indefatigable exertions of the brave officers, assisted by the masters of the merchant ships, with a number of Portuguese Peasants, who were encouraged by Mr. Whitney, the British Consul, from Figuera. All the crew then remaining on the wreck, were brought safe on shore, praising God for a happy deliverance from a shipwreck which has scarcely ever had its parallel. As soon as I stept out of the boat, I found several persons whose humanity prompted them to offer me sustenance, though improperly in spirits, which I avoided as much as possible. Our weak state may be conceived, when it is considered that we received no nourishment from Sunday to Wednesday afternoon, and were continually exposed to the fury of the watery element. After eating and drinking a little, I found myself weaker than before, occasioned, I apprehend, from having been so long without either. Some men died soon after getting on shore, from imprudently drinking too large a quantity of spirits. All were in a very weak and exhausted state, the greater part being badly bruised and wounded. About thirty sail of merchant ships were wrecked at the same time on this dreadful beach. Some ships sunk with all their people, and almost every ship lost from two to twelve men each; yet the situation of the remainder was not equally distressing with that of the crew of the frigate; as the merchant ships drawing a less draught of water, had mostly driven close on shore, and no person remained on board them after the first morning. The masters of the merchant ships had tents upon the beach, and some provisions they had saved from the wrecks, which they generously distributed, and gave every assistance to the Apollo's people. Thus was lost one of the finest frigates in the British navy, with sixty-one of her crew. The number of persons lost in the merchant ships was also very considerable. Dead bodies every day floated ashore, and pieces of the wreck covered the beach for ten miles in extent.

This fatal and unprecedented calamity, is universally ascribed to the carelessness and inattention of the Commodore; and it is asserted, that had it been dark a quarter of an hour longer, the *whole convoy* would have shared the same fate.

[14]

Loss of the *Earl of Abergavenny* East Indiaman

THE WRECK of the *Earl of Abergavenny* was much like that of the *Halsewell* nineteen years before; there were the same well-found Indiaman, the same familiar Channel, the same unfavorable winds, and the same lee shore. The two ships went on rocks only a few miles from each other.

This narrative, taken from Thomas's anthology, is full of puzzles. When the wind failed and the ship was drifting toward shore, why was no attempt made to anchor? The *Halsewell* dropped two anchors and dragged them both. One boat left the *Earl of Abergavenny* and reached shore success-fully, and the pilot boat took some passengers off—both after the ship had beaten over the Shambles. Why did no other boats leave the ship? Perhaps anchors *were* dropped, perhaps boats *were* hoisted out. Cornet Burgoyne, one of the sources, might not have known what was being done to save the ship and the passengers, but certainly Fourth-Officer Gilpin should have known what was going on. One is left with the impression, from this per-haps faulty narrative, that the command of the ship was something less than decisive. And here lies the major interest in this account.

The captain of the *Earl of Abergavenny* was John Wordsworth—not Wadsworth, as the text has it—the older brother of William Wordsworth. The effect of John Wordsworth's death and the way in which the poet learned of the tragedy are the subjects of two articles in *PMLA* (See Intro-duction, Note 1). Briefly, William Wordsworth, greatly shocked at the sudden death of a loved and sympathetic brother, first defended that brother's mem-ory by seizing on all favorable points and denying all condemnations and then used his tragic experience in a kind of sublimation to build greater poetry out of sorrow. Neither article says much of another theory which has been advanced—that John Wordsworth's death and William Wordsworth's subsequent conviction that Nature was less to be trusted than he had thought were responsible for the marked falling off in quality of the later poetry. The judgment of Nature is upheld by Wordsworth's own words in his "Elegiac Stanzas," but that poem is one of his successes in spite of its recog-nition of Nature as a threat to man.

John Wordsworth's death was directly responsible for three of his brother's poems. The relevant passages in them follow.

ELEGIAC STANZAS (composed 1805)

.   .   .

A power is gone, which nothing can restore;
A deep distress hath humanised my Soul.

Not for a moment could I now behold
A smiling sea, and be what I have been:

131

The feeling of my loss will ne'er be old;
This, which I know, I speak with mind serene.

Then, Beaumont, Friend! who would have been the Friend,
If he had lived, of Him whom I deplore,

.   .   .

ELEGIAC VERSES (composed 1805)

.   .   .

Full soon in sorrow did I weep,
Taught that the mutual hope was dust,
In sorrow, but for higher trust,
How miserably deep!
All vanished in a single word,
A breath, a sound, and scarcely heard.
Sea—Ship—drowned—Shipwreck—so it came,
The meek, the brave, the good, was gone;
He who had been our living John
Was nothing but a name.

.   .   .

TO THE DAISY (composed 1805)

.   .   .

Ill-fated Vessel!—ghastly shock!
—At length delivered from the rock,
The deep she hath regained;
And through the stormy night they steer;
Labouring for life, in hope and fear,
To reach a safer shore—how near,
Yet not to be attained!

'Silence!' the brave Commander cried;
To that calm word a shriek replied,
It was the last death-shriek.
—A few (my soul oft sees that sight)
Survive upon the tall mast's height;
But one dear remnant of the night—
For Him in vain I seek.

Six weeks beneath the moving sea
He lay in slumber quietly;
Unforced by wind or wave
To quit the Ship for which he died,
(All claims of duty satisfied;)
And there they found him at her side;
And bore him to the grave.

EARL OF ABERGAVENNY

EAST INDIAMAN

THE universal concern occasioned by the loss of the Earl of Abergavenny, has induced us to lay before our readers an accurate statement of this melancholy disaster, chiefly collected from the accounts which were given at the India-House, by Cornet Burgoyne, of his majesty's eighth regiment of light dragoons, who had the command of the troops on board the above vessel, and by the fourth officer of the ship, (who were among the few who fortunately escaped from the wreck,) and from the best information afterwards received.

On Friday, February the 1st [1805], the Earl of Abergavenny, East-Indiaman, captain Wadsworth [Wordsworth], sailed from Portsmouth, in company with the royal George, Henry Addington, Wexford, and Bombay Castle, under convoy of his majesty's ship Weymouth, captain Draper.

The Earl of Abergavenny was engaged in the company's service for six voyages, and this was the fourth on which she was proceeding.

Her company consisted of

Seamen, &c.	160
Troops, King's and Company's	159
Passengers at the Captain's table	40
Ditto, at the Third Mate's	11
Chinese	32
Total	402

In going through the Needles, they unfortunately separated from the convoy. The fleet, in consequence, lay to nearly the whole of the next day; but seeing nothing of the Weymouth, proceeded under moderate sail towards the next port, in hopes of being joined by the convoy. On the 5th, the convoy not appearing, it was deemed expedient to wait her arrival in Portland Roads, particularly as the wind had become rather unfavorable, having shifted several points from the N.E. Captain Clarke of the Wexford, being senior-commander, and consequently commodore, made the signal for those ships that had taken Pilots on board, to run into the Roads.

The Earl of Abergavenny having at about half past three, P.M. got a pilot on board, bore up for Portland Roads with a steady wind, when on a sudden the wind slackened, and the tide setting in fast, drove her rapidly on the Shambles. The nearer she approached, the less she was under management; and being at last totally ungovernable, was driven furiously on the rocks, off the Bill of Portland, about two miles from the shore. She remained on the rocks nearly an hour, beating incessantly with great violence, the shocks being so great, that the officers and men could scarcely keep their footing on the deck. At four P.M. the shocks became less violent, and in about a quarter of an hour she cleared the rocks. The sails were immediately set, with an intention to run for the first port, as the ship made much water; but the leak increased so fast that the ship would not obey the helm. In this situation, it was considered necessary to fire signal guns of distress. Twenty were fired: the danger did not, however, appear to those on board sufficient to render it necessary for the ship's boats to be hoisted out at this moment, as the weather was moderate, and the ship in sight of the fleet and shore.

The leak increased fast upon the pumps at five, P.M. Soon after striking, the hand pumps started above six inches, and shortly after the water increased from six to eight feet in spite of every exertion at the pumps. All endeavors to keep the water under were found in vain, and night setting in rendered the situation of all on board melancholy in the extreme; the more so, as it was then ascertained that the ship had received considerable damage in her bottom, immediately under the pumps. All hands took their turn at the pumps, alternately bailing at the fore-hatchway. At eight o'clock their situation became still more dreadful, when it was found impossible to save the ship, which was eventually sinking fast, and settling into the water. Signal guns were again discharged incessantly. The purser, with the third officer, Mr. Wadsworth, and six seamen, were sent on shore, in one of the ship's boats, to give notice to the inhabitants of the distressed state of the ship and crew. At this time a pilot boat came off, and Mr. Evans with his daughter, Mr. Routledge, Mr. Taylor, a cadet, and Miss Jackson, passengers, embarked for the shore, notwithstanding a dreadful sea, which threatened them with almost instant destruction.

For a few moments the general attention of the crew was diverted in observing the boats leave the ship; but these unfortunate people were soon reminded of their own approaching fate, by a heavy swell, which baffled almost every attempt to keep the ship above water. Every one seemed assured of his fate, and notwithstanding the unremitting attention of the officers, confusion commenced on board, as soon as it was given out that the ship was sinking. At ten, P.M. several sailors intreated to be allowed more liquor, which being refused, they attacked the spirit-room, but were repulsed by the officers, who never once lost sight of their character, or that dignity so necessary to be preserved on such an occasion, but continued to conduct themselves with the utmost fortitude to the last. One of the officers, who was stationed at the door of the spirit-room, with a brace of pistols to guard against surprise in so critical a moment, at which post he remained even while the ship was sinking, was much importuned by a sailor, while the water poured in on all sides, to grant him some liquor. The man said he was convinced "it would be all one with them in an hour hence." The officer, however, true to his trust in this perilous moment, had courage enough to repulse the man, and bid him go to his duty with his fellow-comrades, observing, "that if it was God's will they should perish, they should die like men."

At half past ten the water had got above the orlopdeck, in spite of the endeavors of the officers and crew who behaved in the most cool and exemplary manner. All on board were now anxiously looking out for boats from the shore, many wishing they had taken refuge in those that had already left the ship, as their destruction on board appeared inevitable. The utmost exertions became necessary to keep the ship above water till the boats came off from the shore. Unfortunately in the general distress and agony of the moment, the ship's boats were not hoisted out, when every soul on board might possibly have been saved. At eleven o'clock, a fatal swell gave the ship a sudden shock: she gave a surge, and sank almost instantaneously, two miles from Weymouth beach; with scarcely five minutes warning, she went down by the head in twelve fathom water, after a heavy heel, when she righted and sank with her masts and rigging standing. Many clung to loose spars, and floated about the wreck, but the majority took refuge in the shrouds. The severe shock of the ship going down, made several let go their hold, whilst others, by the velocity of the ship's descent, had not power to climb sufficiently fast to keep above the water. The Halsewell East Indiaman was wrecked within a few miles from this spot.

When the hull of the ship touched the ground, about one hundred and eighty persons were supposed to be in the tops and rigging: their situation was terrible beyond description: the yards only were above water, and the sea was breaking over them, in the dead of a cold and frosty night. In about half an hour their spirits were revived, by the sound of several boats beating against the waves at a short distance; but, alas! how vain their hopes, when on hailing the boats, not one of them came to their assistance. The sound of them died away, and they were again left to the mercy of the rude waves. By twelve o'clock their numbers had much decreased; the swell had swept off some, whilst others were, from the piercing cold, unable longer to retain their hold. Every moment they perceived some friend floating around them, for awhile, then sinking into the abyss to rise no more.

About this time a sloop was discovered; she had fortunately heard the signal guns, and came to an anchor close by the ship. The weather was moderate, and those who had survived were now promised a speedy delivery. The sloop's boat was immediately manned, and proceeded to the rigging that remained above water, when every person was taken off. The boat returned three times, taking twenty each return. Nothing could be more correct than the conduct of the crew on this occasion: they coolly got into the boat, one by one and those only as they were named by their officers. When it was supposed that every one was brought off, and the boat was about to depart for the last time, a person was observed in one of the tops: he was hailed but did not answer. Mr. Gilpin, the fourth officer, (whose extraordinary exertions on this occasion, as well as throughout the whole of this unfortunate affair, entitled him to the highest commendation,) returned to the wreck, and there found a man in an inanimate state, exhausted from the severe cold. He most humanely brought him down on his back, and took him to the boat; the man proved to be sergeant Heart of the 22nd regiment. Every possible care was taken of him, but to no effect: he died about twelve hours after he had landed. The sloop having now, as was supposed, taken on board all the survivors of the ship, returned to Weymouth. She had not however, proceeded far, before it was perceived that Mr. Baggot, the chief officer, was close astern. The sloop immediately lay to for him; but this noble spirited young man, although certain of securing his own life, disregarded his own safety, on perceiving Mrs. Blair, an unfortunate fellow passenger, floating at some distance from him. He succeeded in coming up with her, and sustained her above water, while he swam towards the sloop; but just as he was on the point of reaching it, a swell came on, and his strength being totally exhausted, he sank and never rose again. The unfortunate Mrs. Blair sank after him, and this generous youth thus perished in vain. It was nearly two o'clock, before the sloop weighed anchor from the wreck, but the wind being favorable she soon reached the port. On mustering those who had landed, it appeared that only one hundred and fifty-five persons had reached the shore out of four hundred and two who had embarked!

The greatest attention was paid to the unfortunate sufferers by the mayor and aldermen as well as the principal inhabitants of Weymouth; and the purser was immediately dispatched to the India House with the melancholy intelligence.

At daylight, February the 6th, the top-masts of the ship were seen from Weymouth. During the time the passengers and crew remained in the tops she appeared to have sunk eight feet, and was considerably lower in the morning; it was therefore conjectured, that she had sunk on a mud-bank. The Greyhound cutter was immediately stationed to guard the wreck, and the boats from the Rover succeeded in stripping the masts of the rigging. On the 7th her decks had not been blown up, and she appeared to remain in exactly the same state in which she had sunk. Her sinking so steadily is attributed to the great weight of her cargo, her floorings consisting chiefly of earthern ware. The cargo of the ship was estimated at two hundred thousand pounds, besides which she had on board dollars to the amount of two hundred and seventy-five thousand ounces, and is supposed to have been one of the richest ships that ever sailed for India. She was of the largest tonnage, and inferior only to the Ganges in the service, being at least fifteen hundred tons burthen, and built for the China trade.

About eighty officers and seamen were saved, eleven passengers, fifteen Chinese, five out of thirty-two cadets and forty-five recruits. The captain was drowned. He was nephew to captain Wadsworth, who formerly commanded the Earl of Abergavenny, and was considered one of the first navigators in the service. He was on his third voyage as captain, and, painful to relate, perished with his ship, disdaining to survive the loss of so valuable a charge: his conduct throughout the distressing scene, has been spoken of in terms of the highest praise. It is an extraordinary fact that he felt such an unaccountable depression of spirits, that he could not be persuaded to go through the usual ceremony of taking leave of the court of directors on the day appointed; and it was not till the Wednesday following, which was specially fixed for that purpose, that he yielded to the wishes of his friends, and reluctantly attended the court! He was a man of remarkably mild manners; his conduct was, in every instance, so well tempered, that he was known among his shipmates, by the title of "the Philosopher." As soon as the ship was going down, Mr. Baggot, the chief officer, went on the quarter deck, and told him, "that all exertions were now in vain; the ship was rapidly sinking." Captain Wadsworth, who, no doubt, expected it, steadfastly looked him in the face, and, at last, with every appearance of a heart-broken man, faintly answered: "Let her go! God's will be done." These were the last words he uttered; from that instant he was motionless. In a few moments the ship sank, and many who were climbing the shrouds endeavored to save him, but without success. In this endeavor Mr. Gilpin was foremost, and made several unsuccessful attempts, at the evident risk of his own life.

Loss of the Brig *Polly*

THE *Polly* was another of those small and unimportant ships remarkable only for the sufferings of those who sailed in her. Seven people died as a result of her capsizing, but the two survivors lived through 191 days and two thousand miles of helpless and agonized drifting before their rescue. Their ingenuity in making a still out of a teakettle and two pistol barrels and the Indian cook's ability to make a fire by rubbing sticks together show rather more ability at coping with disaster than can be found in stories of better-known wrecks.

Poe was so much impressed by the story of the *Polly* that he copied much of this account into his *Narrative of Arthur Gordon Pym,* using this same account from Thomas.

LOSS OF THE

BRIG POLLY.

THE Brig Polly, of one hundred and thirty tons burthen, sailed from Boston, with a cargo of lumber and provisions, on a voyage to Santa Croix, on the 12th of December, 1811, under the command of Capt. W. L. Cazneau—with a mate, four seamen and a cook; Mr. I. S. Hunt, and a negro girl of nine years of age, passengers. Nothing material happened, until the 15th, when they had cleared cape Cod, the shoal of Georges, and nearly, as they supposed, crossed the gulf stream, when there came on a violent gale from the southeast, in which the brig labored very hard, which produced a leak that so gained on the pumps as to sound nearly six feet,—when about midnight she was upset, and Mr. Hunt washed overboard! Not having any reason to hope for her righting, by much exertion the weather-lanyards were cut away, the deck load having been before thrown over, and the lashings all gone; in about half an hour, the mainmast went by the board, and soon after, the foremast, when she righted, though full of water, a dreadful sea making a fair breach over her from stem to stern.—In this situation the night wore away, and daylight found all alive except the passengers, and upon close search, the little girl was found clinging to the skylight, and so saved from drowning in the cabin. The glass and grating of the skylight having gone away, while on her beam ends, the little girl was drawn through the openings, but so much chilled that she survived but a few hours. In this situation they remained, without fire, as near as the captain can recollect, twelve days, when the cook, an Indian from Canton, near Boston, suggested the operation of rubbing two sticks together, which succeeded. Very fortunately, the caboose did not go overboard with the deck load; this was got to windward, a fire kindled, and some provisions cooked, which was the first they had tasted, except raw pork, for the whole time. They now got up a barrel of pork, part of a barrel of beef, and one half barrel of beef. A small pig had been saved alive, which they now dressed, not having any thing to feed it with. But at this time no apprehension was entertained of suffering for meat, there being several barrels stowed in the run, and upwards of one hundred under deck. With this impression, the people used the provisions very imprudently, till they discovered that the stern-post was gone, and the gale continuing for a long time, the barrels had stove, and their contents were all lost forever.

There happened to be a cask of water lashed on the quarter-deck, which was saved, containing about thirty gallons; all the rest was lost. This lasted about eighteen days, when the crew were reduced to the necessity of catching what rain they could, and having no more. At the end of forty days, the meat was all gone, and absolute famine stared them in the face. The first victim to this destroyer was Mr. Paddock, the mate, whose exquisite distress seemed to redouble the sufferings of his companions. He was a man of a robust constitution, who had spent his life in the Bank fishing, had suffered many hardships and appeared the most capable of standing the shocks of misfortune of any of the crew. In the meridian of life, being about thirty-five years old, it was reasonable to suppose that, instead of the first, he would have been the last to have fallen a sacrifice to cold and hunger: but Heaven ordered it otherwise—he became delirious, and death relieved him from his sufferings the fiftieth day of his shipwreck. During all this time, the storms continued, and would often overwhelm them so as to keep them always drenched with sea-water, having nothing to screen them, except a temporary kind of cabin which they built up of boards between the windlass and night-head on the larboard side of the forecastle. The next who sunk under this horrid press of disasters was Howes, a young man of about thirty, who likewise was a fisherman by profession, and tall, spare, and as smart and active a seaman as any aboard. He likewise died delirious and in dreadful distress, six days after Paddock, being the fifty-sixth day of the wreck. It was soon perceived that this must evidently be the fate of all the survivors in a short time, if something was not done to procure water. About this time, good luck, or more probably, kind Providence, enabled them to fish up the tea-kettle, and one of the captain's pistols; and necessity, the mother of invention, suggested the plan of distillation. Accordingly, a piece of board was very nicely fitted to the mouth of the boiler, a small hole made in it, and the tea-kettle, bottom-upwards, fixed to the upper side of the board, the pistol-barrel was fixed to the nose of the kettle and kept cool by the constant application of cold water. This completely succeeded, and the survivors, without a doubt, owe their preservation to this simple experiment. But all that could be obtained by this very imperfect distillation, was a scanty allowance of water for five men; yet it would sustain life and that was all. The impression that there was meat enough under the deck, induced them to use every exertion to obtain it; but by getting up pieces of bone, entirely bare of meat and in a putrid state, they found that nothing was left for them but to rely on Heaven for food, and be contented with whatever came to hand, till relief should come. Their only sustenance now, was barnacles gathered from the sides of the vessel which were eaten raw that the distilling might not be interrupted, which would give them no more than four wine glasses of water each, per day. The next food which they obtained was a large shark caught by means of a running bow-line. This was a very great relief and lasted some time. Two advantages arose from this signal interposition of kind Providence; for while they lived upon their shark, the barnacles were growing larger and more nutritive. They likewise found many small crabs among the sea-weed which often floated around the wreck, which were very pleasant food. But from the necessity of chewing them raw and sucking out the nourishment, they brought on an obstinate costiveness, which became extremely painful and probably much exasperated by the want of water.

On the 15th of March, according to their computation, poor Moho, the cook, expired, evidently from want of water, though with much less distress than the others and in the full exercise of his reason: he very devoutly prayed and appeared perfectly resigned to the will of the God who afflicted him. Their constant study was directed to the improvement of their still, which was made much better by the addition of the other pistol barrel, which was found by fishing with the grain they made by fixing nails into a piece of a stave. With this barrel they so far perfected the still as to obtain eight junk bottles full of water in twenty-four hours. But from the death of Moho to the death of Johnson, which happened about the middle of April, they seemed to be denied every kind of food. The barnacles were all gone, and no friendly gale wafted to their side the sea-weed from which they could obtain crabs or insects. It seemed as if all hope was gone forever, and they had nothing before them but death, or the horrid alternative of eating the flesh of their dead companion. One expedient was left, that was to try to decoy a shark, if happily there might be one about the wreck, by part of the corpse of their ship-mate! This succeeded, and they caught a large shark, and from that time had many fish, till their happy deliverance. Very fortunately, a cask of nails which was on deck, lodged in the lea-scuppers while on their beam ends: with these they were enabled to fasten the shingles on their cabin, which by constant improvement, had become much more commodious, and when reduced to two only, they had a better supply of water.

They had now drifted above two thousand miles, and were in latitude 28 North, and longitude 13 West, when to their unspeakable joy they saw three ships bearing down upon them. The ships came as near as was convenient, and then hailed, which captain Cazneau answered with all the force of his lungs. The ship which hailed, proved to be the Fame, of Hull, captain Featherstone, bound from Rio Janeiro home. It so happened that the three captains had dined together that day and were all on board the Fame. Humanity immediately sent a boat, which put an end to the dreadful thraldom of captain Cazneau and Samuel Badger, the only surviving persons who were received by these humane Englishmen with exalted sensibility. Thus was ended the most shocking catastrophe which our naval history has recorded for many years, after a series of distresses from December 15th to the 20th of June, a period of one hundred and ninety-one days! Every attention was paid to the sufferers that generosity warmed with pity and fellow-feeling could dictate, on board the Fame. They were cherished, comforted, fed, clothed and nursed until the 9th of July, when they fell in with captain Perkins, of the brig Dromo, in the chops of the channel of England, who generously took them on board and carefully perfected the work of goodness begun by the generous Englishmen, and safely landed them in Kennebunk.

It is natural to inquire how they could float such a vast distance upon the most frequented part of the Atlantic and not be discovered all this time? They were passed by more than a dozen sail, one of which came so nigh them that they could distinctly see the people on deck and on the rigging looking at them: but to the inexpressible disappointment of the starving and freezing men, they stifled the dictates of compassion, hoisted sail, and cruelly abandoned them to their fate.

[16]

Shipwreck of the French Frigate *Medusa*

The loss of the *Medusa* and the subsequent sufferings of survivors on a raft make up one of the best-known and most horrible tragedies of the sea. It is one of a few among these narratives frequently chosen for present-day anthologies of shipwrecks, perhaps because of the well-known painting by Gericault.

The cause of the loss of the *Medusa* was very simple. The commander of the ship, knowing nothing of navigation and seamanship himself, took control away from the sailing master and entrusted the ship to one M. Richefort, who promptly, in fine weather, proceeded to run the frigate on the Arguin Bank. That was bad enough, but what happened after the grounding is simply incomprehensible. The ship was badly battered but still holding together; indeed, she was still intact when tardy rescuers reached her fifty-two days after the wreck. She must have had provisions and water, though the holds were probably full of seawater after the battering on the bank. Something could certainly have been done to get casks on deck. Yet 150 people were persuaded to leave the frigate and set out on a crazy raft towed by ship's boats under the command of men who had already proved their incompetence. Of course the hampering raft was soon abandoned by the boats, and only ten men survived the insane conflicts which ensued on that wallowing pile of lumber. Fourteen of seventeen men left on the ship also died; they seem to have spent more time fighting each other than attempting to get provisions from the hold. The whole affair is a mystery.

This narrative is based on an account by two survivors of the raft, Correard and Savigny. It is taken from Charles Ellms's *Shipwrecks and Disasters at Sea,* published in New York by I. J. Rouse in 1836.

SHIPWRECK OF THE

FRENCH FRIGATE MEDUSA,

On the Bank of Arguin, off the Western Coast

of Africa

With an account of the horrid sufferings of those

who embarked on a raft.

THE account of the fatal wreck of the Medusa, and its concomitant events, furnishes a series of horrors almost unparalleled in human suffering and atrocity. It gives a narrative of men, whose affections, in the day of sympathy, were turned to hatred, and pity converted to envy. They preferred their own destruction to the safety of their fellow sufferers; and crushed to atoms the plank under their feet, which divided them from eternity, rather than allow their companions in misfortune the happiness of ever seeing land again.

On the 17th of June, 1816, the Medusa French frigate, commanded by Captain Chaumareys, and accompanied by three smaller vessels, sailed from the island of Aix for the coast of Africa, in order to take possession of the colonies between Cape Blanco and the Gambia, surrendered to France by Great Britain, agreeably to the treaty of 1814. In doubling Cape Finisterre, a man was lost overboard and from the apathy of his companions, and want of promptitude in manoeuvring, was left to perish. On the tenth day of her sailing, there appeared an error of thirty leagues in her reckoning. On the 1st of July the Medusa entered the tropics. The captain gave the charge of the ship to Monsieur Richefort; and with the principal officers and crew, performed the fantastic ceremonies usual on such occasions, with boisterous merriment, while the frigate was surrounded with all the unseen perils of the ocean. A few persons on board, aware of the danger, remonstrated, but without effect, although it was ascertained that the Medusa was on the bank of Arguin. She continued her course without slackening sail. Every thing denoted shallow water; but M. Richefort persisted in saying there were one hundred fathoms. In that very moment six fathoms only were found, and the vessel struck three times, being in about sixteen feet of water. After several attempts to get the frigate afloat were made without success, it was found that her six boats, of different sizes, were not sufficient to contain all the crew, soldiers and passengers. A raft was constructed sixty-five feet long, and twenty-broad. But the only part which could be depended on was the middle, and that was so small that fifteen persons could not lie down upon it. The boats being got out, the captain was one of the first to leave the frigate, by leaping out of the port-hole. As soon as he was in safety, he sent a boat to take a *few,* who he said still remained in the wreck. But what was the surprise of the lieutenant, when he found sixty men left there. All these were carried off with the exception of seventeen; some of whom were drunk, and others refused to leave the frigate.

The raft, after the *one hundred and fifty* passengers destined to be its burden were on board, they stood in a parallelogram, without a possibility of moving; and they were up to their waists in water, and in constant danger of slipping through between the planks.

The plan adopted was, that this raft should be taken in tow by the six boats. On the 5th of July, at 7 A.M., this desperate squadron abandoned the frigate. The weather was calm; the coast was known to be but twelve or fifteen leagues distant; and land was in fact discovered by the boats that very night. After proceeding about two leagues a faulty, if not treacherous manoeuvre broke the tow line of the captain's boat, and all the others let loose their cables. They were not driven to this measure by any new perils; and the cry of *"Nous les abandonnons,"* which resounded through the line, was the yell of a spontaneous and instinctive impulse of cowardice, perfidy and cruelty. The raft then, such as we have described it, was left to the mercy of the waves.

The six boats, after their treacherous exploit of slipping the cables, made all the way they could to the coast of Africa, where they arrived in safety. From the long boat sixty-three of the most resolute were landed with arms, to the north of Cape Blanco, ninety leagues from the settlement. The other boats landed at different places on the coast, and proceeded on the desert towards St. Louis. From St. Louis a goalette sailed in search of the Medusa; but having provisions for only eight days was forced to return. She put to sea again, but in such a disabled state, that after beating about *fifteen* days, she came back a second time. Ten days were employed in repairing her, and at length, having lost thirty-three days, she reached the Medusa on the fifty-second day after the frigate had struck on the bank of Arguin; when, dreadful to relate, three miserable sufferers were found alive. The reader will recollect that seventeen were left on the wreck As long as provisions lasted, they remained in peace. Two of them embarked on a raft of their own construction: the remains were thrown on the coast of Sahara, but the persons on board were never heard of more. One ventured to sea on a hen-coop, but sunk in sight of the frigate. Four remained behind, one of whom died of want. The other three lived in separate corners of the wreck, and never met but to run at each other with drawn knives.

The following is the substance, abridged from MM. Correard and Savigny, of what took place on the raft during thirteen days before the sufferers were taken up by the Argus brig.

After the boats had disappeared, the consternation became extreme. All the horrors of thirst and famine passed before our imagination; besides, we had to contend with a treacherous element, which already covered the half of our bodies. The deep stupor of the soldiers and sailors instantly changed to despair. All saw their inevitable destruction, and expressed by their moans the dark thoughts which brooded in their minds. Our words were at first unavailing to quiet their fears, which we participated with them, but which a greater strength of mind enabled us to dissemble. At last, an unmoved countenance, and our proffered consolations, quieted them by degrees, but could not entirely dissipate the terror with which they were seized.

When tranquillity was a little restored, we began to search about the raft for the charts, the compass, and the anchor, which we presumed had been placed upon it, after what we had been told at the time of quitting the frigate.

These things, of the first importance, had not been placed upon our machine. Above all, the want of a compass the most alarmed us, and we gave vent to our rage and vengeance. M. Correard then remembered that he had seen one in the hands of the principal workman under his command. He spoke to the man, who replied, "Yes, yes, I have it with me." This information transported us with joy, and we believed that our safety depended upon this futile resource. It was about the size of a crown-piece, and very incorrect. Those who have not been in situations in which their existence was exposed to extreme peril, can have but a faint knowledge of the price one attaches then to the simplest objects—with what avidity one seizes the slightest means capable of mitigating the rigor of that fate against which they contend. The compass was given to the commander of the raft, but an accident deprived us of it for ever. It fell, and disappeared between the pieces of wood which formed our machine.

We had kept it but a few hours; and, after its loss, had nothing to guide us but the rising and setting of the sun.

We had all gone afloat without taking any food. Hunger beginning to be imperiously felt, we mixed our paste of sea-biscuit with a little wine, and distributed it thus prepared. Such was our first meal, and the best we had during our stay upon the raft.

An order, according to our numbers, was established for the distribution of our miserable provisions. The ration of wine was fixed at three quarters a day. We will speak no more of the biscuit, it having been entirely consumed at the first distribution. The day passed away sufficiently tranquil. We talked of the means by which we would save ourselves; we spoke of it as a certain circumstance, which reanimated our courage; and we sustained that of the soldiers, by cherishing in them the hope of being able, in a short time, to revenge themselves on those who had abandoned us. This hope of vengeance, it must be avowed, equally animated us all; and we poured out a thousand imprecations against those who had left us a prey to so much misery and danger.

The officer who commanded the raft being unable to move, M. Savigny took upon himself the duty of erecting the mast. He caused them to cut in two one of the poles of the frigate's masts, and fixed it with the rope which had served to tow us, and of which we made stays and shrouds. It was placed on the anterior third of the raft. We put up for a sail the main-top-gallant, which trimmed very well, but was of very little use, except when the wind served from behind; and to keep the raft in this course, we were obliged to trim the sail as if the breeze blew athwart us.

In the evening, our hearts and our prayers, by a feeling natural to the unfortunate, were turned towards Heaven. Surrounded by inevitable dangers, we addressed that invisible Being, who has established, and who maintains the order of the universe. Our vows were fervent, and we experienced from our prayers the cheering influence of hope. It is necessary to have been in similar situations, before one can rightly imagine what a charm is the sublime idea of a God protecting the unfortunate, to the heart of the sufferer.

One consoling thought still soothed our imaginations. We persuaded ourselves that the little division had gone to the isle of Arguin, and that after it had set a part of its people on shore, the rest would return to our assistance. We endeavored to impress this idea on our soldiers and sailors, which quieted them. The night came without our hope being realized; the wind freshened, and the sea was considerably swelled. What a horrible night! The thought of seeing the boats on the morrow, a little consoled our men; the greater part of whom, being unaccustomed to the sea, fell on one another at each movement of the raft. M. Savigny, seconded by some people who still preserved their presence of mind amidst the disorder, stretched cords across the raft, by which the men held, and were better able to resist the swell of the sea. Some were even obliged to fasten themselves. In the middle of the night the weather was very rough; huge waves burst upon us, sometimes overturning us with great violence. The cries of the men, mingled with the flood, whilst the terrible sea raised us at every instant from the raft, and threatened to sweep us away. This scene was rendered still more terrible, by the horrors inspired by the darkness of the night. Suddenly we believed we saw fires in the distance at intervals.

We had had the precaution to hang at the top of the mast, the gunpowder and pistols which we had brought from the frigate. We made signals by burning a large quantity of cartridges. We even fired some pistols; but it seems the fire we saw, was nothing but an error of vision; or, perhaps, nothing more than the sparkling of the waves.

We struggled with death during the whole of the night, holding firmly by the ropes which were made very secure. Tossed by the waves from the back to the front, and from the front to the back, and sometimes precipitated into the sea, floating between life and death, mourning our misfortunes, certain of perishing—we disputed, nevertheless, the remainder of our existence, with that cruel element which threatened to engulf us. Such was our condition till daybreak. At every instant we heard the lamentable cries of the soldiers and sailors. They prepared for death, bidding farewell to one another, imploring the protection of Heaven, and addressing fervent prayers to God. Every one made vows to Him, in spite of the certainty of never being able to accomplish them. Frightful situation! How is it possible to have any idea of it, which will not fall far short of the reality!

Towards seven in the morning the sea fell a little, the wind blew with less fury; but what a scene presented itself to our view! Ten or twelve unfortunates, having their inferior extremities fixed in the openings between the pieces of the raft, had perished by being unable to disengage themselves. Several others were swept away by the violence of the sea. At the hour of repast we took the numbers anew. We had lost twenty men. We will not affirm that this was the exact number; for we perceived some soldiers, who, to have more than their share, took rations for two, and even three. We were so huddled together, that we found it absolutely impossible to prevent this abuse.

In the midst of these horrors, a touching scene of filial piety drew our tears. Two young men raised and recognized their father, who had fallen, and was lying insensible among the feet of the people. They believed him at first dead, and their despair was expressed in the most affecting manner. It was perceived, however, that he still breathed, and every assistance was rendered for his recovery in our power. He slowly revived, and was restored to life, and to the prayers of his sons, who supported him closely folded in their arms. Whilst our hearts were softened by this affecting episode in our melancholy adventures, we had soon to witness the sad spectacle of a dark contrast. Two shipboys and a baker feared not to seek death, and threw themselves into the sea, after having bid farewell to their companions in misfortune. Already the minds of our people were singularly altered. Some believed that they saw land; others, ships which were coming to save us. All talked aloud of their fallacious visions.

We lamented the loss of our unfortunate companions. At this moment we were far from anticipating the still more terrible scene which took place on the following night. Far from that, we enjoyed a positive satisfaction, so well were we persuaded that the boats would return to our assistance. The day was fine, and the most perfect tranquillity reigned all the while on our raft. The evening came and no boats appeared. Despondency began again to seize our men, and then a spirit of insubordination manifested itself in cries of rage. The voice of the officers was entirely disregarded. Night fell rapidly in; the sky was obscured by dark clouds; the wind which, during the whole day, had blown rather violently, became furious and swelled the sea, which in an instant became very rough. The preceding night had been frightful, but this was more so. Mountains of water covered us at every instant, and burst with fury into the midst of us. Very fortunately we had the wind from behind, and the strongest of the sea was a little broken by the rapidity with which we were driven before it. We were impelled towards the land. The men, from the violence of the sea, were hurried from the back to the front. We were obliged to keep to the centre, the firmest part of the raft; and those who could not get there almost all perished. Before and behind the waves dashed impetuously, and swept away the men in spite of all their resistance. At the centre the pressure was such, that some unfortunates were suffocated by the weight of their comrades, who fell upon them at every instant. The officers kept by the foot of the little mast, and were obliged every moment to call to those around them to go to the one or the other side to avoid the waves; for the sea coming nearly athwart us, gave our raft nearly a perpendicular position; to counteract which, they were forced to throw themselves upon the side raised by the sea.

The soldiers and sailors frightened by their danger, seized on casks of wine, and drank till they were void of reason. They now tried to involve all in one common ruin by various acts of destruction, but were prevented by the vigilance of the officers.

One man inspired us all with terror. This was an Asiatic, and a soldier in a colonial regiment. Of a colossal stature, short hair, a nose extremely large, an enormous mouth and dark complexion, he made a most hideous appearance. At first he placed himself in the middle of the raft, and, at each blow of his fist, knocked down every one who opposed him, and none durst approach him. Had there been six such, our destruction would have been certain.

Some men, anxious to prolong their existence, armed and united themselves with those who wished to preserve the raft. Among this number were some subaltern officers and many passengers. The rebels drew their sabres, and those who had none armed themselves with knives. They advanced in a determined manner upon us—we stood on our defence—the attack commenced. Animated by despair, one of them made a stroke at an officer—the rebel instantly fell, pierced with wounds. This firmness awed them for an instant, but diminished nothing of their rage. They ceased to advance, and withdrew, presenting to us a front bristling with sabres and bayonets, to the back part of the raft, to execute their plan. One of them feigned to rest himself on the small railings on the sides of the raft, and with a knife began cutting the cords. Being told by a servant, one of us sprung upon him. A soldier, wishing to defend him, struck at the officer with his knife, which only pierced his coat. The officer wheeled around, seized his adversary, and threw both him and his comrade into the sea.

There had been as yet but partial affairs—the combat became general. Some one tried, to lower the sail: a crowd of infuriated mortals threw themselves in an instant upon the haulyards and the shrouds, and cut them. The fall of the mast almost broke the thigh of a captain of infantry, who fell insensible. He was seized by the soldiers who threw him into the sea. We saved him, and placed him on a barrel; whence he was taken by the rebels, who wished to put out his eyes with a penknife. Exasperated with so much brutality, we no longer restrained ourselves, but pushed in upon them, and charged them with fury. Sword in hand we traversed the line which the soldiers had formed, and many paid with their lives the errors of their revolt. Various passengers, during these cruel moments, evinced the greatest courage and coolness.

M. Correard fell into a sort of swoon; but hearing at every instant the cries, "To arms! with us comrades! we are lost!" joined with the groans and imprecations of the wounded and dying, was soon roused from his lethargy. All this horrible tumult speedily made him comprehend how necessary it was to be upon his guard. Armed with his sabre, he gathered together some of his workmen on the front of the raft, and there charged them to hurt no one, unless they were attacked. He almost always remained with them; and several times they had to defend themselves against the rebels, who, swimming round to that point of the raft, placed M. Correard and his little troop between two dangers, and made their position very difficult to defend. At every instant he was opposed to men armed with knives, sabres and bayonets. Many had carabines, which they wielded as clubs. Every effort was made to stop them, by holding them off at the point of their swords; but, in spite of the repugnance they experienced in fighting with their wretched countrymen, they were compelled to use their arms without mercy. Many of the mutineers attacked with fury, and they were obliged to repel them in the same manner. Some of the laborers received severe wounds in this action. Their commander could show a great number received in the different engagements. At last their united efforts prevailed in dispersing this mass who had attacked them with such fury.

During this combat, M. Correard was told by one of his workmen who remained faithful, that one of their comrades, named Dominique, had gone over to the rebels, and that they had seized and thrown him into the sea. Immediately forgetting the fault and treason of this man, he threw himself in at the place whence the voice of the wretch was heard calling for assistance, seized him by the hair, and had the good fortune to restore him on board. Dominique had got several sabre wounds in a charge, one of which had laid open his head. In spite of the darkness we found out the wound, which seemed very large.

One of the workmen gave his handkerchief to bind and stop the blood. Our care recovered the wretch; but, when he had collected strength, the ungrateful Dominique, forgetting at once his duty and the signal service which we had rendered him, went and rejoined the rebels. So much baseness did not go unrevenged; and soon after he found, in a fresh assault, that death from which he was not worthy to be saved, but which he might in all probability have avoided, if, true to honor and gratitude, he had remained among us.

Just at the moment we finished dressing the wounds on Dominique, another voice was heard. It was that of the unfortunate female who was with us on the raft, and whom the infuriated beings had thrown into the sea, as well as her husband, who had defended her with courage. M. Correard, in despair at seeing two unfortunates perish, whose pitiful cries, especially the woman's, pierced his heart, took a large rope, which he found on the front of the raft, which he fastened round his middle; and throwing himself a second time into the sea, was again so fortunate as to save the woman, who invoked with all her might, the assistance of our Lady of Land. Her husband was rescued at the same time by the head workman, Lavilette. We laid these unfortunates upon the dead bodies, supporting their backs with a barrel. In a short while they recovered their senses. The first thing the woman did, was to acquaint herself with the name of the person who saved her, and to express to him her liveliest gratitude. Finding, doubtless, that her words but ill expressed her feelings, she recollected she had in her pocket a little snuff, and instantly offered it to him; it was all she possessed. Touched with the gift, but unable to use it, M. Correard gave it to a poor sailor, which served him for two or three days. But it is impossible for us to describe a still more affecting scene—the joy this unfortunate couple testified, when they had sufficiently recovered their senses, at finding that they were both saved.

The rebels being repulsed, as it has been stated above, left us a little repose. The moon lighted with her melancholy rays this disastrous raft, this narrow space, on which were found united so many torturing anxieties, so many cruel misfortunes, a madness so insensate, a courage so heroic, and the most generous, the most amiable sentiments of nature and humanity.

The man and wife, who had been but a little before stabbed with swords and bayonets, and thrown both together into a stormy sea, could scarcely credit their senses when they found themselves in one another's arms. The woman was a native of the Upper Alps, which place she had left twenty-four years before, and during which time she had followed the French armies in the campaigns in Italy, and other places, as a sutler. "Therefore preserve my life," said she to M. Correard; "you see I am a useful woman. Ah! if you knew how often I have ventured upon the field of battle, and braved death to carry assistance to our gallant men! Whether they had money or not, I always let them have my goods. Sometimes a battle would deprive me of my poor debtors; but after the victory, others would pay me double or triple for what they had consumed before the engagement. Thus I came in for a share of their victories." Unfortunate woman! she little knew what a horrible fate awaited her among us! They felt, they expressed so vividly that happiness which they, alas! so shortly enjoyed, that would have drawn tears from the most obdurate heart. But in that horrible moment, when we scarcely breathed from the most furious attack, when we were obliged to be continually on our guard, not only against the violence of the men, but a most boisterous sea, few among us had time to attend to scenes of conjugal affection.

After this second check, the rage of the soldiers was suddenly appeased, and gave place to the most abject cowardice. Several threw themselves at our feet, and implored our pardon—which was instantly granted. Thinking that order was re-established, we returned to our station on the centre of the raft, only taking the precaution of keeping our arms. We, however, had soon to prove the impossibility of counting on the permanence of any honest sentiment in the hearts of these beings.

It was nearly midnight; and, after an hour of apparent tranquillity the soldiers rose afresh. Their mind was entirely gone—they ran upon us in despair with knives and sabres in their hands. As they yet had all their physical strength, and besides were armed, we were obliged again to stand on our defence. Their revolt became still more dangerous, as, in their delirium, they were entirely deaf to the voice of reason. They attacked us: we charged them in our turn, and immediately the raft was strewed with their dead bodies. Those of our adversaries who had no weapons, endeavored to tear us with their sharp teeth. Many of us were cruelly bitten. M. Savigny was torn on the legs and the shoulder: he also received a wound on the right arm, which deprived him of the use of his fourth and little finger for a long while. Many others were wounded, and many cuts were found in our clothes from knives and sabres.

One of our workmen was also seized by four of the rebels, who wished to throw him into the sea. One of them had laid hold of his right leg, and had bit most unmercifully the tendon above the heel. Others were striking him with great slashes of their sabres, and with the butt end of their guns, when his cries made us hasten to his assistance. In this affair, the brave Lavilette, ex-sergeant of the foot artillery of the old guard, behaved with a courage worthy of the greatest praise. He rushed upon the infuriated beings in the manner of M. Correard, and soon snatched the workman from the danger which menaced him. Some short while after, in a fresh attack of the rebels, sub-lieutenant Lozach fell into their hands. In their delirium they had taken him for Lieutenant Danglas, of whom we have formerly spoken, and who had abandoned the raft at the moment when we were quitting the frigate. The troop, to a man, eagerly sought this officer, who had seen little service, and whom they reproached for having used them ill during the time they garrisoned the Isle of Rhe. We believed this officer lost; but hearing his voice, we soon found it still possible to save him. Immediately MM. Clairet, Savigny, L'Heureux, Lavilette, Coudin, Correard, and some workmen, formed themselves into small platoons, and rushed upon the insurgents with great impetuosity, overturning every one in their way, and retook M. Lozach and placed him on the centre of the raft.

The preservation of this officer cost us infinite difficulty. Every moment the soldiers demanded he should be delivered to them, designating him always by the name of Danglas. We endeavored to make them comprehend their mistake, and told them that they themselves had seen the person for whom they sought return on board the frigate. They were insensible to every thing we said—every thing before them was Danglas—they saw him perpetually, and furiously and unceasingly demanded his head. It was only by force of arms we succeeded in repressing their rage, and quieting their dreadful cries of death.

Horrible night! thou shrouded with thy gloomy veil these frightful combats, over which presided the cruel demon of despair.

We had also to tremble for the life of M. Coudin. Wounded and fatigued by the attacks which he had sustained with us, and in which he had shown a courage superior to every thing, he was resting himself on a barrel, holding in his arms a young sailor boy of twelve years of age, to whom he had attached himself. The mutineers seized him with his barrel, and threw him into the sea with the boy, whom he still held fast. In spite of his burden, he had the presence of mind to lay hold of the raft, and to save himself from this extreme peril.

We cannot yet comprehend how a handful of men should have been able to resist such a number so monstrously insane. We are sure we were not more than twenty to combat all these madmen. Let it not, however, be imagined, that in the midst of all these dangers we had preserved our reason entire. Fear, anxiety, and the most cruel privations, had greatly changed our intellectual faculties. But being somewhat less insane than the unfortunate soldiers, we energetically opposed their determination of cutting the cords of the raft. Permit us now to make some observations concerning the different sensations with which we were affected. During the first day M. Griffon entirely lost his senses. He threw himself into the sea, but M. Savigny saved him with his own hands. His words were vague and unconnected. A second time he threw himself in; but, by a sort of instinct, kept hold of the cross pieces of the raft, and was again saved.

The following is what M. Savigny experienced in the beginning of the night. His eyes closed in spite of himself, and he felt a general drowsiness. In this condition the most delightful visions flitted across his imagination. He saw around him a country covered with the most beautiful plantations, and found himself in the midst of objects delightful to his senses. Nevertheless, he reasoned concerning his condition, and felt that courage alone could withdraw him from this species of non-existence. He demanded some wine from the master-gunner, who got it for him, and he recovered a little from this stupor. If the unfortunates who were assailed with these primary symptoms, had not strength to withstand them, their death was certain. Some became furious—others threw themselves into the sea, bidding farewell to their comrades with the utmost coolness. Some said, "Fear nothing; I am going to get you assistance, and will return in a short while." In the midst of this general madness, some wretches were seen rushing upon their companions, sword in hand, demanding a wing of a chicken and some bread, to appease the hunger which consumed them. Others asked for their hammocks, to go, they said, between the decks of the frigate, to take a little repose. Many believed they were still on the Medusa, surrounded by the same objects they there saw daily. Some saw ships, and called to them for assistance; or a fine harbor, in the distance of which was an elegant city. M. Correard thought he was travelling through the beautiful fields of Italy. An officer said to him, "I recollect we have been abandoned by the boats; but fear nothing. I am going to write to the governor, and in a few hours we shall be saved." M. Correard replied in the same tone, and as if he had been in his ordinary condition, "Have you a pigeon to carry your orders with such celerity?" The cries and the confusion soon roused us from this languor, but when tranquillity was somewhat restored, we again fell into the same drowsy condition. On the morrow, we felt as if we had awoke from a painful dream; and asked our companions if, during their sleep, they had not seen combats and heard cries of despair. Some replied, that the same visions had continually tormented them, and that they were exhausted with fatigue. Every one believed he was deceived by the illusions of a horrible dream.

After these different combats, overcome with toil, with want of food and sleep, we laid ourselves down and reposed till the morning dawned, and showed us the horror of the scene. A great number in their delirium had thrown themselves into the sea. We found that sixty or sixty-five had perished during the night. A fourth part at least, we supposed, had drowned themselves in despair. We only lost two of our own number, neither of whom were officers. The deepest dejection was seated on every face. Each, having recovered himself, could now feel the horrors of his situation; and some of us, shedding tears of despair, bitterly deplored the rigor of our fate.

A new misfortune was now revealed to us. During the tumult, the rebels had thrown into the sea two barrels of wine, and the only two casks of water which we had upon the raft. Two casks of wine had been consumed the day before, and only one was left. We were more than sixty in number, and we were obliged to put ourselves on half rations.

At break of day the sea calmed, which permitted us again to erect our mast. When it was replaced, we made a distribution of wine. The unhappy soldiers murmured, and blamed us for privations which we equally endured with them. They fell exhausted. We had taken nothing for forty-eight hours, and we had been obliged to struggle continually against a strong sea. We could, like them, hardly support ourselves; courage alone made us still act. We resolved to employ every possible means to catch fish; and, collecting all the hooks and eyes from the soldiers, made fish-hooks of them: but all was of no avail. The currents carried our lines under the raft, where they got entangled. We bent a bayonet to catch sharks: one bit at it, and straightened it; and we abandoned our project. Something was absolutely necessary to sustain our miserable existence; and we tremble with horror at being obliged to tell that of which we made use. We feel our pen fall from our hands; a mortal cold congeals all our members; and our hair bristles erect on our foreheads. Readers! we implore you, feel not indignant towards men already overloaded with misery. Pity their condition, and shed a tear of sorrow for their deplorable fate.

The wretches, whom death had spared during the disastrous night we have described, seized upon the dead bodies with which the raft was covered, cutting them up by slices, which some even instantly devoured. Many nevertheless refrained. Almost all the officers were of this number. Seeing that this monstrous food had revived the strength of those who had used it, it was proposed to dry it, to make it a little more palatable. Those who had firmness to abstain from it took an additional quantity of wine. We endeavored to eat shoulder-belts and cartouch-boxes, and contrived to swallow some small bits of them. Some eat linen; others, the leathers of their hats, on which was a little grease, or rather dirt. We had recourse to many expedients to prolong our miserable existence, to recount which would only disgust the heart of humanity.

The day was calm and beautiful. A ray of hope beamed for a moment to quiet our agitation. We still expected to see the boats or some ships; and addressed our prayers to the Eternal, on whom we placed our trust. The half of our men were extremely feeble, and bore upon their faces the stamp of approaching dissolution. The evening arrived, and brought no help. The darkness of the third night augmented our fears; but the wind was still, and the sea less agitated. The sun of the fourth morning since our departure shone upon our disaster, and showed us ten or twelve of our companions stretched lifeless upon the raft. This sight struck us most forcibly, as it told us we would soon be extended in the same manner in the same place. We gave their bodies to the sea for a grave, reserving only one to feed those who, but the day before, had held his trembling hands, and sworn to him eternal friendship. This day was beautiful. Our souls, anxious for more delightful sensations, were in harmony with the aspect of the heavens, and got again a new ray of hope. Towards four in the afternoon, an unlooked for event happened, which gave us some consolation. A shoal of flying fish passed under our raft, and as there was an infinite number of openings between the pieces which composed it, the fish were entangled in great quantities. We threw ourselves upon them, and captured a considerable number. We took about two hundred, and put them in an empty barrel. We opened them as we caught them, and took out what is called their milt. This food seemed delicious; but one man would have required a thousand. Our first emotion was to give to God renewed thanks for this unhoped for favor.

An ounce of gunpowder having been found in the morning, was dried in the sun during the day, which was very fine. A steel, gun-flints, and tinder, made also part of the same parcel. After a good deal of difficulty we set fire to some fragments of dry linen. We made a large opening in the side of an empty cask, and placed at the bottom of it several wet things, and upon this kind of scaffolding we set our fire; all of which we placed on a barrel, that the sea-water might not extinguish it. We cooked some fish, and eat them with extreme avidity; but our hunger was such, and our portion so small, that we added to it some of the sacrilegious viands, which the cooking rendered less revolting. This some of the officers touched for the first time. From this day we continued to eat it; but we could no longer dress it, the means of making a fire having been entirely lost. The barrel having caught fire, we extinguished it without being able to preserve any thing to rekindle it on the morrow. The powder and tinder were entirely gone. This meal gave us all additional strength to support our fatigues. The night was tolerable, and would have been happy, had it not been signalized by a new massacre.

Some Spaniards, Italians, and negroes, had formed a plot to throw us into the sea. The negroes had told them that they were very near the shore; and that, when there, they would enable them to traverse Africa without danger. We had to take to our arms again, the sailors, who had remained faithful to us, pointing out to us the conspirators. The first signal for battle was given by a Spaniard; who, placing himself behind the mast, holding fast by it, made the sign of the cross with one hand, invoking the name of God, and with the other held a knife. The sailors seized him, and threw him into the sea. An Italian, servant to an officer of the troops, who was in the plot, seeing all was discovered, armed himself with the only boarding axe left on the raft, made his retreat to the front, enveloped himself in a piece of drapery he wore across his breast, and of his own accord threw himself into the sea. The rebels rushed forward to avenge their comrades, and a terrible conflict again commenced. Both sides fought with desperate fury; and soon the fatal raft was strewed with dead bodies and blood, which should have been shed by other hands, and in another cause. In this tumult we heard them again demanding, with horrid rage, the head of Lieutenant Danglas. In this assault the unfortunate sutler was again thrown into the sea. M. Coudin, assisted by some workmen, saved her, to prolong for a little while her torment and her existence. In this terrible night Lavilette failed not to give proofs of the rarest intrepidity. It was to him, and some of those who had survived the sequel of our misfortunes, that we owed our safety. At last, after unheard of efforts, the rebels were once more repulsed, and quiet restored. Having escaped this new danger, we endeavored to get some repose. The day at length dawned upon us for the fifth time. We were now no more than thirty in number. We had lost four or five of our faithful sailors, and those who survived were in the most deplorable condition. The sea water had almost entirely excoriated the skin of our lower extremities; and we were covered with contusions or wounds, which, irritated by the salt water, extorted from us the most piercing cries. About twenty of us only were capable of standing upright or walking. Almost all our fish was exhausted—we had but four days' supply of wine. "In four days," said we, "nothing will be left, and death will be inevitable." Thus came the seventh day of our abandonment. In the course of the day, two soldiers had glided behind the only barrel of wine that was left, pierced it, and were drinking by means of a reed. We had sworn that those who used such means should be punished with death; which law was instantly put in execution, and the two transgressors were thrown into the sea.

This same day saw the close of the life of a child named Leon, aged twelve years. He died like a lamp which ceases to burn for want of aliment. All spoke in favor of this young and amiable creature, who merited a better fate. His angelic form, his musical voice, the interest of an age so tender, increased still more by the courage he had shown, and the services he had performed, (for he had already made, in the preceding year, a campaign in the East Indies), inspired us all with the greatest pity for this young victim, devoted to so horrible and premature a death. Our old soldiers, and all the people in general, did every thing they could to prolong his existence; but all was in vain. Neither the wine which they gave him without regret, nor all the means they employed, could arrest his melancholy doom; and he expired in the arms of M. Coudin, who had not ceased to give him the most unwearied attention. Whilst he had strength to move, he ran incessantly from one side to the other, loudly calling for his unhappy mother, for water and food. He trod indiscriminately on the feet and legs of his companions in misfortune, who, in their turn, uttered the most fearful cries; but these were very rarely accompanied with menaces. They pardoned all which the poor boy had made them suffer. He was not in his senses—consequently could not be expected to behave as if he had the use of reason.

There now remained but twenty-seven of us. Fifteen of this number seemed able to live yet some days; the rest, covered with large wounds, had almost entirely lost the use of their reason. They still, however, shared in the distributions; and would, before they died, consume thirty or forty bottles of wine, which to us were inestimable. We deliberated, that by putting the sick on half allowance, was but putting them to death by halves; but after a council, at which presided the most dreadful despair, it was decided they should be thrown into the sea. This means, however repugnant, however horrible it appeared to us, procured the survivors six days' wine. But after the decision was made, who durst execute it? The habit of seeing death ready to devour us; the certainty of our infallible destruction without this monstrous expedient; all, in short, had hardened our hearts to every feeling but that of self-preservation. Three sailors and a soldier took charge of this cruel business. We looked aside, and shed tears of blood at the fate of these unfortunates. Among them were the wretched sutler and her husband. Both had been grievously wounded in the different combats. The woman had a thigh broken between the beams of the raft, and a stroke of a sabre had made a deep wound in the head of her husband. Every thing announced their approaching end. We consoled ourselves with the belief, that our cruel resolution shortened but a brief space the term of their existence. Ye who shudder at the cry of outraged humanity, recollect that it was other men, fellow-countrymen, comrades, who had placed us in this awful situation.

This horrible expedient saved the fifteen who remained; for when we were found by the Argus brig, we had very little wine left, and it was the sixth day after the cruel sacrifice we had described. The victims, we repeat, had not more than forty-eight hours to live; and by keeping them on the raft, we would have been absolutely destitute of the means of existence two days before we were found. Weak as we were, we considered it as a certain thing, that it would have been impossible for us to have lived only twenty-four hours more without taking some food. After this catastrophe, we threw our arms into the sea: they inspired us with a horror we could not overcome. We only kept one sabre, in case we had to cut some cordage or some piece of wood.

A new event—for every thing was an event to wretches to whom the world was reduced to the narrow space of a few toises, and for whom the winds and waves contended in their fury, as they floated across the abyss—an event happened, which diverted our minds from the horrors of our situation. All on a sudden, a white butterfly, of a species common in France, came fluttering above our heads, and settled on our sails. The first thought this little creature suggested was, that it was the harbinger of approaching land; and we clung to the hope with the delirium of joy. It was the ninth day we had been upon the raft; the torments of hunger consumed our entrails; and the soldiers and sailors already devoured with haggard eyes this wretched prey, and seemed ready to dispute about it. Others looking upon it as a messenger from Heaven, declared that they took it under their protection, and would suffer none to do it harm. It is certain we could not be far from land, for the butterflies continued to come on the following days, and flutter about our sail. We had also, on the same day, another indication not less positive, by a Goeland which flew around our raft. This second visitor left us no doubt that we were fast approaching the African soil; and we persuaded ourselves that we should be speedily thrown upon the coast by the currents.

This same day a new care employed us. Seeing we were reduced to so small a number, we collected all the little strength we had left, detached some planks on the front of the raft, and, with some pretty long pieces of wood, raised on the centre a kind of platform, on which we reposed. All the effects we could collect were placed upon it, and tended to make it less hard; which also prevented the sea from passing with such facility through the spaces between the different planks; but the waves came across and sometimes covered us completely. On this new theatre we resolved to meet death in a manner becoming Frenchmen, and with perfect resignation. Our time was almost wholly spent in speaking of our unhappy country. All our wishes, our last prayers, were for the prosperity of France. Thus passed the last days of our abode upon the raft.

Soon after our abandonment, we bore with comparative ease the immersions during the nights, which are very cold in these countries; but latterly, every time the waves washed over us, we felt a most painful sensation, and we uttered painful cries. We employed every means to avoid it. Some supported their heads on pieces of wood, and made with what they could find a sort of little parapet to screen them from the force of the waves; others sheltered themselves behind two empty casks. But these means were very insufficient; it was only when the sea was calm that it did not break over us.

An ardent thirst, redoubled in the day by the beams of a burning sun, consumed us. An officer of the army found by chance a small lemon, and it may easily be imagined how valuable such a fruit would be to him. His comrades, in spite of the most urgent entreaties, could not get a bit of it from him. Signs of rage were already manifested and had he not partly listened to the solicitations of those around him, they would have taken it by force, and he would have perished the victim of his selfishness. We also disputed about thirty cloves of garlic, which were found in the bottom of a sack. These disputes were for the most part accompanied with violent menaces; and if they had been prolonged, we might perhaps have come to the last extremities. There was found also two small phials, in which was a spirituous liquor for cleaning the teeth. He who possessed them kept them with care, and gave with reluctance one or two drops in the palm of the hand. This liquor, which we think was a tincture of guiacum, cinnamon, cloves, and other aromatic substances, produced on our tongues an agreeable feeling, and for a short while removed the thirst which destroyed us. Some of us found some small pieces of powder, which made, when put into the mouth, a kind of coolness. One plan generally employed was to put into a hat a quantity of seawater, with which we washed our faces for a while, repeating it at intervals. We also bathed our hair and held our hands in the water. Misfortune made us ingenious, and each thought of a thousand means to alleviate his sufferings. Emaciated by the most cruel privations, the least agreeable feeling was to us a happiness supreme. Thus we sought with avidity a small empty phial which one of us possessed, and in which had once been some essence of roses; and every one, as he got hold of it, respired with delight the odor it exhaled, which imparted to his senses the most soothing impressions. Many of us kept our rations of wine in a small tin cup, and sucked it out with a quill. This manner of taking it was of great benefit to us, and allayed our thirst much better than if we had gulped it off at once.

Three days passed in inexpressible anguish. So much did we despise life, that many of us feared not to bathe in sight of the sharks which surrounded our raft; others placed themselves naked upon the front of our machine, which was under water. These expedients diminished a little the ardor of their thirst. A species of molusca, known to seamen by the name of gatere, was sometimes driven by great numbers on our raft; and when their long arms rested on our naked bodies, they occasioned us the most cruel sufferings. Will it be believed, that amids these terrible scenes, struggling with inevitable death, some of us uttered pleasantries, which made us yet smile, in spite of the horrors of our situation? One, besides others, said jestingly, "If the brig is sent to search for us, pray God it has the eyes of Argus," in allusion to the name of the vessel we presumed would be sent to our assistance. This consolatory idea never left us an instant, and we spoke of it frequently.

On the 16th, reckoning we were very near land, eight of the most determined among us resolved to endeavor to gain the coast. A second raft, of smaller dimensions, was formed for transporting them thither; but it was found insufficient: and they at length determined to await death in their present situation. Meanwhile night came on, and its sombre veil revived in our minds the most afflicting thoughts. We were convinced there were not above a dozen or fifteen bottles of wine in our barrel. We began to have an invincible disgust at the flesh, which had till then scarcely supported us; and we may say, that the sight of it inspired us with feelings of horror, doubtless produced by the idea of our approaching dissolution.

On the morning of the 17th the sun appeared free from clouds. After having addressed our prayers to the Eternal, we divided among us a part of our wine. Each, with delight, was taking his small portion; when a captain of infantry, casting his eyes on the horizon, perceived a ship, and announced it to us by an exclamation of joy. We knew it to be a brig, but it was at a great distance: we could distinguish the masts. The sight of this vessel revived in us emotions difficult to describe. Each believed his deliverance sure, and we gave a thousand thanks to God. Fears, however, mingled with our hopes. We straightened some hoops of casks, to the ends of which we fixed handkerchiefs of different colors. A man, with our united assistance, mounted to the top of the mast, and waved these little flags. For more than half an hour, we were tossed between hope and fear. Some thought the vessel grew larger, and others were convinced its course was from us. These last were the only ones whose eyes were not blinded by hope, for the ship disappeared.

From the delirium of joy, we passed to that of despondency and sorrow. We envied the fate of those whom we had seen perish at our sides; and we said to ourselves, "When we shall be in want of every thing, and when our strength begins to forsake us, we will wrap ourselves up as we can; we will stretch ourselves on this platform, the witness of the most cruel sufferings, and there await death with resignation." At length, to calm our despair, we sought for consolation in the arms of sleep. The day before we had been scorched by the beams of a burning sun: to day, to avoid the fierceness of his rays, we made a tent with the mainsail of the frigate. As soon as it was finished, we laid ourselves under it: thus all that was passing without was hid from our eyes. We proposed then to write upon a plank an abridgement of our adventures, and to add our names at the bottom of the recital, and fix it to the upper part of the mast, in the hope it would reach the government and our families.

After having passed two hours, a prey in the most cruel reflections, the master gunner of the frigate, wishing to go to the front of the raft, went out from below the tent. Scarcely had he put out his head, when he turned to us, uttering a piercing cry. Joy was painted upon his face—his hands were stretched towards the sea—he breathed with difficulty. All he was able to say was, "Saved! see the brig upon us!" and in fact it was not more than half a league distant, having every sail set, and steering right upon us. We rushed from our tent: even those whom enormous wounds in their inferior extremities had confined for some days, dragged themselves to the back of the raft, to enjoy a sight of the ship which had come to save us from certain death. We embraced one another with a transport which looked much like madness, and tears of joy trickled down our cheeks, withered by the most cruel privations. Each seized handkerchiefs, or some pieces of linen, to make signals to the brig, which was rapidly approaching us. Some fell on their knees, and fervently returned thanks to Providence for this miraculous preservation of their lives. Our joy redoubled when we saw at the top of the foremast a large white flag; and we cried, "Is it then to Frenchmen we will owe our deliverance." We instantly recognised the brig to be the Argus: it was then about two gun shots from us. We were terribly impatient to see her reel her sails, which at last she did; and fresh cries of joy arose from our raft. The Argus came and lay to on our starboard, about half a pistol shot from us. The crew, ranged upon the deck and on the shrouds, announced to us, by the waving of their hands and hats, the pleasure they felt at coming to the assistance of their unfortunate countrymen.

In a short time we were all transported on board the brig, where we found the lieutenant of the frigate, and some others who had been wrecked with us. Compassion was painted on every face, and pity drew tears from every eye which beheld us.

We found some excellent broth on board the brig, which they had prepared; and when they had perceived us, they added to it some wine, and thus restored our nearly exhausted strength. They bestowed on us the most generous care and attention: our wounds were dressed, and on the morrow many of our sick began to revive. Some, however, still suffered much; for they were placed between decks, very near the kitchen, which augmented the almost insupportable heat of these latitudes. This want of space arose from the small size of the vessel. The number of the shipwrecked was indeed very considerable. Those who did not belong to the navy were laid upon cables, wrapped in flags, and placed under the fire of the kitchen. Here they had almost perished during the course of the night, fire having broken out between decks about ten in the evening; but timely assistance being rendered, we were saved for the second time. We had scarcely escaped, when some of us became again delirious. An officer of infantry wished to throw himself into the sea, to look for his pocket book; and would have done it had he not been prevented. Others were seized in a manner not less frenzied.

The commander and officers of the brig watched over us, and kindly anticipated our wants. They snatched us from death, by saving us from our raft: their unremitting care revived within us the spark of life. The surgeon of the ship, M. Renaud, distinguished himself for his indefatigable zeal. He was obliged to spend the whole of the day in dressing our wounds; and during the two days we were in the brig, he bestowed on us all the aid of his art, with an attention and gentleness which merits our eternal gratitude.

In truth, it was time we should find an end of our sufferings: they had lasted thirteen days in the most cruel manner. The strongest among us might have lived forty-eight hours or so, longer. M. Correard felt that he must die in the course of the day. He had, however, a presentiment we would be saved. He said, that a series of events so unheard of, would not be buried in oblivion: that Providence would at least preserve some of us to tell to the world the melancholy story of our misfortunes.

Such is the fatal history of those who were left upon the memorable raft. Of one hundred and fifty, fifteen only were saved. Five of that number never recovered from their fatigue, and died at St. Louis. Those who yet live are covered with scars; and the cruel sufferings to which they have been exposed, have materially shaken their constitutions.

[17]

Destruction of the *Essex*

The loss of the *Essex* is one of the best-known shipwrecks in all naval history, thanks to Herman Melville, his *Moby-Dick,* and the Melville industrial complex in American literature.

Melville used the loss of the *Essex* for the finale of the action in *Moby-Dick;* he also referred to the story in *Clarel,* Part I, Canto XXXVII. He summarized the tragedy in *Moby-Dick* (as quoted below), but he skirted the facts of the case in a rather gingerly way when he wrote, "After the severest exposure, part of the crew reached the land in their boats." His omissions must have been in his mind when he later remarked in *Clarel* on Captain Pollard's serving as a night watchman on Nantucket and on his quietness and diffidence. Pollard lost the *Essex* to the attack of the whale, and the boats set out on one of the longest cruises recorded for small craft. In Pollard's boat, at the last extremity, the men cast lots to see which of them should be sacrificed for the others. The lot fell on the young cabin boy, Owen Coffin, said in Alexander Starbuck's *History of Nantucket* to have been Captain Pollard's nephew. Impressive as the ending of *Moby-Dick* is, it is still but fiction; there is more tragedy in the short snatch of dialogue in the frail whaleboat lost in the mid-Pacific. Pollard remembered, "I started forward instantly, and cried out, 'My lad, my lad, if you don't like your lot, I'll shoot the first man that touches you.' The poor emaciated boy hesitated a moment or two; then, quietly laying his head down upon the gunnel of the boat, he said, 'I like it as well as any other.' He was soon dispatched, and nothing of him left." Pollard had to go back to Nantucket, tell the story, face and live with the boy's relatives. It was like the judges and accusers and hangmen of the Salem witchcraft, settling down to live as good neighbors with the children and brothers and sisters of the people they had done to death. Pollard was given one other ship and lost it on an uncharted reef in the Pacific. After that he was counted an unlucky man, and no wonder!

It may be interesting to note that in *Clarel* Melville reverses the order of Captain Pollard's shipwrecks, having the loss of the ship to a whale come after the wreck in the Pacific instead of before. Possibly Melville was seeking a kind of climactic order—in *Clarel* cannibalism is mentioned; more likely he simply forgot.

The *Essex* was not the only ship sunk by a whale. The *Union* struck a whale and sank in 1807, and Melville himself mentioned the loss of the *Ann Alexander* just as *Moby-Dick* was about to go to press.

Strong-stomached as our ancestors were, many of the summaries of the *Essex* tragedy left out the cannibalism exactly as did Melville. This narrative is taken from one of the fuller accounts, in the anonymous *Mariner's Chronicle,* New Haven, 1834.

"Look again! Here comes another. Jarl calls it a Bone Shark. . . . To seamen, nothing strikes more terror than the near vicinity of a creature like this. Great ships steer out of its path. And well they may; since the good craft Essex, and others, have been sunk by sea-monsters, as the alligator thrusts his horny snout through a Caribbean canoe."
Mardi, chapter 13.

"My God! Mr. Chace, what is the matter?" I answered, "we have been stove by a whale."
CHACE, *Narrative of the Shipwreck of the Whale Ship Essex.*

First: In the year 1820 the ship Essex, Captain Pollard, of Nantucket, was cruising in the Pacific Ocean. One day she saw spouts, lowered her boats, and gave chase to a shoal of sperm whales. Ere long, several of the whales were wounded; when, suddenly, a very large whale escaping from the boats, issued from the shoal, and bore down directly upon the ship. Dashing his forehead against her hull, he so stove her in, that in less than "ten minutes" she settled down and fell over. Not a surviving plank of her has been seen since. After the severest exposure, part of the crew reached the land in their boats. Being returned home at last, Captain Pollard once more sailed for the Pacific in command of another ship, but the gods shipwrecked him again upon unknown rocks and breakers; for the second time his ship was utterly lost, and forthwith forswearing the sea, he has never tempted it since. At this day Captain Pollard is a resident of Nantucket. I have seen Owen Chace, who was chief mate of the Essex at the time of the tragedy; I have read his plain and faithful narrative; I have conversed with his son; and all this within a few miles of the scene of the catastrophe.
Moby-Dick, chapter xlv.

Retribution, swift vengeance, eternal malice were in his whole aspect, and spite of all that mortal man could do, the solid white buttress of his forehead smote the ship's starboard bow, till men

165

and timbers reeled. Some fell flat upon their faces. Like dis-
lodged trucks, the heads of the harpooneers aloft shook on their
bull-like necks. Through the breach, they heard the waters pour,
as mountain torrents down a flume.

Moby-Dick, chapter cxxxv.

. . . before seeing Chace's ship, we spoke another Nantucket craft
[the *Lima?*] & *gammed* with her. In the forecastle I made the acquaintance of a fine lad of sixteen or thereabouts, a son [William
Henry] of Owen Chace! I questioned him concerning his father's
adventure; and when I left his ship to return again the next
morning (for the two vessels were to sail in company for a few
days) he went to his chest & handed me a complete copy . . . of
the Narrative of the *Essex* catastrophe. This was the first printed
account of it I had ever seen. . . . The reading of this wondrous
story upon the landless sea, & close to the very latitude of the
shipwreck had a surprising effect upon me.

M's memoir of Owen Chase
JAY LEYDA, *The Melville Log*, I:119.

I observe a famine at sea, I observe the sailors casting lots who
shall be kill'd to preserve the lives of the rest,
WALT WHITMAN, "I Sit and Look Out."

DESTRUCTION OF THE

ESSEX

BY A WHALE

As related by her commander,

Captain George Pollard.

My first shipwreck was in open sea, on the 20th of November, 1820, near the equator, about 118 deg. W. longitude. The
vessel, a South Sea whaler, was called the Essex. On that day, as we
were on the look out for sperm whales, and had actually struck two,
which the boats' crews were following to secure, I perceived a very
large one—it might be eighty or ninety feet long—rushing with great
swiftness through the water right toward the ship. We hoped that
she would turn aside and dive under, when she perceived such a balk

in her way. But no! the animal came full force against our sternport: had any quarter less firm been struck, the vessel must have been burst; as it was, every plank and timber trembled throughout her whole bulk.

The whale, as though hurt by a severe and unexpected concussion, shook its enormous head and sheered off to so considerable a distance that for some time we had lost sight of her from the starboard quarter; of which we were very glad, hoping that the worst was over. Nearly an hour afterward we saw the same fish—we had no doubt of this, from her size and the direction in which she came—making again toward us. We were at once aware of our danger, but escape was impossible. She dashed her head this time against the ship's side, and so broke it in that the vessel filled rapidly, and soon became water-logged. At the second shock, expecting her to go down, we lowered our three boats with the utmost expedition, and all hands, twenty in the whole, got into them; seven, and seven, and six. In a little while, as she did not sink, we ventured on board again, and, by scuttling the deck, were enabled to get out some biscuit, beef, water, rum, two sextants, a quadrant, and three compasses. These, together with some rigging, a few muskets, powder, &c. we brought away; and, dividing the stores among our three small crews, rigged the boats as well as we could; there being a compass for each, and a sextant for two, and a quadrant for one, but neither sextant nor quadrant for the third. Then, instead of pushing away for some port, so amazed and bewildered were we, that we continued sitting in our places, gazing upon the ship as though she had been an object of the tenderest affection. Our eyes could not leave her, till, at the end of many hours, she gave a slight reel, then down she sank. No words can tell our feelings. We looked at each other—we looked at the place where she had so lately been afloat—and we did not cease to look till the terrible conviction of our abandoned and perilous situation roused us to exertion, if deliverance were yet possible.

We now consulted about the course which it might be best to take—westward to India, eastward to South America, or south-westward to the Society Isles. We knew that we were at no great distance from Tahiti, but were so ignorant of the state and temper of the inhabitants that we feared we should be devoured by cannibals if we cast ourselves on their mercy. It was determined therefore to make for South America, which we computed to be more than two thousand miles distant. Accordingly we steered eastward, and though for several days harassed with squalls, we contrived to keep together. It was not long before we found that one of the boats had started a plank, which was no wonder, for whale boats are all clinker built, and very slight, being made of half-inch plank only, before planing. To remedy this alarming defect we all turned to, and having emptied the damaged boat into the two others, we raised her side as well as we could, and succeeded in restoring the plank at the bottom. Through this accident some of our biscuit had become injured by the salt water. This was equally divided among the several boats' crews. Food and water, meanwhile, with our utmost economy, rapidly failed. Our strength was exhausted, not by abstinence only, but by the labors which we were obliged to employ to keep our little vessels afloat amidst the storms which repeatedly assailed us. One night we were parted in rough weather; but though the next day we fell in with one of our companion-boats, we never saw or heard any more of the other, which probably perished at sea, being without either sextant or quadrant.

When we were reduced to the last pinch, and out of every thing, having been more than three weeks abroad, we were cheered with the sight of a low uninhabited island, which we reached in hope, but were bitterly disappointed. There were some barren bushes and many rocks on this forlorn spot. The only provisions that we could procure were a few birds and their eggs: this supply was soon reduced; the sea-fowls appeared to have been frightened away, and their nests were left empty after we had once or twice plundered them. What distressed us most was the utter want of fresh water; we could not find a drop any where, till, at the extreme verge of ebb tide, a small spring was discovered in the sand; but even that was too scanty to afford us sufficient to quench our thirst before it was covered by the waves at their turn.

There being no prospect but that of starvation here, we determined to put to sea again. Three of our comrades, however, chose to remain, and we pledged ourselves to send a vessel to bring them off, if we ourselves should ever escape to a Christian port. With a very small quantity of biscuit for each, and a little water, we again ventured out on the wide ocean. In the course of a few days our provisions were consumed. Two men died; we had no other alternative than to live on their remains. These were roasted to dryness by means of fires kindled on the ballast-sand at the bottom of the boats. When this supply was spent, what could we do? We looked at each other with horrid thoughts in our minds, but we held our tongues. I am sure that we loved one another as brothers all the time; and yet our looks told plainly what must be done. We cast lots, and the fatal one fell on my poor cabin boy. I started forward instantly, and cried out, "My lad, my lad, *if you don't like your lot,* I'll shoot the first man that touches you." The poor emaciated boy hesitated a moment or two; then, quietly laying his head down upon the gunnel of the boat, he said, *"I like it as well as any other."* He was soon despatched, and nothing of him left. I think, then another man died of himself, and him too we ate. But I can tell you no more—my head is on fire at the recollection; I hardly know what I say. I forgot to say that we parted company with the second boat before now. After some more days of horror and despair, when some were lying down at the bottom of the boat, not able to rise, and scarcely one of us could move a limb, a vessel hove in sight. We were taken on board and treated with extreme kindness. The second boat was also picked up at sea, and the survivors saved. A ship afterward sailed in search of our companions on the desolate island, and brought them away.

The following particulars respecting the three men left on the island, are extracted from a tract issued by the London Tract Society, in Paternoster Row.

On the 26th of December the boats left the island: this was, indeed, a trying moment to all; they separated with mutual prayers and good wishes, seventeen venturing to sea with almost certain death before them, while three remained on a rocky isle, destitute of water, and affording hardly any thing to support life. The prospects of these three poor men were gloomy; they again tried to dig a well, but without success, and all hope seemed at an end, when providentially they were relieved by a shower of rain. They were thus delivered from the immediate apprehension of perishing by thirst. Their next care was to procure food, and their difficulties herein were also very great; their principal resource was small birds, about the size of a blackbird, which they caught while at roost. Every night they climbed the trees in search of them, and obtained, by severe exertions, a scanty supply, hardly enough to support life. Some of the trees bore a small berry, which gave them a little relief; but these they found only in small quantities. Shell-fish they searched for in vain; and although from the rocks they saw at times a number of sharks, and also other sorts of fish, they were unable to catch any, as they had no fishing tackle. Once they saw several turtles, and succeeded in taking five, but they were then without water; at those times they had little inclination to eat, and before one of them was quite finished, the others were become unfit for food.

Their sufferings from the want of water were the most severe, their only supply being from what remained in holes among the rocks after the showers which fell at intervals; and sometimes they were five or six days without any; on these occasions they were compelled to suck the blood of the birds they caught, which allayed their thirst in some degree; but they did so very unwillingly, as they found themselves much disordered thereby.

Among the rocks were several caves formed by nature, which afforded a shelter from the wind and rain. In one of these caves they found eight human skeletons, in all probability the remains of some poor mariners who had been shipwrecked on the isle, and perished for want of food and water. They were side by side, as if they had laid down and died together! This sight deeply affected the mate and his companions; their case was similar, and they had every reason to expect, ere long, the same end; for many times they lay down at night, with their tongues swollen and their lips parched with thirst, scarcely hoping to see the morning sun; and it is impossible to form an idea of their feelings when the morning dawned, and they found their prayers had been heard and answered by a providential supply of rain.

In this state they continued till the 5th of April following. On the morning of that day they were in the woods as usual, searching for food and water as well as their weakness permitted, when their attention was aroused by a sound which they thought was distant thunder; but looking toward the sea, they saw a ship in the offing, which had just fired a gun. Their joy at this sight may be more easily imagined than described; they immediately fell on their knees and thanked God for his goodness in thus sending deliverance when least expected; then hastening to the shore, they saw a boat coming toward them. As the boat could not approach the shore without great danger, the mate, being a good swimmer, and stronger than his companions, plunged into the sea, and providentially escaped a watery grave at the moment when deliverance was at hand. His companions crawled out farther on the rocks, and by the great exertions of the crew, were taken into the boat, and soon found themselves on board the Surrey, commanded by Captain Raine, by whom they were treated in the kindest manner, and their health and strength were speedily restored.

[18]

Loss of the Ship *Albion*

The story of the loss of the *Albion* is summarized in three short quotations from the narrative by the first mate: "The gale increasing . . . gale increasing . . . gale still increasing." Perhaps stouter masts and spars would have saved the ship, but this seems to be one of the wrecks in which the officers and crew did their duty and the ship was in good condition. The wreck was, in the underwriters' phrase, an Act of God.

One of the passengers, only mentioned in this account, deserves longer comment. General Lefevre Desnouetts, who was using an assumed name and wearing a beard, had been one of Napoleon's generals and had joined his leader after the escape from Elba. Proscribed by the Bourbons after Waterloo, he had escaped to the United States and gone to cotton farming in Alabama while his wife remained in France. He had petitioned the French government for permission to return to that country and had been told to go to Holland and there await the pleasure of the King. He sailed for Europe in the *Albion*.

There are three differing accounts in anthologies of this wreck; the one given here, made up of the two accounts of First Mate Cammyer and Mr. Everhart, was copied by some others. This is Thomas's version.

> ". . . and I thought of the wreck of the gallant Albion, tost
> to pieces on the very shore now in sight . . ."
>
> HERMAN MELVILLE, *Redburn,* chapter xxvii.

LOSS OF THE SHIP

ALBION.

THE following account of this melancholy shipwreck as given by Henry Cammyer, first mate of the vessel.

We sailed from New York on the first of April, 1822, in the ship Albion, of four hundred and forty-seven tons, with a crew, including officers, of twenty-five in number, besides twenty-three cabin, and six steerage passengers; making in the whole fifty-four persons, only nine of whom now live to relate the melancholy tale. For the first twenty days, we continued our voyage with moderate and favorable weather; and at about half past one o'clock, in the afternoon of Sunday the 21st, we made the land. The Fastnet rock bore by compass, E.N.E., distant about three leagues. At two, made cape Clear, bearing east and by north, distance about two leagues. Thick and foggy, blowing fresh, and heavy squalls from the southward. Ship heading up E.S.E., carrying all prudent sail, to crowd the ship off the land. The gale increasing, shortened sail occasionally. At four o'clock, then under double reefed topsails, foresail, and mainsail, carried away the fore-yard, and split the foretopsail. Got the pieces of the yard down, and prepared to get another yard up. Gale increasing, about half past four, took in the mainsail and mizzen-topsail, and set the maintry-sail. Night coming on, cleared the decks for working ship. At half past eight, gale still increasing, with a high sea. Shipped a heavy sea, which threw the ship on her beam-ends, and carried away the main-mast by the deck, the head of the mizzen-mast, and fore-topmast, and swept the decks clear of every thing, including boats, caboose house, bulwarks, and compasses, and stove in all the hatches, state rooms, and bulwarks in the cabin, which was nearly filled with water. At the same moment, six of the crew and one cabin passenger, Mr. A. B. Convers, of Troy, N.Y., were swept overboard.

The ship being unmanageable, and the sea making a complete breach over her, we were obliged to lash ourselves to the pumps, and being in total darkness, without correct compasses, could not tell how the ship's head lay. The axes being swept away, had no means of clearing the wreck. About one o'clock made the light of the Old Head of Kinsale, but could not ascertain how it bore; and at two, found the ship embayed. The captain, anticipating our melancholy fate, called all the passengers up, who had not before been on deck. Many of them had received considerable injury when the sea first struck her, and were scarcely able to come on deck; others had been incessantly assisting at the pumps; and it is an interesting fact, that Miss Powell, an amiable young lady, who was on board, was desirous to be allowed to take her turn. One gentleman, who had been extremely ill during the passage, Mr. William Everhart, of Chester, Penn., was too feeble to crawl to the deck, without assistance, but strange to say, he was the only cabin passenger who was saved.

Our situation at that moment, is indescribable, and I can scarcely dwell upon, much less attempt to detail, its horrors. About three o'clock, the ship struck on a reef, her upper works beat in over the rocks, and in about half an hour after coming in over the first reef, she parted midships, and her quarter-deck drifted in on the top of the inside ledge, immediately under the cliffs. Up to the period of her parting, nearly twenty persons were clinging to the wreck, among whom were two females, Mrs. Pye, and Miss Powell. Captain Williams had, with several others, been swept away soon after she struck; a circumstance which may be attributed to the very extraordinary exertions which he used, to the last moment, for the preservation of the lives of the unfortunate passengers and crew.

A short time before she parted, myself and six of the crew got away from the vessel. After gaining a rock in a very exhausted state, I was washed off, but, by the assistance of Providence, was enabled, before the return of the sea, to regain it; and before I could attempt to climb the cliff, which was nearly perpendicular, I was obliged to lie down, to regain a little strength, after the severe bruises and contusions I had received on the body and feet. One of the passengers, colonel Augustine J. Prevost, reached the rock with me alive, but was, together with one of the stewards, washed off and drowned.

Some of the passengers were suffocated on deck and in the fore rigging, and some must have been destroyed by an anchor which was loose on the forecastle before the ship parted. It is scarcely possible to describe the devastation which followed. The entire cargo, consisting of cotton, rice, turpentine, and beeswax, together with a quantity of silver and gold, to a large amount, was in all directions beaten to pieces by the severity of the sea, without a possibility of saving it.

Very soon after we got upon the cliffs, my poor shipmates and myself found our way to a peasant's cottage. Early in the morning, Mr. James B. Gibbens, of Ballinspittle, came to me from the wreck, where he had been since five o'clock, endeavoring to save some of the lives. He most humanely sent Mr. Everhart, Mr. Raymond, the boy, and myself, to his house, about a mile from the spot, where we experienced the kindest and most hospitable attention. The remaining survivors were taken home by Mr. Purcell, steward of Thomas Rochfort, Esq. of Garretstown, where every attention was paid to them. Coffins were provided by Mr. Purcell, according to the orders of Mr. Rochfort, and the bodies that were found, were interred at Templetrine churchyard, about four miles from Kinsale and one from the fatal spot. The Rev. Mr. Evanson kindly officiated on the occasion. On Tuesday, I went to Kinsale to note a protest, and then first met Mr. Mark, the consul for the United States, who happened to be at Kinsale at that time on other business. He came over and gave directions for clothing the sufferers, who were destitute of every thing.

Unremitting exertions were used daily for the recovery of the goods and specie, but without success, as none of the cargo, and but a small part of the materials of the vessel, were saved, together with property in specie to the amount of about five thousand pounds.

The following is a correct list of the crew and passengers.

Crew. John Williams, captain, drowned; Henry Cammyer, first mate, saved; Edward Smith, second mate, drowned; William Hyate, boatswain, saved; Alexander Adams, carpenter, Harman Nelson, Harman Richardson, Henry Whittrell, William Trisserly, James Wiley, Robert McLellan, and Thomas Goodman, drowned; John Simson, John Richards, Francis Bloom, and Ebenezer Warner, saved; Samuel Wilson and William Snow, boys, drowned; William Dockwood, drowned, body found and interred; Hierom Raymond, saved; Lloyd Potter, Samuel Penny, stewards, and Francis Isaac, boy, blacks, all drowned; Thomas Hill and Adam Johnson, cooks, blacks, both drowned, bodies found and interred.

Cabin Passengers, W. Everhart, Esq., of Chester, Penn., saved; lieutenant-colonel Augustine J. Prevost, major William Gough, of the 68th regiment; Rev. G. R. G. Hill, last from Jamaica; Nelson Ross, of Troy, N.Y.; William H. Dwight, of Boston; Mr. Beynon, of London; professor Fisher, of New-Haven college; Mr. William Proctor, of New York; Mr. and Mrs. Hyde Clark, Mrs. Pye and Miss Powell, of Canada, daughter of Judge Powell, all drowned, found and interred; Mr. A. B. Convers, of Troy, N.Y., and madame Gardiner and son, of Paris, drowned; (madame G.'s body was found and interred;) five French gentlemen, names unknown, (except Mr. Victor Millicent,) drowned, found and interred.

Steerage Passengers. Stephen Chase, of Canada, saved; Mrs. Mary Brereton, and Mary Hunt, drowned, found and interred; Mr. Harrison, carpenter, Mr. Baldwin, cotton spinner, from Yorkshire, England, and Dr. Carver, a veterinary surgeon, drowned.

Four bodies were also found and interred that could not be recognized.

The following account of the wreck of the Albion was communicated to the editor of the Village Record, of Chester, Pennsylvania, by William Everhart, Esq., after his return to the United States. Mr. Everhart, it will be recollected, was the only cabin passenger who was saved, out of twenty-three persons. As his statement affords some additional particulars of the disaster that may be interesting, we publish it entire.

Mr. Everhart says, that up to the 21st of April, the voyage had been prosperous and pleasant for the season, though he had himself suffered much from sea-sickness, and was almost constantly confined to his room. The storm of the day, it was supposed, was over; they were near to the coast, and all hands flattered themselves that in a short time, they should reach their destined harbor; but, about nine o'clock in the evening, a heavy sea struck the ship, swept several seamen from the deck, carried away her masts, and stove in her hatchways, so that every wave which passed over her, ran into the hold without any thing to stop it,—the railings were carried away, and the wheel which aided them to steer. In short, that fatal wave left the Albion a wreck. She was then about twenty miles from the shore, and captain Williams steadily and coolly gave his orders; he cheered the passengers and crew with the hope that the wind would shift, and before morning blow off shore. The sea was very rough, and the vessel unmanageable; and the passengers were obliged to be tied to the pumps, that they might work them. All who could do no good on deck, retired below, but the water was knee deep in the cabin, and the furniture floating about, rendered the situation dangerous and dreadful.

All night long, the wind blew a gale, directly on shore, towards which the Albion was drifting, at the rate of about three miles an hour. The complete hopelessness of their situation was known to few except captain Williams. The coast was familiar to him; and he must have seen in despair and horror, throughout the night, the certainty of their fate. At length, the ocean, dashing and roaring upon the precipice of rocks, told them that their hour was come. Captain Williams summoned all on deck, and briefly told them that the ship must soon strike; it was impossible to preserve her. Mr. Everhart says, that he was the last that left the cabin. Professor Fisher was behind, but he is confident that he never came on deck, but perished below. Some, particularly the females, expressed their terror in wild shrieks. Major Gough, of the British army, remarked that "death, come as he would, was an unwelcome messenger, but that they must meet him like men." Very little was said by the others; the men waited the expected shock in silence. General Lefevre Desnouetts, during the voyage, had evidently wished to remain without particular observation; and to prevent his being known, besides taking passage under a feigned name, had suffered his beard to grow during the whole voyage. He had the misfortune, before the ship struck, to be much bruised, and one of his arms was broken, which disabled him from exertion if it could have been availing. It is not possible to conceive the horrors of their situation.

The deadly and relentless blast impelling them to destruction; the ship a wreck; the raging of the billows against the precipice, on which they were driving, sending back from the caverns and the rocks, the hoarse and melancholy warnings of death, dark, cold, and wet! In such a situation the stoutest heart must have quaked in utter despair. When there is a ray of hope, there may be a corresponding buoyance of spirit. When there is any thing to be done, the active man may drown the sense of danger while actively exerting himself; but here there was nothing to do but to die! Just at the gray of dawn the Albion struck.

The perpendicular precipice of rocks is nearly two hundred feet in height; the sea beating for ages against it has worn large caverns in its base, into which the waves rushed violently, sending back a deep and hollow sound, then, running out in various directions, formed whirlpools of great violence. For a perch or two from the precipice, rocks rise out of the water, broad at bottom and sharp at top; on one of these, the Albion first struck, the next wave threw her further on the rock, the third further still, until, nearly balanced, she swung round, and her stern was driven against another, near in shore. In this situation, every wave making a complete breach over her, many were drowned on deck. A woman, Mr. Everhart could not distinguish who, fell near him and cried for help. He left his hold and raised her up,—another wave came, but she was too far exhausted to sustain herself, and sank on the deck. Fifteen or sixteen corpses, at one time, Mr. Everhart thought, lay near the bows of the ship.

Perceiving now that the stern was higher out of water, and the sea had less power in its sweep over it, Mr. Everhart went aft. He now perceived that the bottom had been broken out of the ship. The heavy articles must have sunk, and the cotton and lighter articles were floating around, dashed by every wave against the rocks. Presently the ship broke in two, and all those who remained near the bow were lost. Several from the stern of the ship had got on the side of the precipice, and were hanging by the crags as well as they could. Although weakened by previous sickness and present suffering, Mr. Everhart made an effort and got upon the rock and stood upon one foot, the only hold that he could obtain. He saw several around him, and among the rest, colonel Prevost, who observed, on seeing him take his station, "here is another poor fellow." But the waves, rolling heavily against them, and often dashing the spray fifty feet above their heads, gradually swept those who had taken refuge one by one away; and one poor fellow losing his hold, grasped the leg of Mr. Everhart, and nearly pulled him from his place. Weak and sick as he was, Mr. Everhart stood several hours on one foot on a little crag, the billows dashing over him, and he benumbed with cold.

As soon as it was light, and the tide ebbed so as to render it possible, the people descended the rocks as far as they could, and dropped him a rope, which he fastened around his body, and was drawn out to a place of safety. Of twenty-three cabin passengers, he alone escaped! Mr. Everhart mentions numerous instances of the kindness shewn by the people to the survivors. A sailor was drawn ashore naked, and one of the peasants, although a cold rain was falling, took the shirt from his own back, and put it on that of the sufferer. Mr. Everhart himself was taken to the hospitable mansion of Mr. James B. Gibbens, where he lay for several weeks exceedingly ill, receiving the kindest attention. "They could not have treated me more tenderly," said Mr. Everhart, "if I had been a brother."

The attentions paid the survivors, were in the style of true Irish hospitality. Such disinterested kindness exalts the human character, and is calculated to have not a limited effect, but will prove of national advantage.

This terrible wreck and loss of lives, and on the part of Mr. Everhart, such a miraculous preservation, excited the public sensibility throughout Europe and America. When he landed at Liverpool, it was difficult for him to get along the streets, the people crowded around in such numbers to see the only passenger saved from the wreck of the Albion.

[19]

Loss of the *Frances Mary*

THIS NARRATIVE is horror story, pure and simple, with much the same macabre interest that attaches to the story of the Donner party trapped in the Sierras. Perhaps worth noting is the fact that the *Frances Mary* was found floating derelict, was refitted, and went to sea again. Ships carrying lumber were unsinkable so long as they held together, and the survivors of the famine on board the *Frances Mary* owed their lives to the cargo of the ship.

Captain Kendall must have written down his recollections for some newspaper or magazine, since he is given as the source of this account; an anonymous "Narrative of the Shipwreck and Sufferings of Miss Ann Saunders" was printed for L. S. Crossman in Providence in 1827 and may include the record of Captain Kendall. Obviously most readers were interested in the redoubtable Miss Saunders rather than in the other survivors.

This narrative is taken from *The Terrors of the Sea,* by an Old Salt, a cheap anthology published by Hurst and Company of New York (no date).

LOSS OF THE

FRANCES MARY.

THE Frances Mary was a new ship, of about four hundred tons burthen, commanded by captain Kendall, and bound from New Brunswick to Liverpool, laden with timber. We publish the following particulars of this dreadful disaster as related by captain Kendall.

Sailed from St. Johns, N.B., January 18, 1826. February 1, strong gales from the W.N.W.; carried away the main-topmast and mizzen-mast head; hove to, got boat's sails in the main rigging, to keep the ship to the wind. At 11, P.M., shipped a heavy sea, which washed away the caboose, jolly-boat, and disabled five men. February 2d, cleared away the wreck and made sail before the wind; strong breezes. February 5, 11, A.M., strong gales, with a heavy sea; clewed up the sails and hove to, head to the southward; shipped a sea, which carried away the long-boat, companion, tiller, the best bower-chain, unshipped the rudder, and washed a man overboard, who was afterwards saved. At 10, P.M. another heavy sea struck us, which stove in our stern. Cut away our foremast and both bower anchors, to keep the ship to the wind. Employed in getting what provision we could, by knocking out the bow-port; saved fifty pounds of bread and five pounds of cheese, which we stowed in the maintop. Got the master's wife and female passenger up, whilst we clearing away below, lightening the ship; most of the people slept in the top. At daylight, found Patric Conney hanging by his legs to the cat-harpins, dead from fatigue; committed his body to the deep.

February 6, at 8, A.M., saw a strange sail standing towards us; made signals of distress,—stranger spoke us, and remained in company twenty-four hours, but gave us no assistance; the American making an excuse that the sea was running too high. Made a tent of spare canvass on the forecastle—put the people on an allowance of a quarter of a biscuit a day. February 8, saw a brig to leeward—strong gales. February 9, 10, A.M., observed the same vessel to windward—made the signal of distress; stranger bore up and showed American colors. February 10, she spoke us, asking how long we had been in that situation, and what we intended to do, if we intended leaving the ship? Answered yes. He then asked if we had any rigging? Answered yes. Night coming on, and blowing hard, saw no more of the stranger. Suffered from hunger and thirst.

On the 11th, saw a large ship to the northward—did not speak her; wore head to the northward. At this time all our provisions were out; suffered much from hunger, having received no nourishment for nine days. February 12, departed this life, James Clark, seaman;— read prayers, and committed his body to the deep. We were at this time on a half gill of water a day, and suffered much from hunger. During the whole period of being on the wreck we were wet from top to toe. February 22, John Wilson, seaman, died at 10, A.M.; preserved the body of the deceased, cut him up in quarters, washed them overboard, and hung them up on pins. February 23, J. Moore died, and was thrown overboard, having eaten part of him, such as the liver and heart. From this date to Saturday, 5th of March, the following number perished from hunger, vis. Henry Davis, a Welsh boy, Alex. Kelly, seaman, John Jones, apprentice boy, nephew of the owner, James Frier, cook, Daniel Jones, seaman, John Hutchinson, seaman, and John Jones, a boy—threw the last named overboard, his blood being bitter.

James Frier was working his passage home, under a promise of marriage to Ann Saunders, the female passenger, who attended on the master's wife, and who, when she heard of Frier's death, shrieked a loud yell, then snatching a cup from Clerk, the mate, cut her late intended husband's throat and drank his blood! insisting that she had the greatest right to it. A scuffle ensued, but the heroine got the better of her adversary, and then allowed him to drink one cup to her two.

February 26, on or about this day an English brig hove in sight; hoisted the ensign downward; stranger hauled his wind towards us, and hauled his foresail up when abreast of us; kept his course about one mile distant—set his foresail, and we soon lost sight of him—fresh breeze with a little rain—the sea quite smooth, but he went off, having shown English colors. Had he at this time taken us off the wreck, much of the subsequent dreadful sufferings would have been spared us.

March 7. His B.M. ship Blond came in sight, and to our relief, in latitude 44, 43, north, longitude 31, 57, west. Words are quite inadequate to express our feelings, as well as those which Lord Byron and our deliverers most evidently possessed, when they had come to rescue six of their fellow-creatures, two of them females, from a most awful, lingering, but certain death. It came on to blow during the night a fresh gale, which would no doubt have swept us all overboard. Lieutenant Gambier came in the ship's cutter to bring us from the wreck. He observed to us, "You have yet, I perceive, fresh meat." To which we were compelled to reply, "No, sir, it is part of a man, one of our unfortunate crew,—it was our intention to put ourselves on an allowance even of this food, this evening, had not you come to our relief." The master's wife, who underwent all the most horrid sufferings which the human understanding can imagine, bore them much better than could possibly have been expected. She is now, although much emaciated, a respectable, good-looking woman, about twenty-five years of age, and the mother of a boy seven years old. But what must have been the extremity of want to which she was driven, when she ate the brains of one of the apprentices, saying it was the most delicious thing she ever tasted; and it is still more melancholy to relate, that the person, whose brains she was thus forced by hunger to eat, had been three times wrecked before, but was providentially picked up by a vessel, after being twenty-two days on the wreck, water-logged; but in the present instance, he perished, (having survived similar sufferings for a space of twenty-nine days,) and then became food for his remaining shipmates!

Ann Saunders, the other female, had more strength in her calamity than most of the men. She performed the duty of cutting up and cleaning the dead bodies, keeping two knives for the purpose in her monkey jacket; and when the breath was announced to have flown, she would sharpen her knives, bleed the deceased in the neck, drink his blood, and cut him up as usual. From want of water, those who perished drank their own urine and salt water. They became foolish, and crawled upon their hands round the deck when they could, and died, generally, raving mad!

After floating about the ocean for some months, this ill-fated vessel was fallen in with by an English ship, and carried into Jamaica, where she was refitted, and again went to sea. The putrid remains of human bodies, which had been the only food of the unfortunate survivors, was found on board the vessel.

[20]

Loss of the *Helen McGregor*

THIS NARRATIVE of an explosion aboard the *Helen McGregor* was printed in nearly all the anthologies published after 1830; probably it was thought to be typical of a large number of similar disasters which occurred on American rivers.

The introduction of steam engines added still another hazard to the already danger-filled life of the nineteenth-century traveler, though eventually, of course, the power of steam and the larger ships made possible by that power resulted in much greater safety. As with all innovations, there were hazards which had to be learned.

This account of the wreck of the *Helen McGregor* (spelled variously) is taken from *Shipwrecks and Disasters at Sea,* compiled by Charles Ellms, 1836.

FATAL EXPLOSION OF THE BOILER

ON BOARD

THE STEAM BOAT

HELEN MACGREGOR,

At Memphis, on the Mississippi.

THE following is a description, by a passenger, of one of the most fatal steam boat disasters that has ever occurred on the western waters.

On the morning of the 24th of February, 1830, the Helen Mc-Gregor stopped at Memphis, on the Mississippi river, to deliver freight and land a number of passengers, who resided in that section of Tennessee. The time occupied in so doing could not have exceeded three quarters of an hour. When the boat landed, I went ashore to see a gentleman with whom I had some business. I found him on the beach, and after a short conversation, I returned to the boat. I recollect looking at my watch as I passed the gang-way. It was half past eight o'clock. A great number of persons were standing on what is called the boiler deck, being that part of the upper deck situated immediately over the boilers. It was crowded to excess, and presented one dense mass of human bodies. In a few minutes we sat down to breakfast in the cabin. The table, although extending the whole length of the cabin, was completely filled, there being upwards of sixty cabin passengers, among whom were several ladies and children. The number of passengers on board, deck and cabin united, was between four and five hundred. I had almost finished my breakfast, when the pilot rung his bell for the engineer to put the machinery in motion. The boat having just shoved off, I was in the act of raising my cup to my lips, the tingling of the pilot bell yet on my ear, when I heard an explosion, resembling the discharge of a small piece of artillery. The report was perhaps louder than usual in such cases; for an exclamation was half uttered by me, that the gun was well loaded, when the rushing sound of steam, and the rattling of glass in some of the cabin windows, checked my speech, and told me too well what had occurred. I almost involuntarily bent my head and body down to the floor—a vague idea seemed to shoot across my mind that more than one boiler might burst, and that by assuming this posture, the destroying matter would pass over without touching me.

The general cry of, "a boiler has burst," resounded from one end of the table to the other; and, as if by a simultaneous movement,

all started on their feet. Then commenced a general race to the ladies' cabin, which lay more towards the stern of the boat. All regard
to order or deference to sex seemed to be lost in the struggle for
which should be first and farthest removed from the dreaded boilers.
The danger had already passed away. I remained standing by the
chair on which I had been previously sitting. Only one or two persons staid in the cabin with me. As yet no more than half a minute
had elapsed since the explosion; but, in that brief space, how had the
scene changed! In that "drop of time" what confusion, distress, and
dismay! An instant before, and all were in the quiet repose of security—another, and they were overwhelmed with alarm or consternation. It is but justice to say, that in this scene of terror, the ladies
exhibited a degree of firmness worthy of all praise. No screaming, no
fainting—their fears, when uttered, were not for themselves, but for
their husbands and children.

I advanced from my position to one of the cabin doors for the
purpose of inquiring who were injured, when, just as I reached it, a
man entered at the opposite one, both his hands covering his face,
and exclaiming, "Oh God! oh God! I am ruined!" He immediately
began to tear off his clothes. When stripped, he presented a most
shocking spectacle: his face was entirely black—his body without a
particle of skin. He had been flayed alive. He gave me his name,
and place of abode—then sunk in a state of exhaustion and agony on
the floor. I assisted in placing him on a mattress taken from one of
the berths, and covered him with blankets. He complained of heat
and cold as at once oppressing him. He bore his torments with manly
fortitude, yet a convulsive shriek would occasionally burst from him.
His wife, his children, were his constant theme—it was hard to die
without seeing them—"it was hard to go without bidding them one
farewell." Oil and cotton were applied to his wounds; but he soon
became insensible to earthly misery. Before I had done attending to
him, the whole floor of the cabin was covered with unfortunate sufferers. Some bore up under the horrors of their situation with a degree of resolution amounting to heroism. Others were wholly overcome by the sense of pain, the suddenness of the disaster, and the
near approach of death, which even to them was evident—whose pangs
they already felt. Some implored us, as an act of humanity, to complete the work of destruction, and free them from present suffering.
One entreated the presence of a clergyman, to pray by him, declaring
he was not fit to die. I inquired—none could be had. On every side
were heard groans, and mingled exclamations of grief and despair.

To add to the confusion, persons were every moment running
about to learn the fate of their friends and relatives—fathers, sons,
brothers—for in this scene of unmixed calamity, it was impossible to
say who were saved, or who had perished. The countenances of many

were so much disfigured as to be past recognition. My attention, after some time, was particularly drawn towards a poor fellow, who lay unnoticed on the floor, without uttering a single word of complaint. He was at a little distance removed from the rest. He was not much scalded; but one of his thighs was broken, and a principal artery had been severed, from which the blood was gushing rapidly. He betrayed no displeasure at the apparent neglect with which he was treated—he was perfectly calm. I spoke to him: he said "he was very weak, but felt himself going—it would soon be over." A gentleman ran for one of the physicians. He came, and declared that if expedition were used, he might be preserved by amputating the limb; but that, to effect this, it would be necessary to remove him from the boat. Unfortunately the boat was not sufficiently near to run a plank ashore. We were obliged to wait until it could be close hauled. I stood by him, calling for help. We placed him on a mattress, and bore him to the guards. There we were detained some time from the cause we have mentioned. Never did any thing appear to me so slow as the movements of those engaged in hauling the boat.

I knew, and he knew, that delay was death—that life was fast ebbing. I could not take my gaze from his face—there all was coolness and resignation. No word or gesture indicative of impatience escaped him. He perceived by my loud, and perhaps angry tone of voice, how much I was excited by what I thought the barbarous slowness of those around: he begged me not to take so much trouble—that they were doing their best. At length we got him on shore. It was too late—he was too much exhausted, and died immediately after the amputation.

So soon as I was relieved from attending on those in the cabin, I went to examine that part of the boat where the boiler had burst. It was a complete wreck—a picture of destruction. It bore ample testimony to the tremendous force of that power which the ingenuity of man had brought to his aid. The steam had given every thing a whitish hue; the boilers were displaced; the deck had fallen down; the machinery was broken and disordered. Bricks, dirt, and rubbish, were scattered about. Close by the bowsprit was a large rent, through which I was told the boiler, after exploding, had passed out, carrying one or two men in its mouth. Several dead bodies were lying around. Their fate had been an enviable one compared with that of others: they could scarcely have been conscious of a pang ere they had ceased to be. On the starboard wheel-house lay a human body, in which life was not yet extinct, though apparently there was no sensibility remaining. The body must have been thrown from the boiler-deck, a distance of thirty feet. The whole of the forehead had been blown away: the brains were still beating. Tufts of hair, shreds of clothing, and splotches of blood might be seen in every direction. A piece of skin was picked up by a gentleman on board, which appeared to have been pealed off by the force of steam. It extended from the middle of the arm down to the tips of the fingers, the nails adhering to it. So dreadful had been the force, that not a particle of the flesh adhered to it. The most skilful operator could scarcely have effected such a result. Several died from inhaling the steam or gas, whose skin was almost uninjured.

The number of lives lost, will, in all probability, never be distinctly known. Many were seen flung into the river, most of whom sunk to rise no more. Could the survivors have been kept together until the list of passengers was called, the precise loss would have been ascertained. That, however, though it had been attempted, would, under the circumstances, have been next to impossible.

Judging from the crowd which I saw on the boiler-deck immediately before the explosion, and the statement which I received as to the number of those who succeeded in swimming out after they were cast into the river, I am inclined to believe that between fifty and sixty must have perished.

The cabin passengers escaped, owing to the peculiar construction of the boat. Just behind the boilers were several large iron posts, supporting, I think, the boiler-deck: across each post was a large circular plate of iron of between one and two inches in thickness. One of these posts was placed exactly opposite the head of the boiler which burst, being the second one on the starboard side. Against this plate the head struck, and penetrated to the depth of an inch; then broke, and flew off at an angle, entering a cotton bale to the depth of a foot. The boiler head was in point blank range with the breakfast table in the cabin; and had it not been obstructed by the iron post, must have made a clear sweep of those who were seated at the table.

To render any satisfactory account of the cause which produced the explosion, can hardly be expected from one who possesses no scientific or practical knowledge on the subject, and who previously thereto was paying no attention to the management of the boat. The captain appeared to be very active and diligent in attending to his duty. He was on the boiler deck when the explosion occurred, was materially injured by that event, and must have been ignorant of the mismanagement, if any there were.

From the engineer alone could the true explanation be afforded; and, if indeed it was really attributable to negligence, it can scarcely be supposed he will lay the blame on himself. If I might venture a suggestion in relation thereto, I would assign the following causes:— That the water in the starboard boilers had become low, in consequence of that side of the boat resting upon the ground during our stay at Memphis; that, though the fires were kept up some time before we shoved off, that the head which burst had been cracked for a considerable time; that the boiler was extremely heated, and the water, thrown in when the boat was again in motion, was at once converted into steam: and the flues not being sufficiently large to carry it off as soon as it was generated, nor the boiler head of a strength capable of resisting its action, the explosion was a natural result.

[21]

Loss of the *Isabella*

Little comment is necessary on the loss of the *Isabella*. She put to sea when other and wiser captains stayed at anchor; her captain sent away a lifeboat when the ship was in manifest danger, would not believe that the ship had been holed by the rocks on which she struck, and was saved from his own folly only by the crew of the lifeboat. Here again a severe storm and the narrow waters of the Channel did their work, as they had done earlier with the *Halsewell* and the *Earl of Abergavenny*.

This account is taken from Thomas.

ISABELLA,

Off Hastings, England.

THE details below were furnished by one of the passengers, in a letter to a friend, dated

Eastbourne, March 15, 1833.

This wreck is still visible; she was a fine ship of 340 tons, and offers an awful evidence of the power of nature over the noblest works of art. My heart still sickens with dismay at the recollection of the dreadful trials I have passed through. I have not before had health and strength enough to give you an outline of the particulars, and, even now, I tremble as they pass in review before me.

All our valuable furniture, plate, books, manuscripts, outfit and necessaries had been put on board the Isabella in the docks, when she dropped down to Gravesend, where I joined her on the evening of Saturday the 16th of February, with my wife and three children, a girl of eighteen months, and two boys of four and six years. We were opposed by contrary winds, and put our pilot on shore on Monday evening. On Tuesday, the wind freshened into a gale; and the dreadful enervating sickness usually attending these scenes, dispossessed my wife and myself of all energy and strength. The wind was now directly against us, and every hour increasing its fearful power; but our captain, full of intrepidity and confidence, determined to proceed, although he left behind a fleet of perhaps an hundred sail. As night closed, the tempest raged yet more fearfully. Our gallant ship was but as a feather on the wave's surface, and all was fearfully dark as any night in the black catalogue of tempests; the wind right ahead; there was equal peril now in advancing or receding; the captain, however, gave his orders with as much precision as if he were exhibiting in a state pageant. The loud voice of the speaking-trumpet was the only sound that could be heard amid the wild roar of contending elements. Between three and four o'clock, our captain entered the cabin; he spoke little. I saw the distressed workings of his mind, and one or two questions constituted all the interruptions I offered. He took brandy and water, threw off his saturated dress, and having sat a little in dry clothes, retired.

From this time, the ship seemed to me to labor and strain more than before, and the hurricane to drive and lay down the ship lower on her side; but as the captain was taking rest, I had fancied more security, and had lain myself on the floor of the cabin in the hope of getting also some repose. I had been lying down I suppose thirty minutes, when I thought I heard or felt the keel of the ship drag. I had been to this time, sick to death. I was exhausted and listless, almost lifeless, when the dreadful suspicion and announcement of "shore" alarmed me; I was ill no more. I jumped up, and was rushing through the cabin to mention my fears, when the ship beat twice on a rock, and I heard the cry of "The ship has struck!" I called the captain. The dreadful shock and loud cries of alarm, combined to summon all on deck, excepting the ladies and the poor children, who had been roused, at last, by the general crash and these I would not allow to leave their berths lest they might interrupt the exertions making above. Here, indeed, was redoubled energy. The rudder was unshipped when we first struck, and was abandoned. Now was the loud cry for the speaking-trumpet—now for the axes, which for a time could not be found. I asked if there were no guns to fire signals of distress? No guns. No rockets to let off to acquaint the coast-guard with our condition? No rockets. It was manifest our captain had been, as Napoleon said of Massena, a spoiled child of fortune! Always happy and successful in his adventures, his voyages deservedly fortunate, had superseded all contemplation of disaster. Every effort was now made, by manoeuvring the sails, to force the ship once more to sea, and made in vain—we were constrained to wait until daylight enabled us to appreciate our real situation, and procure for us, from the shore, the necessary assistance.

It is difficult to judge of distance on water, but I believe we lay nearly half a mile from the beach. Every succeeding wave raised the ship several feet, and subsiding, we beat with tremendous violence on the rock. An immense quantity of bricks had been shipped in lieu of ballast; between these and the rock, the ship's bottom might represent the metal works between the anvil and the hammer, and strange it would have been had it not severely suffered. Every wave was a fearful mountain, while the hurricane momentarily threatened to shiver us into atoms. Such a storm has not been felt on these shores during the last fifty years. As the ungoverned state of the rudder was now breaking up all within its range, the binnacles were removed below for security, and the rudder lashed to the boom; but the cords were soon rent asunder like threads. After lying in this situation nearly two hours, sometimes fancying we saw boats approaching to our assistance, sometimes that we saw lights as signals, the dawn at length assured us we were descried from the shore, where we saw a general activity corresponding to the peril of our unhappy condition. Not a boat

could, however, venture to put out through the frightful surf, and I
own I felt little hopes of relief while the elements continued their
frightful ravages. The shore was now lined with spectators, but their
sympathy could avail us nothing. While this was our condition without, within the ship all was devastation. At each new concussion
something was strained and gave way. Bedsteads, lamps, tables and
trunks were hurled from side to side with frightful noise, which made
the females believe, in spite of our assurances, the ship was breaking
up. But now beamed suddenly forth in our extremity, the dawn of
our deliverance. We had watched a team laboring along the beach
conveying to windward a boat. It was launched, and, in the same
moment, manned. It was the God-like life-boat, equipped with the
most intrepid crew that ever deserved their country's gratitude. In
half an hour of unequalled struggles they were alongside, and boarded
us; and now, indeed, I saw countenances where the glad gleam of joy
endeavored to penetrate through a mass of suffering and despair; but
we had scarcely interchanged congratulations, when I was told the
boat had left the ship. I could not believe it. I ran aloft and found
it true. I felt I had now a duty to perform to my family, and I asked
the captain, if the boat were dismissed, what could be his plan? I
represented that as our rudder was useless, he could have no command
of the ship if she floated with the coming flood; and if her bottom
was pierced, of which there could be no doubt, we must expect
that if she dipped into deep water, she would fill and go down, and
all would inevitably perish—that it would be impossible, in her present crippled state, to work her into any port, and I submitted therefore, that our safety should be consulted above all things. Our captain
firmly answered, our safety was his principal duty and first care; that
I might rely on his word, that he would not hazard our lives; and that
if the ship was not in a condition to leave the shore, he would not attempt it. I own I returned to my family with a heavy heart to announce the fearful experiment.

The flood-tide was rolling in, and the trumpet of our vigilant
captain was again in full activity. After many mighty workings, an
awful blast drove us over the reef, and hurried us to sea. Hope
beamed again, but it was found that the ship had made five feet of
water in ten minutes. The signal of distress was hoisted, and every
possible effort made to put the ship's head to the shore, but without
the assistance of her rudder, she was wholly unmanageable, and very
soon became water-logged. I now caught the captain's eye; he mo-
tioned me, and gave the dreadful intelligence that the ship was sinking, and I must prepare my wife and children for any event! I asked
how long it might be before she would go down? He said, "Some time

yet." Without making any communication, I conveyed my family on deck, and watched the progress of the ship visibly made in sinking. Efforts were again made to put the ship about, but they were fruitless.

Happily for our safety, the life-boat, better acquainted with the distressing features of disaster, had kept hovering around. I had grieved at its dismissal, but now suddenly heard it hailing the captain to let go the remaining anchor. After dragging a little, it held on, and threw her stern round; but the ship was water-logged, and made little progress. She was now so low that every wave rolled in one side and discharged itself on the other. We had thrown out a line to the boat, but it had quickly snapped, and we threw others, in the hope of keeping them at a short distance. As it appeared we must in a few seconds go down, I was preparing cords for the safety of my family, when a squall, a hundred times more frightful than any that had yet assailed us, gave hopes, and the crew cried out, "Now—now the masts must go." But still they stood, to our great danger and annoyance. The ship had, however, felt the impulse received from the last blast, and been impelled forward;—and now a shock succeeded which gave the glad, auspicious tidings of shore. The men clasped their hands, and looked towards Heaven with emotions of gratitude. The last nearly overwhelming gale had lifted us forward, and proved our deliverance; and now the exertions of the crew of the boat were increased tenfold, and they were quickly under our stern. Our intrepid captain, lashing himself for security, jumped over the ship's side, and, though overwhelmed by every wave, called aloud for the children first. I had taken them below, lest the fall of the masts should injure them. I flew down, and in an instant my eldest son was in the arms of the captain.—The lifeboat was now riding on the brink of the wave, and now was lost in the abyss; but as she was descending my son was caught as the captain loosed his arm, by a dozen eager arms raised for his safety. The second boy met with more facility, and the infant was thrown and caught, when the whole crew, with generous sympathy, cried out, "Now the mother." The mother was soon with her children, and seemed to us protected by these our worldly saviors from destruction. The other females were then handed down, with a youth of fourteen, and I next followed, in agonizing anxiety to share with those I felt dearer to me than life, the yet remaining perils.

Lifted sometimes mountains high, sometimes hidden from all view in the depths into which we descended, we at last reached the shore. The people upon the beach rushed into the surf to receive us, and braved its perils for our security. The boat was soon lighted, and a cart stood ready to convey us to an adjoining house, where dry clothing was soon exchanged for garments long saturated with brine.

The captain and crew were left on the wreck with one passenger, and two hours elapsed before the boat could succeed in extricating these from the dangers assailing them. For a considerable period, the sea had been covered with floating packages, carried by the storm and tide many miles along the beach, but at nightfall, began the active work of plunder, and that which had resisted other violence was soon conveyed away from observation.

Loss of the *Lady of the Lake*

THIS NARRATIVE is reprinted to remind readers that the *Titanic* was not the first ship to fall prey to an iceberg. Here again the captain, after doing his poor best for his people, saved his own life and left many passengers on a sinking vessel. "The last time I saw the brig, (the ice coming between her and us) she was sunk up to the tops, and about thirty of the passengers in the main-top-mast rigging." Fortunately, they could not have lived long in that freezing Atlantic. One gets an idea of the crowded shipping lanes of the time from the fact that the survivors reached the sinking *Harvest Home,* were picked up by a brig bound for Newfoundland, and were the next day transferred to the *Amazon.* If the *Lady of the Lake* had had enough boats and time, all those on board might have been saved.

This account is taken from Thomas.

LOSS OF THE

LADY OF THE LAKE

THE ship Lady of the Lake, sailed from Belfast, on the 8th of April 1833, bound to Quebec, with two hundred and thirty passengers. The following particulars were furnished by captain Grant.

On the 11th May, in latitude 46. 50, north, and longitude 47. 10, west, at five A.M., steering per compass W.S.W. with a strong wind at N.N.E. we fell in with several pieces of ice; at eight, A.M. the ice getting closer, I judged it prudent to haul the ship out to the eastward under easy sail to avoid it; while endeavoring to pass between two large pieces, a tongue under water in the lee ice struck our starboard bow and stove it entirely in. We immediately wore the ship round, expecting to get the leak out of the water, but did not succeed; the ship now filling fast, the mate, with seven or eight of the crew, got into the stern boat—after getting bread, beef, compass, &c. &c. we pulled away to the northwest—the scene that then took place is beyond description; after getting the long-boat out, the passengers crowded into her with such mad desperation, that she was twice upset alongside, drowning about eighty of them. I now attempted to save my own life and succeeded in getting the boat clear of the ship half full of water, with thirty-three souls in her, without oars, sails, or a mouthful of provisions. The last time I saw the brig, (the ice coming between her and us) she was sunk up to the tops, and about thirty of the passengers in the main-top-mast rigging. We then tried to pull after the other boat, with the bottom boards and thufts, but got beset with the ice. We now expected a worse fate than those who were in the vessel, viz. to perish with cold and hunger. The next morning the wind changed to the westward and we got clear of most of the ice. We then pulled to the eastward, in the faint hope of some vessel picking us up, and at noon saw a brig lying-to under her two top-sails—at four got on board of her, and found the crew just leaving her, the brig in the same state as our own, sinking. We, however, got some provisions out of her, and there being a boat lying on her decks, I got part of the passengers out of our own boat into it. In the course of the night it came on to blow from the south-west and the other boat foundered. All that now remained alive, to the best of my belief or knowledge, out of a crew and passengers of two hundred and eighty, is myself, one seamen, two boys, nine male passengers and two female, fifteen in all. At noon on the 14th, we fell in with the master and mate of the brig Harvest Home, of Newcastle, the vessel we had previously been on board of; and on the evening of the same day both got on board of a loaded brig bound to St. Johns, Newfoundland, after we had been seventy-five hours in an open boat, half-dressed, wet, and frost bitten; next morning, I, with the remainder of the crew and passengers, left the brig and was kindly received on board the ship Amazon, of Hull, bound to Quebec, where we arrived in safety.

[23]

DESTRUCTION OF THE *Ben Sherod*

THIS NARRATIVE, put together from a number of accounts, gives a curious and daunting picture of the hazards of travel in the early nineteenth century. Our ancestors built wooden steamers, piled a couple of thousand bales of cotton around the decks, took on board barrels of gunpowder, piled cordwood close around an overheated furnace, set out a barrel of whiskey for crewmen who felt the need for stimulants, started a race with a faster boat—and expected to reach port in safety. And when a passenger found himself in the river, his chances were about even when another steamer approached; he might be pulled aboard, but he might be run over. Weak as our safety regulations may be in the twentieth century, we have come a long way since 1837.

This account is taken from *Steamboat Disasters and Railroad Accidents in the United States,* Worcester, 1846.

BEN SHEROD,

By Fire and Explosion, on the Mississippi River,

while on her Passage from New Orleans for Louisville,

May 8, 1837;

by which Terrible Catastrophe nearly Two Hundred Persons

lost their Lives.

The steamer Ben Sherod, Captain Castleman, left New Orleans on Sunday morning, May 7, bound to Louisville; and on the night of the 9th, when about thirty miles below Natchez, she was discovered to be on fire, and in a few minutes after, the whole boat was enveloped in flames.

Being in the stream, and her wheel-ropes burnt off, it was impossible to run her ashore; and no alternative was left to the persons on board, but to jump into the water, and attempt to save themselves by swimming, or floating on such articles as they could find, or to perish in the flames. In the confusion and alarm, many, who could not swim, sprang overboard, without taking the precaution to provide themselves with a plank or box, and were drowned; but many more, it is feared, were burnt to death.

So rapid was the spread of the fire, and so destitute were those on board of all means of escape, that nothing could be saved, not even the register of the boat; thus rendering it impossible to state with certainty how many were lost, or what were their names.

The fire is believed to have originated from the fuel being piled up near the boiler. The story of the disaster was related to us by a young man, who was a cabin passenger: it is awfully interesting, and his own escape almost miraculous. When he awoke, he put on his clothes, and leaped into the yawl, which was hanging at the stern, and was followed by about forty other men, one of whom cut the rope connecting the stern of the steamer to the bow of the yawl, when the latter canted over, and hung in a perpendicular position, the bow towards the water. All on board were precipitated into it, and are believed to have been drowned, with the exception of the narrator,— and he saved himself by clinging to the thwarts.

In a few minutes, about twenty of the crew made their way to the stern of the steamer, and placed themselves in the boat, suspended as she was. One of them imprudently took out his knife, and cut the rope which attached the steamer to the stern of the yawl, and she plunged, as might have been expected, full twenty feet under water. All that had been hanging to her were missing, except four, and the individual who relates the story. He says, that when he rose to the surface, he found himself under the yawl, which was lying bottom up. Being strong, active, and expert at swimming, he worked his way from underneath and mounted on her bottom, where he was soon joined by the other four men who had saved themselves; and in this situation they floated twelve miles down the river, before they were picked up by the Columbus.

There was some powder on board,—in what quantities was not known; but the knowledge that it was there, seemed to have paralyzed the efforts of the crew, and its explosion added to the deep horrors of the scene. There were nine ladies on board, only two of whom were rescued.

The survivors of this terrible disaster have unanimously concurred in their expressions of gratitude to the commanders of the steamers Columbus and Statesman, for their activity in saving them from a watery grave, and for their kindness to them while on board their boats. On the conduct of Captain Littleton, of the steamboat Alton, the public censure of the surviving sufferers was published in the newspapers of the day. The reckless manner in which he drove his vessel through the crowd of exhausted sufferers, thereby drowning many, even while calling for help, and turning a deaf ear to the cries and pleadings of all, cannot soon be forgotten by an indignant community, or the record of its truth be obliterated from public print.

The following is the statement, alluded to above, from a part of the surviving passengers:—

"We, the undersigned, part of the passengers saved from the wreck of the steamer Ben Sherod, on the night of the 9th inst., feel it a duty we owe to the officers of the steamboats Columbus and Statesman, to say that they deserve the praise of every friend of humanity for their untiring exertions in rescuing the suffering passengers whom they found afloat in the current. Many of the passengers owe their lives to the kindness of the officers of these boats.

"We feel it also due to the public to state,—and our hearts sicken within us when we assert it,—that the steamboat Alton, Capt. Littleton, passed through the midst of the sinking crowd, all hands crying for help, and, although within a few feet of some, covering them with her waves, she did not even stop her headway until she arrived at Fort Adams, ten miles below, where she could have rendered no assistance.

"Signed,

HUGH SIMPSON, *Carlinsville, Tenn.*
THOMAS DUVALL, *Shelby Co., Ind.*
JOHN BLANC, *New Orleans.*
JOHN P. WILKINSON, *Richmond, Va.*
EPHRAIM STANFIELD, *Richmond, Va.*
DANIEL MARSHALL, *Moscow, Ind.*
ROSSON P. ANDRUS, *Natchez.*
ASA S. SMITH,   *do.*
CHARLES W. ANDRUS,   *do.*
M. M. ORME,   *do.*

"Natchez, May 18, 1837."

There were two hundred and thirty-five persons on board, of whom not more than sixty escaped; leaving upwards of one hundred and seventy five drowned and burnt, including the captain's father and two children,—his wife was picked up by a flat boat badly injured. The following are the names of some of the ladies who were lost:— Mrs. M'Dowell, of Belfont, Ala.; Mrs. Gamble, and three children, of New Orleans; Miss Frances Few, of Belfont, Ala.

This awful occurrence should teach the community the immense importance of the character of a steamboat. After the wanton disregard of life evinced by the captain of this boat some weeks ago at Vicksburg, by which ten or twelve persons were drowned, not a single individual, who had any regard for his life, should have ventured on that same boat while under such a reckless commander. A man who would refuse to bring his boat to, for the purpose of landing a dozen individuals, would not scruple to run a race with two hundred passengers on board, and fire his boat by the red heat of his boilers. The Ben Sherod had been on fire twice during the race on that same night, previous to the final conflagration.

Captain Castleman subsequently published the following vindication of his conduct:—

"Merely to show how things will be exaggerated, not that it can alter in any way the circumstances, I would mention that the number of persons on board the Ben Sherod, at the time that she was burnt, did not exceed from one hundred and fifty to one hundred and sixty. I think one hundred and fifty would probably come the nearest to it, including the crew, children, and servants, and all; and from all I could learn before I left New Orleans, and at Natchez on my way up, I do not think there were more than sixty or sixty-five lost, instead of from one hundred to two hundred, as is stated in so many different reports. I, myself, clung to the hope of getting the boat to the shore, and saving all, until it was too late to save my own family, and thereby lost my father and two children, and got my wife burnt so badly that she was not expected to live. I was burnt myself slightly; one child was burnt to death and in my wife's arms when I got hold of her, and the other drowned.

"As to the report of my officers and crew being in a state of intoxication, the barrel of whiskey with the head knocked out, or set out for the men to have access to,—it is all in the imagination. Drunkenness is the only misdemeanor for which I allowed a man to be discharged without first consulting me; but the clerks, the mates, the engineers, all had full authority to drive any man of the crew off the boat, either in or out of the port, if he was the least drunk, as was the case the first trip, when we first made up our crew. Some of that crew got drunk, and were discharged, and replaced by sober men, until we had a good crew; and I feel positive that we had not had a drunken man amongst our crew for three months before the fatal accident.

"I had not left the deck in the fore part of the night. The firemen were singing and dancing about, as they always do when on duty, but there were none of them the least intoxicated, so far as I could see; and the watch that were on duty at the time (the first watch having retired) had not been out of their beds long enough to get drunk, if they had wanted to. *We always gave our men, black or white, as much as they wanted, kept a barrel of whiskey tapped on the boiler deck for them, have always done so, and generally let one of the watch that was on duty, go to it and draw for his watch, whenever they wanted it.* He is called the captain of the watch. I have always done the same for the last ten years, and my acquaintances, I think, will vouch for my discipline about drunkenness, as well as other things, being severe and rigid enough. Indeed, I am generally blamed for being too particular about such things, and too rigid with my hands."

We give some further particulars, gathered from various sources:—

One gentleman, Mr. Cook, floated down the river some miles before he was picked up. He hailed some wretched and dispicable character, who had put off in a yawl from the shore, and begged his assistance. The infamous scoundrel, who was intent only on picking up boxes, &c., asked him with the utmost *sang froid,* "How much will you give me?" To the entreaties of others for help, he replied, "O, you are very well off there! Keep cool, and you'll come out comfortable!" Whether the captain of the Alton deserves the censure that has been heaped upon him, we know not, nor will we pretend to say positively until we have seen his statement; but it does appear that if the captain of the Columbus had acted in a similar manner to that of the Alton, there would not have been half a dozen souls left to tell the tale of the calamity.

Mr. Davis, the pilot, who was at the wheel during the fire, was conversing with a friend, just before he left the city, about the burning of the St. Martinville, and the burning of her tiller-rope, three or four years since. "If ever I'm in a boat that takes fire," said Davis, "if I don't run her ashore, it will be because I shall be burnt up in her!" Poor fellow! His statement was verified; he *was* burnt up in the Ben Sherod.

Out of the nine ladies that were on board, only two have been saved, the captain's wife and Mrs. Smith, of Mobile. Their husbands threw hen-coops into the river, and jumped off the wheel-house; the ladies followed their example, and were saved.

One scene was distressing in the extreme: a young and beautiful lady, whose name we could not learn, on hearing the cry of fire, rushed out of the ladies' cabin, in her loose dress, in search of her husband, at the same time holding her infant to her bosom; in endeavoring to go forward, her dress caught fire, and was torn from her back to save her life; after witnessing her husband fall into the flames in the forward part of the boat, unable to reach him, she leaped with her child into the water, seized a plank, and was carried by the current within eighty yards of the Columbus; but just as she had seized a rope thrown from the steamboat, both mother and child sunk to rise no more.

It is impossible to enumerate the various heart-rending sights occasioned by this calamitous affair. The captain, for instance, saved his wife, but saw his two children perish. Mr. Smith saved his wife and one child, and saw the nurse rush madly through the flames with his daughter, and both perish. Mr. Gamble's wife, we understand, was burnt to death; he escaped, although very badly burnt. One young man, who had reached the hurricane-deck in safety, heard the cries of his sister; he rushed back to the cabin, clasped her in his arms, and both were burnt to death. One of the clerks, one of the pilots, and the first mate were burnt. All the chamber-maids and women employed in the boat perished. Out of thirty-five negroes, that were known to have been on board, only two escaped. The Ben Sherod had the largest crew of any boat on the river, and out of about fifty who were saved, only thirty belonged to the boat. Of the sixty or seventy cabin passengers, there were but ten or twelve left alive. One of the officers of the boat stated that, in addition to the cabin passengers, there were at least sixty or more deck passengers, of whom scarce six were saved.

Altogether, this is one of the most serious disasters that ever happened in the annals of Mississippi steamboat navigation; there being at least one hundred and fifty families deprived by it of some dear and beloved member, and over one hundred being hurried by it, out of time into eternity, with scarce a moment's warning.

We understand that three different explosions took place on board the boat whilst burning—first, barrels of whiskey and brandy; then the boilers blew up with a fearful explosion, and, lastly, thirty-nine barrels of gunpowder exploded, which strewed the surface of the river with fragments.

At the time the Ben Sherod took fire, she was engaged in a race with the steamer Prairie; and the fire took from the great heat of the boilers, caused by raising her steam to its extreme power. A barrel of whiskey was placed on deck for the use of the hands during the race, who drank to excess, and became intoxicated.

At about 12 o'clock at night, the furnace became so heated that it communicated fire to the wood, of which there was on board about sixty cords. When the crew discovered the fire, they all left their posts, and ran for the yawl without giving any alarm to the passengers, who were all asleep in their berths. The captain, for a time, attempted to allay the extreme confusion, by stating that the fire was extinguished; twice he forbade the lowering of the yawl, which was attempted by the deck hands and passengers.

The shrieks of nearly three hundred persons on board now rose wild and dreadful. The cry was, *"to the shore! to the shore!"* The boat made for the starboard shore, but did not gain it, the wheel-rope having given way, and the pilot driven by the flames from his station. The steam was not let off, and the boat kept on. The scene of horror now beggared all description.

The yawl, which had been filled with the crew, had sunk, and the passengers had no other alternative than to jump overboard, without taking even time to dress. There were nine ladies on board, who all went overboard without uttering a single scream, some drowning instantly, and others clinging to planks,—two of the number were finally saved. Many of the passengers were supposed to have been burnt. One man, by the name of Ray, from Louisville, hung to a rope at the bow of the boat, until taken up by the yawl of the steamboat Columbus, which arrived about half an hour after the commencement of the disaster, on her downward passage.

The steamboat Alton arrived soon after the Columbus; but from the carelessness or indiscretion of those on board, was the means of drowning many persons who were floating in the water. She drove into the midst of the exhausted sufferers, who were too weak to make longer exertion, and, by the commotion occasioned by her wheels, drowned a large number. A gentleman, by the name of Hamilton, from Alabama, was floating on a barrel, and sustaining also a lady, when the Alton drove up and washed them both under; the lady was drowned, but Mr. Hamilton came up, and floated down the river fifteen miles, when he was taken up by the steamer Statesman.

Mr. M'Dowell attributes the drowning of his wife to the indiscretion of the managers of the Alton, as she was floating safely on a plank at this time. He sustained himself some time against the current, so that he only floated two miles down the river, when he swam ashore ten miles above Fort Adams. Besides the loss of his wife, Mr. M'Dowell lost his son, a young lady who was under his protection, and a negro servant.

The following interesting narrative was written by a passenger:—

"On Sunday morning, the 7th of May, 1837, the steamboat Ben Sherod, under the command of Captain Castleman, was preparing to leave the levee at New Orleans. She was thronged with passengers. Many a beautiful and interesting woman that morning was busy in arranging the little things incident to travelling, and they all looked forward with high and certain hopes to the end of their journey. Little innocent children played about the cabin, and would run to the guards, now and then, to wonder, in infantine language, at the next boat, or the water, or something else that drew their attention. 'O, look here, Henry, I don't like that boat Lexington.' 'I wish I was going by her,' said Henry, musingly. The men, too, were urgent in their arrangement of the trunks, and the getting on board sundry articles, which a ten days' passage rendered necessary. In fact, all seemed hope, and joy, and certainty.

"The cabin of the Ben Sherod was on the upper deck, but narrow in proportion to her build, for she was, what is technically called, a Tennessee cotton boat. To those who have never seen a cotton boat loaded, it is a wondrous sight. The bales are piled up from the lower guards, wherever there is a cranny, until they reach above the second deck,—room being merely left for passengers to walk outside the cabin. You have regular alleys left amid the cotton, in order to pass about on the first deck. Such is a cotton boat, carrying from one thousand five hundred to two thousand bales.

"The Ben Sherod's finish and the accommodation of the cabin were by no means such as would begin to compare with the regular passenger boats. It being late in the season, and but few large steamers being in port, in consequence of the severity of the times, the Ben Sherod got an undue number of passengers; otherwise she would have been avoided, for her accommodations were not enticing. She had a heavy freight on board, and several horses and carriages on the forecastle. The build of the Ben Sherod was heavy—her timbers being of the largest size.

"The morning was clear and sultry—so much so that umbrellas

were necessary to ward off the heat of the sun. It was a curious sight to see the hundreds of citizens hurrying on board to leave letters, and to see them coming away. When a steamboat is going off on the southern or western waters, the excitement is fully equal to that attendant upon the departure of a Liverpool packet.

"About nine o'clock, A.M., the ill-fated steamer pushed off upon the turbid current of the Mississippi, as a swan upon the waters. In a few minutes, she was under way, tossing high in air bright and sunny clouds of steam at every revolution of her engine. Talk not of your northern steamboats! A Mississippi steamer of seven hundred tons burden, with adequate machinery, is one of the sublimities of poetry. For thousands of miles that great body forces its way through a desolate country, against an almost resistless current, and all the evidence you have of the immense power exerted, is brought to your sense by the everlasting and majestic burst of exertion from her escapement pipe, and the careless stroke of her paddle wheels. In the dead of night, when, amid the swamps on either side, your noble vessel winds her upward way—when not a soul is seen on board but the officer on deck—when nought is heard but the clang of the fire doors amid the hoarse coughing of the engine, imagination yields to the vastness of the ideas thus excited in your mind; and, if you have a soul within you, you cannot help feeling strongly alive to the mightiness of art in contrast with the mightiness of nature. Such a scene—and hundreds such have been realized with an intensity that cannot be described—always makes me a better man than before. I never could tire of the steamboat navigation of the Mississippi.

"On Tuesday evening, the 9th of May, 1837, the steamer Prairie, on her way to St. Louis, bore hard upon the Ben Sherod. It was necessary for the latter to stop at Fort Adams, during which the Prairie passed her. Great vexation was manifested by some of the passengers, that the Prairie should get to Natchez first. The subject formed the theme of conversation for two or three hours, the captain assuring them that he would beat her *any how*.

"The Prairie was a very fast boat, and, under equal circumstances, would have beaten the Sherod. As soon as the business was transacted at Fort Adams, for which she stopped, orders were given to the men to keep up the fires to the extent. It was now a little past 11 o'clock, P.M. The captain retired to his berth with his clothes on, and left the deck in charge of an officer. During the evening, a barrel of whiskey had been turned out, and permission given to the hands to do as they pleased. As may be supposed, they drew upon the barrel quite liberally. It is the custom of all the boats to furnish the firemen with liquor, though a difference exists as to the mode. But it is due to the many worthy captains now on the Mississippi, to state that the practice of furnishing spirits is gradually dying away, and where they are given, it is only done in moderation.

"As the Sherod passed on above Fort Adams, towards the mouth of the Homochitta, the wood piled up in front of the furnaces several times caught fire, and was once or twice imperfectly extinguished by the drunken hands. It must be understood by those who have never seen a western steamboat, that the boilers are entirely above the first deck, and that, when the fires are well kept up for any length of time, the heat is almost insupportable. Were it not for the draft occasioned by the speed of the boat, it would be very difficult to attend the fire.

"The boat went on her way at a tremendous rate, quivering and trembling her full length at every revolution of the wheels. The steam was created so fast, that it continued to escape through the safety-valve, and, by its sharp singing, told a tale that every prudent captain would have understood.

"As the vessel rounded the bar that makes off the Homochitta,—being compelled to stand out into the middle of the river in consequence,—the fire was discovered. It was about 1 o'clock in the morning. A passenger had got up previously, and was standing on the boiler-deck, when, to his astonishment, the fire broke out from the pile of wood. A little presence of mind, and a set of men unintoxicated, could have saved the boat. The passenger seized a bucket, and was about to plunge it overboard for water, when he found it locked. An instant more, and the fire increased in volume. The captain was now awakened. He saw the fire had seized the deck. He ran aft, and announced the ill tidings.

"No sooner were the words out of his mouth, than the shrieks of mothers, sisters and babes, resounded, in the wildest confusion, throughout the hitherto silent cabin. Men were aroused from their dreaming cots to experience the hot air of approaching fire. The pilot, being elevated on the hurricane-deck, at the instant of perceiving the flames, put the head of the boat towards the shore. She had scarcely got under way in that direction, before the tiller ropes were burnt off. Two miles at least from the land, the boat sheered and, borne up by the current, made several revolutions, until she struck off across the river. A bar brought her up for the moment.

The flames had now extended fore and aft. At the first alarm, several deck passengers had got into the small boat that hung suspended by the davits. A cabin passenger, endowed with some degree of courage and presence of mind, expostulated with them, and did all he could to save the boat for the ladies. But all was useless. One took out his knife and cut away the forward tackle. The next instant, and they were all launched into the angry waters. They were seen no more.

"The boat being lowered from the other end, filled, and was useless. Now came the trying moment. Hundreds leaped from the burning deck into the water. Mothers were seen standing on the guards, with dishevelled hair, praying for help,—their dear little innocents clung to their sides, and seemed, with their tiny hands, to beat away the burning flames. Sisters called out to their brothers in unearthly voices, 'Save me, O my brother!' Wives crying to their husbands to save their children, in total forgetfulness of themselves. Every moment or two the desperate plunge of some poor victim would fall on the appalled ear. The dashing to and fro of the horses on the forecastle, groaning audibly in their fierce agony,—the continued puffing of the engine, for still it continued to go,—the screaming mother who had leaped overboard, in the desperation of the moment, with her only child,—the heat and the crackling of the lurid fire, as its greedy flames darted with horrible rapidity from one portion to another of the devoted vessel,—shall I ever forget that scene, that hour of horror and alarm? Never, were I to live till memory forgot all else that ever came to the senses. The short half hour, that separated and plunged into eternity *two hundred human beings,* has been so indelibly burnt into the memory, that nothing can have power to efface it.

"I was swimming to the shore with all my might, endeavoring to sustain a mother and child. My strength failed me,—the babe was nothing—a mere cork. 'Go, go,' said the brave mother, 'save my child, save my——,' and she sunk to rise no more. Nerved by the resolution of that woman, I reached the shore in safety. The babe I saved. Ere I reached the beach, the Sherod had swung off the bar, and was slowly floating down, the engine having ceased running. In every direction, heads dotted the surface of the river. A new and still more awful appearance, the burning wreck now wore: mothers were seen clinging with the energy of expiring hope to the blazing timbers, and dropping off one by one. The screams had ceased. A sullen silence rested over the devoted vessel. The flames seemed tired of their work of destruction.

"While I sat, dripping and overcome, upon the beach, a steamboat, the Columbus, hove in sight, and bore for the wreck. It seemed like one last ray of hope gleaming across the dead gloom of that night. Several were saved. And still another, the Statesman, came in sight. More, more were saved. A moment, to *me,* only had elapsed, when high in the heavens the cinders flew, and the country was lighted all around. Still another boat came booming on. I was happy that help had come. After an exchange of words with the Columbus, it continued on its way, under full steam. O, how my heart sunk within me! The waves created by that boat sent many a poor mortal to his long home. A being by the name of Littleton was its reckless and merciless commander. Long may he be remembered!

"My hands were burnt, and I now began to experience severe pain. The scene before me,—the loss of my two sisters, and a brother, whom I had missed in the confusion,—all had steeled my heart.

"Again—another explosion! and the waters closed slowly and suddenly over the scene of disaster and death. Darkness resumed her sway, and silence was only interrupted by the distant efforts of the Columbus and Statesman in their laudable exertions to save human life.

"Captain Castleman lost, I believe, a father and child. Some argue this was punishment enough; no, it was not. He had the lives of hundreds under his charge. He was careless of his trust; he was guilty of a crime that nothing will ever wipe out. The blood of two hundred victims is crying out from the waters for retribution and vengeance. Neither society nor law will give it. His punishment is yet to come. May I never meet him!

"It was more than three weeks after this terrible occurrence before I could shed a tear. All the fountains of sympathy had been dried up, and my heart was as the stone. As I lay on my bed, the twenty-fourth day after, tears, salt tears, came to my relief, and I felt the loss of my sisters and brother more deeply than ever. Peace be to their spirits! They found a watery grave."

[24]

LOSS OF THE STEAM PACKET *Home*

THIS NARRATIVE of the loss of the *Home* is quite typical of one type of report of American shipwrecks of the mid-nineteenth century, with its overwritten, sententious introduction and its quite matter-of-fact story from the captain. Captain White, protecting his owners, said nothing about the condition of the ship, though he did report the breakdown of an engine. The anonymous author of the introduction, on the other hand, was convinced that the *Home* should never have been sent to sea at all. This narrative, taken from *Steamboat Disasters*, proves that a pair of weak engines and a reputation for fast passages were no guarantee of safety in an October hurricane off Cape Hatteras. I have not felt that it was necessary to afflict readers with the elegiac poem which, again quite typically, ends the account of the loss of the *Home* in my source.

LOSS OF THE

STEAM PACKET HOME,

ON HER PASSAGE FROM NEW YORK TO CHARLESTON,

OCTOBER 9, 1837,

by which Melancholy Occurrence

Ninety-Five Persons perished.

AN occurrence so awful as the loss of the steam packet HOME, excites in the mind of the civilized and human community a most intense and painful interest. In a vessel for passage, whole countries are represented among those who have trusted their lives upon the deep, divided from eternity by a single plank, and directly committed to His providence who holds the waters in the hollow of his hand; but who sometimes sees fit, for purposes in his dispensation beyond the ken of mortals, to visit the wanderer upon the deep with sudden and awful death.

The loss of a vessel engaged in the common pursuits of commerce, with no more souls on board than are requisite to her guidance and management, is a painful event, which calls forth the commiseration of all to whose ears the tidings are borne. The parents, the wives, and the children, whose hopes and whose dependence are all enbarked with "them that go down to the sea in ships, that do business in great waters," are stricken to the earth by the tidings of their loss; but the great public can only pity the little circle of mourners, without sharing their sorrows. Not so, when, from the climes of the sunny south—from the towns and cities of the north—from the valley of the father of waters, and from the cities on the seaboard, a company are gathered together, it would seem for destruction, as in the case of the ill-fated boat of whose loss we speak. The funeral wail rises from one extremity of the country to the other—every state, and almost every community, has a claim to assert in the loss of persons connected by ties of blood, of friendship, or of business. The awful realities of the dangers to which a large portion of the human family is daily exposed are brought home to every bosom; and the sympathies of the whole public are touched. It is the intense interest felt in the fate of the Home, that has induced us to present to the public as full and accurate account of the disaster as we have been able to glean from the various sources at our command.

The steam packet Home was launched in April, 1836, and finished in January, 1837. Her length on deck was about two hundred and twenty feet, with twenty-two feet beam, twelve feet depth of hold; and measuring five hundred and fifty tons burthen. That she was not the kind of vessel to withstand the tempestuous gales of the Atlantic, has proved fearfully true. We have no evidence that, in her model or timbers, any reference was had to a capacity for encountering the perils of the ocean; but candor compels us to say that her model, the time of her lying unemployed, and other circumstances, induce the conviction that she *never was intended* for a sea boat. If she was so intended, then those who had charge of her construction should never again attempt to plan a vessel. In the minor points of elegance and convenience,—minor compared with the great consideration of safety,— the Home was all that could have been wished, and would have made an elegant and safe steamer for the river, or the summer navigation of the sound. She was calculated to accommodate one hundred and twenty persons with berths or state rooms. In her appointments and finish, she ranked with the "floating palaces" for which our American waters are famed; and in speed, another characteristic of American ship-building, she was unsurpassed.

Her second passage to Charleston was made in sixty-four hours— a shorter passage than was ever made before by any vessel. Communication with Charleston was regarded as almost as direct as that with the nearer cities, which are brought within a day's travel by steamboat and railroad. Numbers who, under other circumstances, would hardly venture upon a journey from one city to the other, were induced, by the rapidity and comfort of the conveyance, to make the jaunt; and circumstances had warranted us in supposing that the north and south were thus to be connected by the annihilation of distance; and pride in our national enterprise and resources pointed exultingly to the fact, that a distance which had occupied our ancestors weeks in its passage, could now be compassed in less than three days. It was even hinted, *after she was finished,* that the Home would essay a trip across the Atlantic, in advance of the completion of a line of packets designed for that great route. The public mind anticipated great things from the success of the first trips of the new and splendid vessel; and became so much familiarized with the subject of ocean steam communication, and so devoid of fear as to its danger, that the whisper of apprehension was met with a reproving smile.

It was on the 7th of October, 1837, that the steam packet Home, under the command of Captain Carleton White, left New York for Charleston, S.C., on her third trip. Owing to the speed of the boat, her very excellent accommodations, and the high character of the captain as a commander, the number of passengers who started in her on this, her last and ill-fated voyage, was very great. She had on board, as near as could be gathered from her berth-book, and judging also from the numbers who took passage at the last moment, without previously securing berths, *ninety* passengers. Her crew, including officers and servants, male and female, numbered *forty-five,* comprising in all about *one hundred and thirty-five* souls; among whom were between thirty and forty females

Gentlemen from the north going south, and southern gentlemen returning from excursions of business, pleasure, or health, at the north; ladies impatient to return to the friends from whom circumstances had separated them, buoyant with hope, and confident of safety and a quick passage from the reputation which the packet had thus early acquired; children, trusting in their parents, and willing to leave to them all questions as to danger or safety,—a happier company never assembled together. It seemed more like a departure upon a pleasure excursion, than the commencement of what was once deemed a serious voyage. With hope elate, and with the sorrow of parting with friends here swallowed up in joyous anticipation of meeting others at the end of a short and pleasant passage, the passengers on board the Home bade adieu to New York. Little did they dream that the adieus made were their last, or that those who looked at them while leaving port, "should see them no more forever."

The weather was fine, with a light breeze from the south-west, and the packet proceeded gaily on her way till she had passed the Narrows. The buoyancy of hope was somewhat depressed, and the consciousness of security rather enfeebled, when the vessel, very soon after, was found to be aground upon the Romer shoal, where she remained three or four hours. The accident was occasioned by mistaking one of the bouys, designating Captain Gedney's new channel, for the buoy on the Romer. It was thought that the boat had sustained no injury by the accident; but escape from all injury we conceive could hardly have been possible.

We give the following extract from a detailed account by Captain White, published shortly after the occurrence of the disaster:—

"On leaving my office, after examining the list of passengers, I found that the boat headed off to the eastward, and the headway nearly stopped. I then ran up to the man at the wheel, and ordered the helm hard a-port; he answered, 'The helm is hard a-port, sir, but she won't mind her helm.' By this time the boat had entirely stopped on the Romer shoal; the ebb tide setting strong to the eastward, and a light westerly wind, to which cause I attribute the grounding of the boat. At this time the engine was working forward. The engineer inquired whether he should continue to work her so or back her off. I ordered him to keep on, under the impression that she was so near the eastern edge of the shoal that she would go over; but finding she did not go ahead, I ordered him to back her off; at the same time ordered the wood and cable to be shifted to the larboard side, in order to list the boat; in backing her, found she slued a little, but would not work off the shoal. There was now no alternative but to remain until the tide rose.

"The passengers, at tea, made many inquiries as to any danger from being aground; apprehended none myself, as the water was entirely smooth, and the wind light. I endeavored to make them easy. About 7 o'clock, P.M., were boarded by a Sandy Hook pilot, who coincided in the opinion that the boat could receive no injury where she lay, until she should float. He inquired if he could be of any service; I replied, that, as he was on board, I preferred that he should remain until we had passed the Hook. At half past 10 o'clock, P.M., the tide having risen, the square-sail was hoisted and laid aback; we started the engine, and succeeded in backing her off, having the flood tide to aid us.

"We then proceeded on our course past the Hook; and, about a quarter past 11 o'clock, the pilot left us for town. The boat and machinery appearing to be in good order, we made rapid progress, and were abreast of Barnegat light on Sunday, between 4 and 5 o'clock, A.M. We continued with fine weather until towards noon, when the wind hauled north-east, with indications of a storm. In the after part of the day the wind increased, occasioning a heavy sea. Between 7 and 8 o'clock, P.M., Mr. Hunt, the chief engineer, informed me that the feeder-pipe of the forward boiler had opened at the joint, so that it forced more of the water into the hold than into the boiler; consequently, there was not a supply for that boiler: we then run with one boiler, and set the square-sail. I inquired if he could repair the pipe at sea; to which he answered that it was possible, if we kept the vessel off before the wind and sea. I accordingly put her before the wind, which both eased the vessel and enabled me to reach the mouth of Chesapeake Bay, in case it should become necessary to make a harbor. About midnight, the chief engineer reported to me that he had succeeded in repairing the feeder-pipe; and then we again put both boilers in operation, and resumed our course for Charleston, continuing, occasionally, to heave the lead, shoaling the water gradually, from twenty to eleven fathoms. When we got into eleven fathoms, at 4 o'clock, A.M., the mate and his watch were called; we took in the square sail, and hauled her course to south-south-east, this being the course along the land; we continued this course until 7 o'clock, at which time it lighted up a little, and we saw the land about fifty miles to the northward of Hatteras. The gale continuing to increase, I ordered the second mate, Mr. White, to reef the jib and foresail, to have them ready for use if we should want them. At about 9 o'clock, A.M., on Monday, the second engineer, Mr. Conro, came to me at the wheel-house, and reported that the boilers had given out, and said, 'We can do nothing more for you with steam.'

"The land being then in sight, I ordered the jib and foresail set, and headed the vessel in for shore, with the intention of beaching her. I ordered the reef turned out of the foresail, and then went down to the chief engineer, Mr. Hunt, in the engine-room, and asked him whether the boilers had indeed given out; he replied, 'No, it is the feeder-pipe,' which had again started; and that the report of the second engineer arose from a mistake of the fireman. Mr. Hunt having 'woulded' the joint again, I asked him whether it would stand to work the boat off shore; he answered, yes, that he thought it would. I then ordered him to fire up, and to get more steam on, to force her off shore; I then returned to the wheel-house, and ordered the foresail taken in, and again hauled the vessel off shore to resume our former course. Before we got to the Wimble Shoals, when I was at the wheel-house, I observed Mr. Lovegreen (a passenger) very busy about the small boat on the after upper deck. I went aft to see what he was doing; he told me he 'was getting the boats ready for launching, in case we should want them, and was fixing life-lines, and lashing the oars in the boat.' I said, 'Very well, sir, but cast off *none of the lashings.*'

"In consequence of running in, for the purpose of beaching her, as above stated, we were brought within the Wimble Shoals. In passing these shoals we received the shock of three heavy rollers on our larboard beam, which stove in our after gangway, several of the larboard state-room windows, and one of the dining-room windows. Mr. Matthews, about this time, remarked, 'We are through this.' I answered, *'Yes, we are over that part of it,'* meaning the passing of the shoals. Captain Hill, a passenger, came to the forward deck, and hailed me, to know whether 'we had not better knock away the forward bulwarks, that the sea might have a fair breach over her,' as he was afraid that we might ship some of those seas and fill the deck and cabin. I told him there was no necessity for it, as some of the boards had already been burst off; however, I had no objection to his knocking off some more, if he chose to do it; he did knock off some of the boards, and, with the assistance of the steward, Mr. Milne, unshipped the starboard gangway.

"During this time, our course was south-south-east to south-east; and, finding the vessel pressed too much to leeward, I ordered the jib to be taken in. About this period, Captain Salter, of Portsmouth, N.H., a passenger, came on the forward deck and hailed me, I being at the wheel-house on the upper deck, and said, 'Captain White, had not some of us better look out for some place to beach her?' I answered, 'No, Captain Salter, I do not intend to beach her yet, nor as long as I can keep off shore.' He expressed his surprise, and replied, 'No! Do you think you can work her off?' I answered, *'Yes.'* Between 2 and 3 o'clock, P.M., Mr. Hunt, the engineer, sent to the wheel-house for me; I went to the engine-room; he told me that 'the boat had commenced leaking badly.' I asked if it were not possible to keep her free with the engine-pumps. He said, 'You had better send men to the hand-pumps, and perhaps we may then keep her free.' I ordered the mate to send men to the pumps, which was immediately done. I then returned to the wheel-house.

"About this time Captains Salter and Hill came on the forward deck, and asked me if I would not get a light, and go down with them and try to find the leak. I ordered a lantern and marlinspike, which were brought. I then went down into the forward cabin with them, took up the floor scuttles, went down into the hold, found *no water* over the platform, broke some holes in the platform with the marlinspike, and then found *no water.* Whilst in the forehold, Captain Salter remarked, that the boat 'was ceiled with nothing but thin, common pine plank, whereas she should have been ceiled throughout with *seven inch* oak timber, champered down to the edges.' We then returned to the deck, and went to the after cabin, where they proceeded to open the scuttle, and I returned to the wheel-house. I now ordered the mates to set the crew to bailing from the engine-room. The passengers now scuttled the aftercabin floor, and commenced taking out the coal for the purpose of bailing, as they had previously found water aft. At this time the water was gaining on the pumps; some of the passengers and waiters went on to bailing from the aftercabin. The water, in front of the furnaces, having risen several inches in depth, washed the coals about, by the rolling of the vessel, rendering it impracticable to feed the fires with coal. I therefore directed the mate to have wood passed along, as we would keep steam up altogether with wood; which we continued to burn until the water quenched the fires in the furnaces. About 3 o'clock, P.M., Captain Salter again came to the forward deck, and said, 'Captain White, we had better go around Hatteras Shoals, and not attempt to go through inside.'

"Whilst the passengers and crew were at work with the pumps and buckets, I frequently went down to see that they continued at work. In passing the engineroom I remarked to Mr. Hunt, 'If we can keep the water down, so as not to reach the furnaces, I think we will go *round* the shoals; as the risk would be greater in going inside.' My reason for this conclusion was, that if, in an attempt to pass inside, with such a heavy sea and thick weather, the vessel should strike, probably every life would be lost. I again went up to the wheel-house, and Mr. Matthews asked me, 'if I was going round the shoals.' I answered in the affirmative. Captain Salter now came forward and said, 'it was the best way to track the shoals around by the lead.' We had all along been occasionally heaving the lead, and had from nine to eleven fathoms water. I continued to run so as to pass the outer shoal, until I deepended the water from eleven to twenty fathoms, and hauling up her course gradually to the south-west, until we judged ourselves round the shoals; then hauled up by degrees until we brought her up to a north-north-west course, for the purpose of getting under the lee of the shoals, believing that, as we got into smooth water, the leak would decrease, and that we should be enabled to run up under the lee of Cape Hatteras. The leak continued to gain upon us, and I soon after altered our course to north-west, and ordered the jib to be set. After heading her for the land, at the solicitation of Mr. Matthews, I left him in charge, and went to my room to get some rest. I examined one of my charts, threw off my wet coat, sat down on my trunk, and leaned my head against the berth; but, after remaining some time, found it impossible to get any rest. I went on deck and proceeded aft, where I found the water was fast gaining on us. I then went to the wheel-house and took my trumpet; the crew and passengers being still occupied in bailing and pumping, and the engine-pumps working; although these often had to be cleared of the shavings, &c., which the suction drew in; but we had to depend mostly upon the hand-pumps and bailing. About 8 o'clock, P.M., Mr. Hunt came to me at the wheel-house, and told me that the 'furnace fires were out.'

"All hope was now abandoned of making a harbor under the lee of Hatteras; and our only alternative was to run her on shore, for the purpose of saving our lives. I then directed the mate to have the square-sail set, to press her in to the land. In a few minutes the lee leach of the square sail split from foot to head, and it was lowered down. The vessel being water-logged, we consequently made but slow progress towards the shore. The weather became more moderate. Shortly after, I went below to my room and put on my pea-jacket; went aft, and saw them bailing and pumping. Whilst passing among the passengers, some of them asked me if there was a probability of their being saved. I replied, that I feared the chance was but small; as the boats would be of no service, and that there must be a heavy surf running on the beach which we were approaching. I then walked to the after starboard quarter-deck, and hove the lead, and found nine fathoms water; I laid the lead in, and remained by the rail, thinking of our condition, and calculating our chances for our lives. I now went forward, and, in passing the dining-room (which was on deck and over the after cabin) door, saw the ladies and many of the gentlemen sitting in there, and in great distress and anxiety. This was the last time I went aft, on the lower deck. I then passed on by the entrance to the after cabin; I found the stairway completely occupied with men in passing up water. I then passed forward, and went up to the wheel-house: by this time we were not far from the shore.

"About 10 o'clock, Mr. Matthews, then standing on the lower deck, asked me if I meant to put her head on; I answered, 'Yes, certainly.' Some one now ran forward, and called out that the water was over the cabin floor. Captain Salter cried out, 'Bail away, bail away, boys.' Captain Salter also asked Mr. Matthews if the boats were all clear, that they might be all lowered away without confusion, after she struck. Mr. Matthews said, 'The boats are all ready.' We now made the breakers on the starboard bow, and ahead. Mr. Matthews was standing forward, and said, 'Off the starboard bow it looks like a good place to beach her.' I ordered Trost, the man at the helm, to port his helm; and said to him, 'Mind yourself; stand clear of that wheel when she strikes, or she will be breaking your bones;' he answered 'Yes, sir, I'll keep clear.'

"The boat immediately struck on the outer reef, slued her head to the northward; the square sail caught aback; she heeled off shore, exposing the deck and upper houses to the full force of the sea. The square-sail halyards were let go, but the sail would not come down, as it was hard aback against the mast and rigging; it had previously been split, and was now blown to ribbons. The passengers, ladies and gentlemen, placed themselves along the in-shore side of the boat, seeking protection from the breaking of the sea. At this time, Mr. Matthews came up to me, on the upper deck, and asked me if I was going in the boats. I replied, 'No; I think there is no possibility of any person being saved in them, but you had better go aft and see to the launching them.' He went aft, on the upper deck, and I saw them launching the large boat off of it. The larboard quarter-boat having been lowered before and upset, they succeeded in getting the large boat alongside; many of the passengers, and both mates, got into her, several others clinging to her gunwales; she upset before she had gone ten yards from the vessel. The starboard quarter-boat had been previously stove, as well as the houses and bulwarks on that side. I went forward, pulled off my pea-jacket, vest, and boots, and threw them into the door of the wheel-house; then went a few feet aft, unshipped a small ladder, found a strand of rope lying on the deck, made one end of it fast around the middle step, took the other end around my hand, then placed myself on the forward part of the upper deck, took hold of a chimney-brace with the other hand, awaiting the event of the breaking up of the vessel.

"About the time I went aft, as above stated, the mast had gone about twenty feet from the head. The boat was now fast breaking to pieces—the dining-cabin gone—the starboard state-rooms all stove in—the upper deck breaking up. Whilst standing with the ladder in in my hand, Mr. Hunt came up to me. I said, 'Mr. Hunt, we little thought this would be our fate when we left New York.' I shook hands with him, and added, 'I hope we may all be saved.' He turned and went to the gallows frame, where there were many others collected with him. The forward smoke chimney fell in shore, across the side houses on the upper deck, close by where I was standing. Mr. Holmes, a passenger saved, was standing by me with a piece of board and rope, prepared to jump. The most of the passengers, who had placed themselves along the guards, had, by this time, been washed off; their shrieks and cries, during this time, were appalling and heart-rending beyond description. The deck, on which Mr. Holmes and myself were standing, was breaking up; we threw away our ladder and board, simultaneously, and jumped off the deck, and made for the top-gallant forecastle, which appeared to be our best place for safety. In running forward, I stepped into the fore-hatch, which was open, and fell in, but caught by the remnants of the sail which were hanging down by the hatch, and which saved me from falling quite down. I got up, by the aid of the sail, on to the deck, and made for the forecastle, which I gained, where I found a number of persons had already placed themselves.

"The first one whom I recognized, or heard, was Captain Salter, who said, 'Captain White, *my dear fellow,* I am glad to see you here.' I was at this time holding on the forestay, which lay across the forecastle; and he further said, 'Come forward here; take the other end of this rope; it is long enough for both of us.' I went and took the rope; he then added, 'I picked out this place for myself, long before the boat went ashore.' I lashed myself to the next stanchion: this deck now began to work loose from the main part of the boat; the deck settling, the starboard bow heaving up. I remarked, 'I don't like this being tied fast to stanchions; for if the bow falls over on us, we have no means to clear us from being crushed by it.' I proposed casting ourselves loose from the stanchions; we did so; and then I took a piece of small rope, passed it round a small cleat, and held one end in my hand. At this time Captain Salter was washed off from the forecastle, but succeeded in regaining it, and was a second time washed off, when one of the men, named Jackson, caught him, and assisted him to get on the forecastle. I then handed the other end of the rope, which I fastened to the cleat, to Salter. The sea, which had washed Salter off, broke off the stanchions to which he had first been lashed. All this time a Mr. Lovegreen was on the gallows frame, tolling the bell.

"The forecastle deck now broke loose and floated towards the shore, with the six persons besides myself. Very soon one man jumped off and gained the beach; we all followed. I washed ashore with only shirt, pantaloons, stockings, and hat. We proceeded along the beach towards the light. We soon found another survivor; afterwards we met Mr. Lovegreen. We continued our steps towards the lighthouse; next, found Captain Hill, apparently very much exhausted; asked for assistance to help him along, as he could not proceed without. Finding the lighthouse at a greater distance than was at first believed, I persuaded one of the crew to remain with me, to go along the surf, in order to give assistance to those who might be washed ashore; whilst the other above-mentioned persons continued their course to the lighthouse."

CHECKLIST

OF NARRATIVES

OF SHIPWRECKS AND DISASTERS

OBVIOUSLY, shipwrecks and disasters at sea have been mentioned or reported in thousands of books, chapbooks, pamphlets, magazine articles, and newspaper stories. It would be impossible for anyone to discover and list them all. The number of such works in which the shipwrecks or other maritime disasters have been the *primary* concern of the editors or authors is much smaller. I have listed here all such items I could locate, though there must be hundreds, perhaps thousands, of which I have never heard. My primary sources have been the *Catalogue of the Books, Manuscripts, and Prints and other Memorabilia in the John S. Barnes Memorial Library of the Naval History Society* (1915), E. G. Cox's *A Reference Guide to the Literature of Travel* (1938), Robert Albion's *Naval and Maritime History/An Annotated Bibliography* (1963 plus additions), and the catalogues of antiquarian booksellers. E. G. Cox in his *Reference Guide* paid tribute to the help he had received from the catalogues of Maggs Brothers; I should like to express the same gratitude for the interesting and valuable catalogues of Francis Edwards, Ltd., London; Alfred W. Paine, Bethel, Connecticut; James Thin, Edinburgh; and Paul P. B. Minet, Newport Pagnell. I am personally indebted to Carola W. Paine of Bethel, Connecticut, and Francis M. O'Brien of Portland, Maine.

The chronological arrangement of this list is arbitrary. It seemed more sensible than an alphabetical listing because of the large number of anonymous items. Nearly all of the major anthologies were published in the early nineteenth century. At the very end of the list I have grouped a small number of entries published without dates.

I made no deliberate attempt to discover items in foreign languages, though a few sources of translated narratives are listed. Narratives of piracies and of naval battles—made up as they are of catastrophes—present something of a problem, but they are largely covered in detailed histories and bibliographies. I have, therefore, listed only a couple of wrecks that occurred after naval battles and the single account of the piracies of Gibbs and Wansley, with its impressive title page.

I have included some doubtful items, preferring to err on the side of inclusiveness. A short list of general collections of voyages and travels precedes the checklist proper. Anyone who wishes to know more about these interesting and important narratives should consult the *Reference Guide* of E. G. Cox.

General Collections of Voyages and Travels

There were dozens of such compilations in English, to say nothing of those in other languages. I have listed only those collections most often referred to in books on shipwrecks and disasters.

Ramusio, Giovanni Battista
Navigationi et Viaggi . . .
Venice, 1550
Cited as a model for Hakluyt and read by James Stanier Clarke, compiler of *Naufragia*, 1805.

Hakluyt, Richard
Principall Navigations, Voiages, and Discoveries of the English Nation
London, 1589–1600, and many subsequent editions

De Bry
Collection of Voyages (Latin text)
  Grand Voyages—Frankfurt, 1590–1634
  Petits Voyages—Frankfurt, 1598–1628
  Elenchus—London, 18th Century

Purchas, Samuel
Hakluytus Posthumus, or Purchas His Pilgrimes
London, 1625

Morisoto, Claude Barthelmy
Orbis Maritimi sive Rerum in Mari et Littoribus Gestarum Generalis Historia
Dijon, 1643

Harris, John
Navigantium . . . or, a Complete Collection of Voyages and Travels
London, 1705, 2 vols.

Astley, Thomas [John Green?]
A New General Collection of Voyages and Travels
London, 1745–47, 4 vols.

Churchill, A. and J.
A Collection of Voyages and Travels
London, 1752, 8 vols.
Apparently based on a collection of 1745 by Thomas Osborne.

Knox, J.
A New Collection of Voyages, Discoveries, and Travels
London, 1767, 7 vols.

Moore, John Hamilton
A New and Complete Collection of Voyages and Travels . . .
London, 1778, 2 vols.

Mavor, William
Historical Account of the most celebrated Voyages, Travels, and Discover-
    ies . . .
London, 1796, 20 vols.
Another edition, London, 1810, was in 28 vols.

Pinkerton, John
A General Collection of the Best and Most Interesting Voyages and Trav-
    els . . .
London, 1808–14

Kerr, Robert
General History and Collection of Voyages and Travels . . .
Edinburgh, 1811–1824, 18 vols.

Narratives of Shipwrecks and Disasters

1550

1. Ramusio, Giovanni Battista (1485–1557)
    Navigationi et Viaggi . . .
    Venice, 1550
Mentioned as read by James Stanier Clarke, editor of *Naufragia* (#67).

1610

2. Anonymous
    A True Declaration of the State of the Colonie in Virginia
    London, 1610
A pamphlet which includes material on the cruise of Sir George Somers, whose
    Sea Venture was wrecked on the Bermudas. This pamphlet and the next item
    are believed to have been used by Shakespeare as bases for *The Tempest.*

3. Jourdain, Sylvester
    A Discovery of the Bermudas, otherwise called the Ile of Devils . . .
    London, 1610
Another pamphlet telling the story of Somers's wreck. Another source for *The
    Tempest* may have been a letter written in 1610 by William Strachey, published
    in *Purchas His Pilgrimes* (1625) as "A True Reportory of the Wrack and Re-
    demption of Sir Thomas Gates Knight." Strachey had been a member of
    Somers's expedition.

1612

4. Anonymous
    Relation of an Englishman Shipwrecked on the Coast of Camboya . . .
    London, 1612
    Cox, II, 451. Stated to be cited in Pinkerton, XVII.

1632

5. LALEMANT, CHARLES (b. 1587)
   "The Shipwreck of Father Charles Lalemant, Philibert Noyrot, and
      others, off Cape Breton"
   In Champlain's *Voyages*, Paris, 1632
The wreck occurred in 1629.

1641

6. ANONYMOUS
   Sad News from the Seas . . . Loss of the good Ship called the Merchant
      Royall . . . cast away ten leagues from the Lands end, on . . . 23
      Septem. 1641
   London, 1641
   Cox, II, 451

1664

7. JOHNSON, WILLIAM
   Sermon and Narrative of the Dangers and Deliverances at Sea
   London, 1664
   Third edition titled *Deus Vobiscum,* 1672; sixth edition, 1769.
   Wreck of the *William and John* of Ipswich on the coast of Norway and
      other escapes of the author.
   Cox, II, 452

1671[?]

8. ANONYMOUS
   A Description of a Great Sea Storm, that happened to some Ships in the
   Gulph of Florida, in September last
   London, [1671?]
   A broadsheet in verse, published by Putlick and Simpson.
   Cox, II, 452

1675

9. JANEWAY, JAMES (1636–1674)
   Mr. J. J.'s Legacy to his Friends, containing twenty-seven famous in-
      stances of God's Providence in and about Sea-Dangers and Deliver-
      ances; with the names of several that were Eye-Witnesses to them
   London, 1675
A later edition was titled *A Token for Mariners,* London, 1708, and is stated to have
   included the narratives of twenty-nine wrecks. This is the first anthology of
   shipwreck narratives that I have located. Cox, II, 452

1682

10. SMITH, WILLIAM, AND HARSHFIELD, JOHN
    A Full Account of the late Shipwreck of the Ship called the President,
       which was cast away in Montz-Bay in Cornwall on the 4th of Febru-
       ary . . . 1682
    London, 1682. 8 pp.
    Cox, II, 453

1699

11. DICKINSON, JONATHAN
    God's Protecting Providence Man's Surest Help and Defence in the
       Times of the greatest difficulty and most imminent Danger
    Philadelphia, Jansen, 1699
Wreck of the barkentine *Reformation* on the coast of Florida, Sept. 22–23, 1696.
    There were many later editions including a modern reprint, *Jonathan Dick-
    inson's Journal*, Yale University Press, New Haven, 1961.

1704

12. ANONYMOUS
    The Storm: or, A Collection of the most Remarkable Casualties and
       Disasters which happened in the Late Dreadful Tempest, both by
       Sea and Land
    [London], G. Sawbridge, 1704. 8 + 272 pp. 8vo.

13. [DEFOE, DANIEL]
    A Collection of the most remarkable Casualties and Disasters, which
       happened in the late dreadful Tempest, both by Sea and Land, on
       Friday the twenty-sixth of November, 1703
    London, George Sawbridge: J. Nutt, [1704?]. Second edition
The two items above are probably the first and second editions of the same text.

14. ANONYMOUS
    Exact Relation of the Late Dreadful Tempest: or, A Faithful Account
       of the most remarkable Disasters which hapned . . . in the City
       and Country; the number of Ships, Men and Guns, that were lost,
       etc.
    [London], A. Baldwin, 1704. 24 pp.

1708

15. GEARE, ALLEN
    Eben-Ezer . . . being a true Account of a late miraculous Preservation
       of 9 Men in a small Boat . . . in their voyage in the Ship called
       the Langdon Frigate
    London, [1708]. 8 pp.
    Cox, II, 454

1711

16. DEAN, JOHN
    A True Account of the Voyage of the Nottingham Galley of London
       . . . from the River Thames to New England. Near which place
       she was cast away on Boon-Island, Dec. 11. 1710 . . . the whole
       attested upon oath, by Christopher Langman, Mate, Nicholas Mil-
       ler, Boatswain, and George White, Sailor in said Ship
    London, [1711]. 36 pp. Another edition, Boston, 1727

17. LANGMAN, CHRISTOPHER
    A True Account of the Voyage of the Nottingham Galley, J. Dean,

Commander, from the Thames to New England . . . by C. Langman, N. Mellen and G. White
London, 1711
This item and the preceding pamphlet by John Dean are the bases for Kenneth Roberts's novel *Boon Island,* New York, 1956.

1720

18. BURCHETT, JOSIAH
A Complete History of the Most Remarkable Transactions at Sea
London, 1720
I have not seen this item. It may not include narratives of shipwrecks and disasters, but the title is inclusive enough to allow the possibility.

19. FALCONER, RICHARD (Captain)
Voyages, Dangerous Adventures and Imminent Escapes of Captain Richard Falconer . . . in his Shipwreck . . . intermixed with the Voyages and Adventures of Thomas Randal, his Shipwreck in the Baltic . . .
London, [1720]
Cox, II, 455. According to Halkett and Laing, the author was W. R. Chetwood.

1726

20. URING, NATHANIEL
A History of the Voyages and Travels of Nathaniel Uring (A relation of the late intended settlement of the Islands of St. Lucia and St. Vincent, in right of the Duke of Montagu)
London, 1726. Other editions, 1727, 1749. Reprinted 1928.

1732

21. MAY, CHARLES
An Account of the Wonderful Preservation of the Ship Terra Nova of London
[London?], 1732
Cox, II, 457. Stated to be reprinted in Churchill, VI, 343–54.

1735

22. GOMES DE BRITO, BERNARDO (b. 1688)
Historia Tragico-maritima . . .
Lisbon, 1735–36
Reprinted as *The Tragic History of the Sea, 1589–1622,* Hakluyt Society, II, 112

1740

23. DEAN, JOHN
A True and Genuine Narrative of the Whole Affair relating to the Ship Sussex . . . wrecked on the Bassas de India . . . by John Dean, the only surviving person of them all
London, 1740

1742

24. CRESPEL, EMMANUEL
    Voyages of Rev. Father Emmanuel Crespel, in Canada, and his Ship-
    wreck, While returning to France. Published by Sieur Louis
    Crespel, his brother
    Frankfort-on-the-Meyn, 1742
    Reprinted in John Gilmary Shea, *Perils of the Ocean and Wilder-
    ness . . .*
    Boston, Patrick Donahoe, n.d. (preface dated 1856)

1743

25. BUCKLEY, JOHN, AND CUMMINS, JOHN
    A Voyage to the South-Seas, in the Year 1740–1, containing a Faithful
    Narrative of the Loss of His Majesty's Ship the Wager on a Deso-
    late Island . . .
    London, Jacob Robinson, 1743

1751

26. YOUNG, JOHN
    An Affecting Narrative of the Unfortunate Voyage and Catastrophe of
    His Majesty's Ship Wager . . . one of Commodore Anson's Squad-
    ron . . .
    London, 1751
    Cox, II, 274

1761

27. SUTHERLAND, JAMES (Lieutenant)
    A Narrative of the Loss of His Majesty's Ship, the Litchfield, Captain
    Barton, on the Coast of Africa . . .
    London, 1761. Another edition, 1768
    Cox, II, 461

1762

28. BY A SAILOR [Falconer, William]
    The Shipwreck: A Poem in Three Cantos
    London, 1762. Many other editions
Based on Falconer's own experiences in the loss of the *Britannia* on the coast of
    Greece. He was later lost at sea.

1766

29. HARRISON, DAVID (Captain)
    The Melancholy Narrative of the Distressful Voyage and Miraculous
    Deliverance of Captain David Harrison of the Sloop Peggy, of New
    York . . . until relieved by Captain Evers of the Virginian Trade.
    Written by himself
    London, 1766
    Cox, II, 461

30. PURNELL, THOMAS
The Following is a True and Faithful Account of the Loss of the
Brigantine Tyrrell, Arthur Coghlan, Commander . . . By Thomas
Purnell, Chief Mate Thereof
Hoxton, 1766. Another edition, London, 1776. 8 pp.

1768

31. BYRON, JOHN
The Narrative . . . containing an account of the Great Distresses
. . . on the Coast of Patagonia 1740 . . . Loss of the Wager Man
of War . . .
London, 1768. 257 pp.

32. DUBOIS-FONTANELLE, JEAN GASPARD (1737–1812)
The Shipwreck and Adventures of Monsieur Pierre Viaud . . .
Bordeaux and Paris, 1768. Translation from the French by Mrs. Griffith,
London, 1771. Another edition of Mrs. Griffith's translation,
Dover, N.H., 1799
The wreck occurred on the coast of Florida in 1766.

1774

33. LeROY, P. L.
Narrative of the Singular Adventures of Four Russian Sailors, cast away
on the desert island of East-Spitzbergen
London, 1774. pp. 41–118, 8vo.
Bookseller's note: "Complete in itself, though originally issued as a supplement
to Staehlin's 'Account of the New Northern Archipelago.'"

34. VIAUD, PIERRE
The Surprising and yet Real and True Voyages and Adventures of
Monsieur Pierre Viaud, a French Sea Captain, to which is added
The Shipwreck, a Sentimental and descriptive Poem in three Cantos
by William Falconer, an English Sailor
Philadelphia, printed by Robert Bell in Third Street, MDCCLXXIV
[1774]
Bell also published the Viaud book separately in 1774. Probably this was the
Griffith translation of Dubois-Fontanelle cited above.

1780[?]

35. ANONYMOUS
Dreadful Wreck of the Brig "St. Lawrence," from Quebec to New York,
1780, which struck on an Island of Ice near the Gulph of St. Law-
rence . . .
London, n.d. [1780?] Wrappers
Barnes Catalogue

1781

36. ANONYMOUS
Extracts from the *Westminster Magazine*, 1781. Pamphlet No. 2,
"Dreadful Hurricane in the West Indies, with losses of ships of the
Royal Navy"
Barnes Catalogue

37. DEPERTHES, JEAN LOUIS HUBERT SIMON
Relations d'infortunes sur mer
Rheims, 1781. Later edition, Paris, 1789, 3 tom. English translation,
1833

1782

38. PRENTICE, S. W.
Narrative of a Shipwreck on the Island of Cape Breton in a voyage
from Quebec, 1780. By S. W. Prentice, Ensign of the 84th Regi-
ment of Foot
London, 1782. Second and third editions, 1783
Cox, II, 462

1783

39. DALRYMPLE, ALEXANDER
An Account of the Loss of the Grosvenor Indiaman, commanded by
Captain John Coxon, on the 4th of August, 1782 . . . on the coast
of Africa . . . being the Report given in to the East India Com-
pany by Alexander Dalrymple
London, 1783
Cox, II, 463

40. INGLEFIELD, . . . [Captain]
Narrative Concerning the Loss of His Majesty's Ship the Centaur, of 74
Guns . . .
London, 1783
Cox, II, 463

1786

41. MERITON, HENRY, AND ROGERS, JOHN
A Circumstantial Narrative of the Loss of the Halsewell East-Indiaman,
Captain Richard Pierce, which was unfortunately wrecked at Sea-
combe in the Isle of Purbeck . . .
London, 1786
Cox, II, 463

1787

42. BOYS, WILLIAM
An Account of the Loss of the Luxborough Galley, by Fire on her Voy-
age from Jamaica to London . . . in the Year 1727
London, 1787
Cox, II, 464

43. HAWKINS, JAMES [Captain]
Account of the Loss of His Majesty's Ship Deal Castle . . . off the Island of Porto Rico, during the Hurricane in the West Indies, in
1780
London, 1787. 48 pp.

1788

44. ANONYMOUS
    An Account of the Loss of H.M.S. Deal Castle off the Island of Porto
    Rico, 1787[?]
    Captain Inglefield's Narrative concerning the Loss of H.M.S. the
    Centaur, 1783[?]
    Smith, C.
    A Narrative of the Loss of the Catherine, Venus, and Piedmont [trans-
    ports] and the Thomas, Golden Grove and Aeolus [merchant ships]
    near Weymouth, 1796
Cox (II, 463) states that these three narratives are printed in *The Habitable World
Described*, London, 1788. Since the Smith narrative is dated 1796, perhaps a
later edition of *The Habitable World* is the source.

45. KEATE, GEORGE (F.R.S.)
    An Account of the Pelew Islands . . . in August, 1783, [and those who]
    were there shipwrecked in the "Antelope"
    London, 1788[?]. Second edition, London, 1788; Dublin, 1788; chap-
    book edition, Perth, 1788; third edition, London, 1789; Dublin,
    1793

46. WILSON, HENRY
    The Wreck of the Antelope . . .
    [London?], 1788
    Cox, II, 302–3

1789

47. BYRON, THE HONORABLE JOHN
    The Narrative of the Honorable John Byron, Commodore in a Late
    Expedition round the World . . . a Relation of the Loss of the
    Wager Man-of-War
    London, 1789
Perhaps a later edition of #31.

1791

48. CARTER, G.
    A Narrative of the Loss of the Grosvenor, East Indiaman, wrecked
    upon the Coast of Caffraria . . .
    London, 1791
    Cox, II, 465

1792

49. BLIGH, WILLIAM
    A Voyage to the South Sea . . .
    London, 1792
The mutiny on the *Bounty* has been the subject of almost innumerable books,
notably the novels of Nordhoff and Hall. S. A. Spence's *Captain William Bligh
1754–1817 and Where to Find Him*, 1970, is a convenient list of the major
sources. One little-known American item is Edward Everett Hale's *Stories of the
Sea, Told by Sailors*, Boston, 1880, which tells of the wreck of the American
ship *Wild Wave* on Pitcairn's Island.

50. SAUGNIER AND BRISSON
Voyages to the Coast of Africa, by Messrs. Saugnier and Brisson: Containing an Account of their Shipwreck on board different vessels, and subsequent slavery,—and interesting details of the manners of the Arabs of the Desert, and of the Slave Trade, as carried on at Senegal and Galam
London, for G. G. and J. Robinson, 1792. 8vo., folding map

51. THUNBERG, KARL PETER (1743–1828)
Travels in Europe, Africa and Asia, made between the Years 1770 and 1779
Berlin, 1792–1794. London, 3rd. edition, F. & C. Rivington, 1795–96, 4 vols.
J. S. Clarke, *Naufragia*, cites Vol. I, pp. 270–75, a shipwreck on the coast of South Africa, and says the account was inserted in Vol. III of the *Naval Chronicle*.

1793

52. HAMILTON, G.
A Voyage around the World in H.M.'s Frigate "Pandora" performed under the direction of Captain Edwards, 1790–92, with the discoveries made in the South-Sea and the many distresses experienced by the crew from shipwreck and famine in a voyage of 1100 miles in open boats between Endeavor Straits and the Island of Timor
Berwick, 1793

1795

53. ANONYMOUS
Authentic Narratives of Affecting Incidents at Sea, in a Series of Letters, interspersed with Poetry and Moral Observations . . . published by subscription for the benefit of a poor lame boy
Printed by B. & W. Wilson, Scarborough, 1795. 32 pp.

1796

54. SMITH, C.
A Narrative of the Loss of the Catherine, Venus, and Piedmont Transports, and the Thomas, Golden Grove, and Aeolus Merchant Ships . . .
London, 1796

1797

55. CRESPEL, EMANUEL
Travels in North America . . . with a Narrative of his Shipwreck and Extraordinary Hardships and Sufferings on the Island of Anticosti . . . and of the Shipwreck of His Majesty's Ship Active, and Others
London, 1797
Cox, II, 174
Only the first part is by Crespel, of course.

1798

56. ANONYMOUS [Benjamin Stout]
   A Narrative of the Loss of the Ship Hercules, Commanded by Captain
      Benjamin Stout on the Coast of Caffraria, the 16th of June, 1796
   Hudson, N.Y., 1798
   Cox, II, 467

57. MACKEY, WILLIAM
   A Narrative of the Shipwreck of the Juno, on the Coast of Aracan . . .
   London, 1798. German translation, 1800
This narrative, read at school and probably later reobtained, was used by Byron
as one of the sources for Canto II of *Don Juan.*

1799

58. ANONYMOUS
   The Naval Chronicle containing the Current History of the Royal
      Navy, with Original Papers, Biographies, Lists of Ships, &c with
      numerous Portraits and Views
   [London], 1799–1818. Complete in 40 vols. Royal 8vo.
Barnes Catalogue states: ". . . the other contents include narratives . . . of ship-
wrecks and disasters of former periods." This magazine may well have been
the primary source for many later narratives and anthologies.

1800

59. PARDOE, MICHAEL
   The Shipwreck and Sea-Fight of the Amazon Frigate, Capt. Reynolds,
      and the Indefatigable, Sir Edward Pellew, Commander
   [London?], c. 1800. Wrappers, 36 pp.
The action occurred in 1797 and is described in "The Loss of the *Droits de
l'Homme.*"

1802

60. SAUNDERS, DANIEL, JR.
   A Journal of the Travels and Sufferings of Daniel Saunders, Jr., a
      mariner on board the Ship "Commerce" of Boston, Samuel John-
      son, Commander, which was cast away near Cape Morebet, on the
      coast of Arabia, July 20, 1792
   New Haven, 1802. 143 pp. Other editions, Hudson, N.Y., 1805; Salem,
      Mass., printed by Joshua and John D. Cushing, 1824
   Barnes Catalogue

1803

61. GRANGER, WILLIAM, AND OTHERS
   New Wonderful Museum and Extraordinary Magazine, Being a Com-
      plete Repository of all the Wonders, Curiosities, and Rarities of
      Nature and Art . . .
   [London], Alex. Hogg & Company, Paternoster Row, 1803–1808, 6
      vols.

This magazine contains a few accounts of contemporary shipwrecks, though it is primarily directed to those interested in distinguished misers, murderers, horned ladies, and monstrosities of every kind.

1804

62. DUNCAN, ARCHIBALD

The Mariner's Chronicle, Being a Collection of the most Interesting Narratives of Shipwrecks, Fires, Famines, and other Calamities Incident to a Life of Maritime Enterprise, by Archibald Duncan, Esq. Late of the Royal Navy

London, printed and published by James Cundee, 1804

As noted earlier, the dates are puzzling. The British Museum Catalogue lists the first edition as in 6 volumes, 1804–[1808], and the second edition in 4 volumes, 1804–05. There was another London edition in 6 volumes in 1810 and two Philadelphia editions, each in 4 volumes, in 1806 and 1810. This anthology seems to have been the source from which most later editors borrowed.

63. WOODARD, DAVID (Captain)

Narrative of Captain David Woodard, and Four Sailors, who lost their Ship while in a Boat at Sea and surrendered themselves up to the Malays in the Island of Celebes . . . their Sufferings, Escape . . . and an Appendix containing Narratives of various Escapes and Shipwrecks

London, 1804. Portrait, two maps and plates

Another edition, London, 1805, is stated to contain narratives of the mutiny on the *Bounty*, the wrecks of the *Antelope* and the *Pandora*, and the sufferings of the crew of the *Shah Homazier* in Torres Strait.

1805

64. ANONYMOUS

The Loss of the Earl of Abergavenny, East Indiaman, off Portland, on the Night of fifth February, 1805 . . . Corrected from the official returns at the East India House

London, John Stockdale, Feb. 13, 1805. Pamphlet, 49 pp.

65. ANONYMOUS

An Authentic Narrative of the Loss of the Earl of Abergavenny East Indiaman, Captain John Wordsworth . . . by a Gentleman in the East India House

London, Minerva Press, Feb. 21, 1805

66. ANONYMOUS [Thomas Page?]

Narrative of the Loss of the Ship Fanny, on her Passage from Bombay to China &c. In a Letter from Thomas Page, Second Officer

London, 1805. Second edition, iv, 36 pp., 8vo.

67. CLARKE, JAMES STANIER, F.R.S.

Naufragia: or Historical Memoirs of Shipwrecks and of the Providential Deliverance of Vessels, by James Stanier Clarke F.R.S., Chaplain of the Prince's Household and Librarian to His Royal Highness

London, printed by I. Gold, Shoe Lane, Fleet Street, for J. Mawman, 22 Poultry, MDCCCV. Vol. I, 1805, Vol. II, 1806

Spine title: Memoirs of Shipwrecks

1806

THE NEXT SEVERAL ITEMS present bibliographical difficulties. All should probably appear under 1808–1809, but a Barnes Catalogue entry requires some kind of explanation. Between 1805 and 1810 Thomas Tegg, 111 Cheapside, London, a dealer in remaindered books and a successful but not very pretentious publisher, produced a series of pamphlets on shipwrecks. These were all, so far as I can determine, of 28 pages, and each had a folding aquatint as frontispiece. Tegg's anonymous compilers used one, two, or three disasters to fit the 28-page format. These pamphlets are usually found separately, and the title page is undated, but the aquatints are dated. Booksellers usually print the aquatint dates in brackets as the publication date. In the Barnes Catalogue, however, appears a volume of collected pamphlets said to be bound together by Tegg and dated 1806, though that date must be incorrect. There are a number of errors in the Barnes Catalogue, including those noted below, but I have decided to give the material as the Barnes Catalogue lists it, and then add the individual Tegg items I have found.

68. ANONYMOUS

A series of narratives, with folding plates in aquatint. 12 mo. 28 pages each. Half-calf gilt, bound by Thomas Tegg, Cheapside, 1806 [?] [Number f below, with its engagement that took place in 1808, makes the 1806 date impossible.]

    a. Loss of the "Wagner" [Wager], 1744
    b. Wallis and his Crew at Otaheite, 1776
    c. Adventures of Captain Stedman in Surinam, 1773
    d. Wreck of the St. Lawrence—Quebec to New York, 1780
    e. Wreck of the "Phoenix" off Cuba. Also, "Pirard de Laval" on the Maldivia, 1601
    f. Loss of the "Ville de Paris" captured by Rodney, 1782. Engagement between the H.M.S. "Amethyst" and the French "La Thetis," 1808
    g. Loss of the "Halsewell" on the Isle of Purbeck, 1786
    h. Loss of the "Bounty," 1789, and the adventures of the mutineers
    i. Adventures of Captain Woodward [Woodard] among the Malays, 1791
    j. Loss of the "Duke [Earl] of Abergavenny" off Portland Bill, 1805
    k. Loss of the "Duke of Cumberland," Coast of Antigua, 1804
    l. Capture of the "General Washington," Captain Boyle, by Barbary Corsairs
    m. Loss of the E. J. [I] Company's Ship "Hindostan" off Margate, 1803

69. ANONYMOUS

Piratical Seizure of the Brig Admiral Trowbridge by part of her crew while lying at anchor off the Island of Sooloo, Aug. 21, 1807 . . . communicated by Captain Alexander Wallace. Also, The captivity and cruel treatment of M. de Brisson on the Coast of Barbary London, Thomas Tegg, [1808]. 12 mo., 28 pp., fldg. frontis.

70. ANONYMOUS
    The Loss of His Majesty's Frigate Anson . . . Dec. 1807. . . . Also, An
        authentic narrative of the Loss of the Sydney . . . May 1806
    London, Thomas Tegg, [1808]

71. ANONYMOUS
    Destruction of the Boyne . . . by a most rapid and tremendous Fire
        . . . May 4, 1795. . . . Also, The Embarrassments of Mons. Pierre
        Viaud and Md. La Couture
    London, Thomas Tegg, [1808]. 12 mo., 28 pp., fldg. plate

72. ANONYMOUS
    Shipwreck and Captivity of Captain Donald Campbell, on leaving Goa
        for Madras, 1782 . . .
    London, Thomas Tegg, [1808]. 12 mo., 28 pp. fldg. frontis.

73. ANONYMOUS
    Correct Statement of the Loss of the Earl of Abergavenny, East India-
        man, John Wordsworth, Commander . . . February 5, 1805. . . .
        Also, The Shipwreck of Occum Chamnan, a Siamese Noble
    London, Thomas Tegg, [1808]

74. ANONYMOUS
    Interesting Narrative of the Loss of the Halsewell, East Indiaman . . .
        at Seacombe . . . January 6, 1786. . . . Also, An Account of the
        Destruction of the New Hoorn, Dutch East Indiaman, by Fire
    London, Thomas Tegg, [1808]. 8vo.[?], 28 pp., fldg. frontis.

75. ANONYMOUS
    Shipwreck and Death of Lord Royston, and other Persons of distinc-
        tion . . . Passengers in the Agatha . . . near Memel, April 7,
        1808. . . . Also, The Loss of the Portuguese ship Bowaniong,
        Calcutta to China, June 17, 1807
    London, Thomas Tegg, [1808]. 12 mo., 28 pp., fldg. frontis.

76. ANONYMOUS
    Dreadful Explosion of H.M.S. Frigate Amphion . . . Sept. 22, 1798.
        . . . Also, The Loss of a Spanish Frigate on the Coast of Mexico,
        in 1678
    London, Thomas Tegg, [1809]

77. ANONYMOUS
    Authentic Narrative of the Recent Loss of His Majesty's Ship Crescent,
        John Temple, Captain, which struck . . . 1808, off the Coast of
        Jutland. . . . Also, The Shipwreck and Adventures of Nathaniel
        Uring, in the beginning of November, 1711
    London, Thomas Tegg, [1809]

78. ANONYMOUS
    Melancholy Loss of the Lady Hobart Packet . . . William Dorset
        Fellows, Esq., which struck on an Island of Ice in the Atlantic
        Ocean, June 28, 1803. . . . Also, Curious particulars of Emmanuel
        Jose [Manuel de Sousa?] and his wife . . . who were shipwrecked
        on the East Coast of Africa
    London, Thomas Tegg, [1809]. 12 mo., 28 pp., fldg. frontis.

79. ANONYMOUS
    Authentic Account of the Recent Loss of the Travers, Indiaman, Cap-

r

tain Collins. . . . Also, The Shipwreck of the Sparrow-Hawk, a Dutch East-Indiaman
London, Thomas Tegg, [1809]. 8 vo. [?], 28 pp., fldg. frontis.

80. ANONYMOUS
Authentic Narrative of the Wreck of His Majesty's Ship Sceptre of 64 Guns, Captain Valentine Edwards, in Table Bay . . . November 6, 1799. . . . Also, The Sufferings of Don Joseph Pizarro, &c.
London, Thomas Tegg, [1809]

81. ANONYMOUS
Affecting Narrative of the Loss of the Thames Smack, Captain Craiggy . . . on the Nore Sand . . . February 8, 1809. . . . Also, The Sufferings of Alexander Selkirk . . .
London, Thomas Tegg, [1809]. 12 mo., 28 pp., fldg. frontis.

82. ANONYMOUS
Loss of the Wager Man of War . . . in the Year 1744, and the Consequent Embarrassments of the Crew . . . and other Distresses which they endured upwards of Five Years
London, Thomas Tegg, [1809]. 12 mo., 28 pp., fldg. engr.

1808

83. RAY, WILLIAM
Horrors of Slavery: or, The American Tars in Tripoli. Containing an Account of the Loss and Capture of the United States Frigate "Philadelphia" . . . interspersed with interesting remarks, anecdotes and poetry, on various subjects. Written during upwards of nineteen months' imprisonment and Vassalage among the Turks
Troy [N.Y.], printed by Oliver Lyons for the author, 1808. 12 mo., 280 pp.
Barnes Catalogue

1809

84. MARTIN, MARIA
History of the Captivity and Sufferings of Maria Martin, who was Six Years a Slave in Algiers . . . Written by Herself
Philadelphia, printed and sold by Joseph Rakestraw, 1809. 12 mo., 107 pp. Another edition, New York, 1812

1810

85. ANONYMOUS
Narrative of Calamitous and Interesting Shipwrecks &c., with Authentic Particulars of the Sufferings of the Crews . . .
Philadelphia, published by Mathew Carey, printed by A. Small, 1810. iv, 92 pp.

1812

86. ANONYMOUS
Narrative of the Shipwrecks and other Calamities, incident to a life of

> Maritime Enterprise . . . Loss of the Wager Man of War . . .
> and also the Loss of the Halsewell East Indiaman
> New Haven, 1812. 16 mo., 107 pp.

87. DALYELL, SIR J. G.

> Shipwrecks and Disasters at Sea, or Narratives of Noted Calamities and
> Deliverances Resulting from Maritime Enterprise . . .
> Edinburgh, 1812. 3 vols. Other editions: London, 1846–54, 1866

Apparently the chief rival of Duncan's *The Mariner's Chronicle*. Cox (II, 468)
states that Byron borrowed from this anthology for the second canto of *Don
Juan*. As noted in the introduction, every borrowing I have seen listed could
have been made from some other source.

88. LUCE, JOHN

> Narrative of a Passage from the Island of Cape Breton across the Atlan-
> tic Ocean, with other interesting occurrences in a letter to a friend
> London, 1812

Barnes Catalogue states: ". . . case of shipwrecks, disasters, and rescues"

1813

89. ANONYMOUS

> Analectic Magazine: Containing Selections from Foreign Reviews and
> Magazines, together with Original Miscellaneous Compositions and
> a Naval Chronicle
> Philadelphia, 1813–20

90. ANONYMOUS

> Narrative of the Capture of the United States Brig "Vixen" of 14 Guns,
> by the British Frigate "Southampton," and of the subsequent Loss
> of both Vessels on a Reef of Rocks off Conception Island: with
> some account of the sufferings of the crew, their manner of deliver-
> ance and final deposit in the prison ships at Port Royal, Jamaica.
> The whole interspersed with various remarks, relative to the treat-
> ment shown to and conduct observed by the prisoners. By one of
> the "Vixen's" crew, in a letter to his friend
> Charleston, S. C., Gazette Office, printed and published by the author,
> 1813. 8vo. 35 pp.
> Barnes Catalogue

91. ANONYMOUS

> Remarkable Shipwrecks, or A Collection of Interesting Accounts of
> Naval Disasters, with many particulars of the Extraordinary Ad-
> ventures and Sufferings of the Crews of Vessels wrecked at Sea and
> of their Treatment on distant Shores, together with an Account of
> the Deliverance of Survivors. Selected from Authentic Sources
> Hartford, published by Andrus and Starr, John Russell, Jr., Printer,
> 1813

This volume lists at the end the names of about 4,000 subscribers. One bookseller
states that the book is almost always found "read to pieces."

92. SOREN, JOHN

> Case of John Soren, proprietor of the Ship "Enterprise," at the time of
> of her seizure in the act of saving nearly three hundred of His
> Majesty's troops from sinking in the Atlantic Ocean
> London, printed by Cox and Bayliss, July 1813
> Barnes Catalogue

1814

93. FLINDERS, CAPTAIN MATTHEW, R.N.
    A Voyage to Terra Australis; undertaken for the purpose of completing
    the discovery of that vast country, 1801–1803, in H.M.S. "Investi-
    gator" . . . with an account of the shipwreck of the "Porpoise"
    . . .

    [London?], 1814. 2 vols. with 8 plates, plus atlas with 16 large-scale
    maps. 3 vols. in all

1815

94. ANONYMOUS
    Narrative of the Heroic Enterprise of William Hanson. . . . Also, The
    shipwreck and sufferings of Occum Chamnan, a Siamese Mandarin,
    in 1674
    London, Champante and Whitron, [1815?]

1816

95. ADAMS, ROBERT
    The Narrative of Robert Adams, a Sailor who was wrecked on the
    Western Coast of Africa, 1810 . . .
    London, John Murray, 1816. Another edition, Boston, Wells and Lilly,
    1817

96. ALLEN, MRS. SARAH
    A Narrative of the Shipwreck and Unparalleled Sufferings of Mrs. Sarah
    Allen
    Boston, Benjamin Marston, 1816. 24 pp. Second edition, Boston, M.
    Brewer, 1816

97. CAMPBELL, ARCHIBALD
    A Voyage Around the World, from 1806 to 1812 . . . including a Nar-
    rative of the Author's Shipwreck on the Island of Sannack . . .
    Edinburgh, 1816. 219 pp. Second edition, New York, 1819

1817

98. CORREARD, ALEXANDRE, AND SAVIGNY, HENRI
    Naufrage de la fregate le Meduse faisant partie de l'expedition du
    Senegal en 1816 . . .
    Paris, Correard, 4th edition, 1821. [First edition 1817?] Another edi-
    tion by J. B. Henry Savigny and Alexander Correard, London, H.
    Colburn, 1818
    A narrative of the loss of the *Medusa* by two of the fifteen survivors from the raft.

99. MCLEOD, JOHN
    Narrative of a Voyage in H.M.S. Alceste along the Coast of Corea to
    the Island of Lewchew, with an Account of her subsequent Ship-
    wreck
    London, John Murray, 1817. Second edition, 1818; another edition,
    Philadelphia, Carey, 1818

100. PATTERSON, SAMUEL
   Narrative of the Adventures and Sufferings experienced in the Pacific
   Ocean and many other parts of the world, with an account of the
   Feejee and Sandwich Islands
   Palmer, Mass., 1817. Repr. Fairfield, Washington, 1967
Voyage to Fiji and wreck in 1818.

101. RILEY, JAMES
   Sufferings in Africa: Captain Riley's Narrative—an Authentic Narrative of the Loss of the American Brig Commerce, wrecked on the
   western Coast of Africa in the Month of August, 1815. With an
   Account of the Sufferings of her surviving Officers and Crew, who
   were enslaved by the wandering Arabs on the great African Desert,
   or Zahahrah: and Observations historical, geographical, &c. made
   during the Travels of the Author while a Slave to the Arabs, and
   in the Empire of Morocco. By James Riley, late Master and Super-
   cargo
   New York, Riley, 1817. Other editions, 1820, 1828, 1850, 1859, 1965.
   French edition, Paris, Le Normant, 1818

1818

102. PADDOCK, JUDAH
   A Narrative of the Shipwreck of the Ship Oswego on the Coast of South
   Barbary, and of the Sufferings of the Master and the Crew while
   in Bondage among the Arabs; interspersed with numerous remarks upon the Country and its Inhabitants, and concerning the
   peculiar Perils of that Coast. By Judah Paddock, her late Master
   New York, published by Captain James Riley. J. Seymour, Printer,
   1818. Another edition, New York, published by Collins and Company, 1818 (listed in Barnes Catalogue)

103. ROBBINS, ARCHIBALD
   A Journal, comprising an account of the Loss of the Brig Commerce,
   of Hartford, (Con.) James Riley, Master, upon the western Coast
   of Africa, August 28th, 1815; also of the Slavery and Sufferings of
   the Author and the rest of the Crew, upon the Desert of Zahara,
   in the years 1815, 1816, 1817 . . .
   Hartford, 3rd edition, published by Silas Andrus, 1818; 7th edition,
   1818; another edition, 1821; reprint, Greenwich, Conn., 1937
I suspect the numbering of those editions; either the editions must have been
very small, or the publisher hoped that indications of a large sale would result
in one.

1820

104. ANONYMOUS
   A Narrative of the Loss of the Waterton East Indiaman, wrecked on
   the Coast of Madagascar in 1792 . . .
   Edinburgh, 1820
   Cox, II, 468

105. ANONYMOUS
   The Shipwreck: showing what sometimes happens on the seacoasts,
   etc.

New York, American Tract Society, 1820. Another edition, London,
1830
In verse. May be all or part of Falconer's *The Shipwreck,* or something quite
different.

1821

106. BRADLEY, ELIZA
An Authentic Narrative of the Shipwreck and Sufferings of Mrs. Eliza
Bradley, the Wife of Captain James Bradley of Liverpool, Com-
mander of the Ship Sally which was wrecked on the Coast of
Barbary, in June, 1818 . . .
Boston, printed by James Wald, 1821

107. CHASE, OWEN
Narrative of the Most Extraordinary and Distressing Ship Wreck of
the Whale Ship Essex of Nantucket
New York, W. B. Gilley, 1821
As noted in the introduction, this narrative by Owen Chase provided Melville with
the main plot line and the climax of *Moby-Dick.*

108. COCHELET, CHARLES
Naufrage du Brick Francais La Sophie, 1819, sur la Cote Occidentale
d'Afrique . . .
Paris, 1821. 2 vols., map, plates. Another edition, *Narrative of the
Shipwreck of the* "Sophia" . . . London, 1822, "With engravings
by Charles Cochelet, ancient paymaster in Catalonia, and one of
the sufferers."
Barnes Catalogue

1822

109. ANONYMOUS
Wonderful Escapes, containing the Narrative of the Shipwreck of the
Antelope Packet, the Loss of the Lady Hobart Packet, on an Island
of Ice, etc. . . .
Dublin, 1822. 180 pp.

1823

110. ANONYMOUS [William Allen]
Accounts of Shipwrecks and other Disasters at Sea, designed to be inter-
esting and useful to Mariners . . . compiled by a friend to Seamen
Brunswick, Maine, published by Griffin, 1823

111. CRAMP, W. B.
Narrative of a Voyage to India; of a Shipwreck on board the Lady
Castlereagh; & a description of New South Wales
London, 1823

1824

112. ANONYMOUS
Slaves Wrecked in the Portuguese Ship called "The Donna Paula" . . .

in the neighborhood of Tortola . . .
n.p., 1824. 2 reports, 10 pp., map

113. DARD, CHARLOTTE (née Charlotte Adelaide Picard)
La Chaumiere Africaine; ou, Histoire d'une Famille Francaise jetee sur
la cote occidentale de l'Afrique, a la suite du naufrage de la Fregate
la Meduse
Dijon, 1824. 12 mo. Another edition, translated from French by Patrick
Maxwell for Constable's Miscellany XI, *Perils and Captivity* . . . ,
Edinburgh, 1827
An account of the wreck of the *Medusa* by a survivor who escaped in one of the
boats.

114. POTTER, ISRAEL
Life and Remarkable Adventures of Israel R. Potter
Providence, [R.I.], printed by Henry Trumbull, 1824
This small book, the source of Herman Melville's novel *Israel Potter*, tells in a
paragraph the story of the loss by fire of an unnamed vessel.

115. ANONYMOUS [A Passenger]
A Narrative of the Loss of the Kent East Indiaman by Fire in the Bay
of Biscay on the 1st March 1825 by a Passenger
Edinburgh, 1825. Other editions, Edinburgh, 1826; London, 1837;
Dublin, before 1837

116. ANONYMOUS [?]
Unnamed tract on the loss of the whale ship *Essex*, stated to have been
issued "by the London Tract Society in Paternoster Row," and
quoted in *The Mariner's Chronicle,* New Haven, 1834
London, [1825?]

1827

117. ANONYMOUS
Narrative of the Shipwreck and Sufferings of Miss Ann Saunders, who
was a Passenger on board the Ship "Francis Mary," foundered at
Sea on the 5th of February, 1826. Survivors subsisted 22 Days on
the dead bodies of the Crew who died of Starvation, one of whom
she was engaged in Marriage.
Providence, printed for L. S. Crossman, 1827
Barnes Catalogue

118. ANONYMOUS
Perils and Captivity; comprising the Sufferings of the Picard Family
after the Medusa Shipwreck in 1816, the Captivity of M. de Brisson in 1765, and the Voyage of Madame Godins along the Amazons
in 1770
Edinburgh, Constable's Miscellany Vol. XI, 1827

119. MURRAY, H.
Adventures of British Seamen in the Southern Ocean
Edinburgh, 1827
Includes the mutiny on the *Bounty,* Bligh's voyage in an open boat, discovery of
the mutineers by the *Pandora* and the *Briton,* and Barry's account of the
massacre of the crew of the *Boyd* on the coast of New Zealand, 1809.

1828

120. LAY, W., AND HUSSEY, C. M.
Narrative of the Mutiny on Board the Whaleship Globe . . . in the
Pacific Ocean, Jan. 1824 . . . Residence of Two Years on the
Mulgrave Islands . . .
New London, Conn., Lay and Hussey, 1828

1829

121. BARNARD, CAPTAIN CHARLES H.
Narrative of Sufferings and Adventures in a Voyage Round the World,
1812–1816
New York, 1829

122. The Sailors' Magazine and Naval Journal, published by the American
Seamen's Friend Society . . . monthly . . .
New York, published at the Society's Office, 1829–1849
Barnes Catalogue states: "replete with naval anecdotes . . . shipwrecks . . ."

1831

123. FOWLER, J.
Journal of a Tour in the State of New York in the year 1830: Remarks
on agriculture in those parts most eligible for settlers and a return to England by the Western Islands, in consequence of being
shipwrecked in the Robert Fulton . . .
London, Whittaker, Treacher and Arnot, 1831. 333 pp.

124. GIBBS, CHARLES [?]
Mutiny and Murder. Confession of Charles Gibbs, a native of Rhode
Island, who, with Thomas J. Wansley, was doomed to be hung in
New-York on the 22nd of April last, for the murder of the Captain
and Mate of the Brig Vineyard, on her passage from New Orleans
to Philadelphia, in November 1830. Gibbs confesses that within
a few years he has participated in the murder of nearly 400 human
beings! Annexed, is a solemn Address to Youth.

> *Youths! by their example learn to shun their fate*
> *(How wretched is the man who's wise too late!)*
> *Ere innocence, and fame, and life be lost,*
> *Here purchase wisdom cheaply at their cost!*

Providence, printed for and published by Israel Smith, 1831

1832

125. ANONYMOUS
Horrible Shipwreck and Dreadful Loss of Lives [Steamship *Helen Mc-
Gregor*]
London, J. Catnach, [1832?]

126. TYERMAN, DAVID
Journal of Voyages and Adventures

New York, Crocker and Brewster for the Missionary Society of London,
1832
Cited in Hochling, *Great Ship Disasters,* New York, 1971, as containing a narrative
of the wreck of the *Essex.* May be the same as #116, [1825?]

1833

127. ANONYMOUS [J. Deperthes?]
A History of Shipwrecks and Disasters at Sea, from the most Authentic
Sources. "The wreck, the shores, the dying, and the drown'd."
Falconer. In Two Volumes. Vol. I, The Northern and Polar Seas;
Vol. II, the Atlantic and Southern Seas
London, Whittaker, Treacher, & Co., Ave-Maria Lane, MDCCCXXXIII
[1833]. Constable's Miscellany, Vols. LXXVIII, LXXIX
The preface, signed by Cyrus Redding, refers to an earlier volume or volumes of
which this item is a continuation.

128. ANONYMOUS
Stories of Voyages: being authentic narratives of the most celebrated
voyages from Columbus to Parry, with accounts of remarkable
shipwrecks and naval adventures
Boston, 1833. Illustrated, 12 mo.
Barnes Catalogue

1834

129. ANONYMOUS
The Mariner's Chronicle: Containing Narratives of the Most Remark-
able Disasters at Sea, such as Shipwrecks, Storms, Fires, and Fam-
ines. Also Naval Engagements, Piratical Adventures, Incidents of
Discovery, and other Extraordinary and Interesting Occurrences
New Haven, stereotyped by A. Chandler, published by Durrie and
Peck, 1834. Another edition, Columbus, 1837
Barnes Catalogue contains a citation of the same title published by George W.
Gaston in New Haven in 1834. In view of the popularity of this title for books
of this type, there is probably some question as to whether the book published
by Gaston and the putative Columbus reprint are really identical with the
Durrie and Peck volume. This book contains 39 narratives of shipwrecks and
disasters and 8 stories of battles and piracies.

130. MATHEWS, MRS.
Shipwreck and Remarkable Instances of the Interposition of Divine
Providence, in the Preservation of the Lives of 12 unfortunate
Persons, who were shipwrecked on the 3rd. of December last on
their Passage from Portsmouth England to Bombay . . .
n.p. 1834. 24 pp.

1835

131. MACY, OBED
The History of Nantucket; Being a Compendious Account of the First
Settlement of the Island by the English, together with the Rise
and Progress of the Whale Fishery . . .

Boston, Hilliard, Gray, 1835
Contains a few individual narratives, including accounts of the *Globe* mutiny and the loss of the *Essex*.

132. THOMAS, R. (A.M.)
Interesting and Authentic Narratives of the Most Remarkable Ship-wrecks, Fires, Famines, Calamities, Providential Deliverances, and Lamentable Disasters on the Seas in most Parts of the World
New-York, published by Ezra Strong, 1836. Copyright 1835
This book was published as a single volume and also combined into a thick octavo with the following:
THOMAS, R. (A.M.)
An Authentic Account of the Most Remarkable Events; Containing the Lives of the Most Noted Pirates and Piracies
New-York, published by Ezra Strong, 1836. Copyright 1835
My copy of the combined edition has the piracy narratives first, though both frontispiece illustrations are of shipwrecks.

1836

133. DICKINSON, CAPTAIN THOMAS, R.N.
A Narrative of the operations for the recovery of the public stores and treasure sunk in the H.M.S. Thetis, at Cape Frio, on the coast of Brazil, on the 5th of December, 1830. To which is prefixed a concise account of the loss of that ship
London, Longman, Rees, Orme, Brown, Greene, and Longman, MDCCCXXXVI [1836]

134. ELLMS, CHARLES [Compiled by]
Shipwrecks and Disasters at Sea; or, Historical Narratives of the Most Noted Calamities and Providential Deliverances from Fire and Famine, on the Ocean.

> "Ye lost companions of distress, adieu!
> Your toils and pains, and dangers are no more.
> The tempest now shall howl unheard by you,
> While ocean smites in vain the trembling shore."
> FALCONER

With a sketch of the various expedients for preserving the lives of mariners by the aid of life-boats, life-preservers, &c.
New York City, I. J. Rouse, 1836. Other editions, 1844, 1860
Like Thomas, Ellms also put together an anthology of piracies.

135. ANONYMOUS
Diary of the Wreck of His Majesty's Ship Challenger, on the Western Coast of South America in May, 1835, with an account of . . . encampment of the officers and crew . . . on the South Coast of Chile
London, Rees, 1836. 8vo., 160 pp., 4 pl.

136. ANONYMOUS
Histoire Complete des Naufrages Evenements et Aventures de Mer
Paris, 1836. 2 vols., 12 mo., 267, 275 pp., 6 engr., plates, large fldg. map
Bookseller's catalogue states: "Most wrecks are 19th Century, hence *not* Deperthes."

137. HOLDEN, HORACE
A Narrative of the Shipwreck, Captivity, and Sufferings of Horace Holden and Benjamin H. Nute; who were cast away in the Ameri-

can Ship "Mentor" on the Pelew Islands, and were subjected to unheard-of suffering
Boston, 1836. 12 mo., 133 pp.
Barnes Catalogue

1837

138. Anonymous
The Loss of the Kent, East Indiaman. New Edition
London, printed for the Society for Promoting Christian Knowledge, sold at the depository, Great Queen Street, Lincoln Inn Fields, 1837
Stated to have been originally prepared and published by the "Society for Promoting the Education of the Poor in Ireland, held in Kildare Place, Dublin." This item may be identical with #115, 1825.

139. Anonymous
Narrative of the Capture, Sufferings and Miraculous Escape of Mrs. Eliza Fraser
New York, Charles Webb, 1837

140. Anonymous
Shipwreck of Mrs. Fraser and the Loss of the Stirling Castle
London, Dean & Munday, 1837

141. Anonymous [?]
Tales of Travellers or A View of the World
n.p., September, 1837
Cited in Michael Alexander, Mrs. Fraser on the Fatal Shore (New York, Simon and Schuster, 1971, p. 29) as presenting one version of Mrs. Fraser's story.

142. King, Captain Phillip P.
A Voyage to Torres Strait in search of the Survivors of the Ship Charles Eaton, which was wrecked upon the Barrier Reefs, in the Month of August, 1834, in His Majesty's Colonial Schooner Isabella, C. M. Lewis, Commander
Sydney, Australia, George William Evans, 1837

143. [Manby, Geo. W.]
Reflections on Shipwreck, with historical facts and suggestions for diminishing that calamity . . .
Yarmouth, [1837]. 8vo., 31 pp., 4 pl.

1838

144. Anonymous
Chronicles of the Sea; or, Faithful Narratives of Shipwrecks, Fires, Famines, and Disasters Incidental to a Life of Maritime Enterprise; together with Celebrated Voyages, Interesting Anecdotes
[London?]. Portrait and 119 finely engraved text illustrations. 2 vols., 4to, 1838–1840
119 weekly numbers beginning on Jan. 6, 1838, and "published every Saturday, price one penny." 442 narratives

145. Anonymous
On September 6, 1838, the Forfarshire was wrecked on a voyage from Hull to Dundee, 38 out of 53 people being drowned. James Darling, lighthouse keeper on Outer Fern Isle, and his daughter Grace put off in a coble to attempt a

rescue. Grace Darling became a widely renowned heroine, the subject of innumerable street ballads and pamphlets. (Charles Hindley, *The Life and Times of James Catnach*, London, Reeves and Turner, 1878, p. 343.)

146. CURTIS, JOHN
The Shipwreck of the Stirling Castle
London, George Virtue, 1838

147. STORMS, REID (Lt. Col. W.)
An Attempt to Develop the Law of Storms by means of Facts, etc. . . . with folding charts and woodcuts
n.p., John Weale, 1838. Roy. 8vo., 436 pp.
Bookseller's note: "a fascinating work, full of wrecks and hurricanes."

1839

148. ANONYMOUS
The Eventful History of the Mutiny and Piratical Seizure of H.M.S. Bounty: its Cause and Consequences
London, John Murray, Albemarle Street, and Thomas Tegg, Cheapside, MDCCCXXXIX [1839]. Family Library Series XXV
Barnes Catalogue

149. GOODRIDGE, CHARLES MEDYETT
Narrative of a Voyage to the South Seas, and the Shipwreck of the Princess of Wales Cutter with an Account of a Two Years' Residence on an Uninhabited Island
Exeter [England], 1839

1840

150. ANONYMOUS
Awful Calamities: or, the Shipwrecks of December, 1839, being a full account of the Dreadful Hurricanes of December 15, 21, 27 on the Coast of Massachusetts, in which were lost more than 90 Vessels and nearly 200 dismasted, and more than 150 lives destroyed. Also the dreadful disasters at Gloucester
Boston, 1840
Barnes Catalogue

151. ANONYMOUS
Loss of the Steamboat "Lexington" in Long Island Sound, on the Night of January 13th, 1840. A full and particular account with all circumstances attending
Providence, 1840
Barnes Catalogue

152. ANONYMOUS
The Mariner's Library, or Voyager's Companion, containing Narratives of the Most Popular Voyages . . . with Accounts of Remarkable Shipwrecks . . .
Boston, C. Gaylord, 1840

153. ANONYMOUS
A Narrative of the Loss of H.M.S. Royal George, of 108 Guns, sunk at Spithead August 29th, 1782 . . .
Portsmouth, 1840
Cox, II, 468

154. COMSTOCK, WILLIAM
The Life of Samuel Comstock, the Terrible Whaleman. Containing an Account of the Mutiny and Massacre of the Officers of the Ship Globe, of Nantucket . . .
Boston, J. Fisher, 1840

155. HOWLAND, S. A.
Steamboat Disasters and Railroad Accidents in the United States . . . and Accounts of Recent Shipwrecks, Fires at Sea, . . . &c.
Worcester, Dorr, Howland, 1840 [2nd edition]
Another edition of what seems to be the same work is anonymous, labeled "Revised and Improved," and was published in Worcester by Warren Lazell, 1846.

1841

156. ANONYMOUS [S. Horsey, Jun.?]
A Narrative of the Loss of the Royal George, at Spithead, August, 1782; including Tracey's attempt to raise her in 1783. Also, Col. Pasley's operations in removing the Wreck, by explosions of gunpowder, in 1839–1840–41
Portsea, S. Horsey, Jun., 151 Queen St., printed and published by S. Horsey, Sen., 43 Queen St.; Whittaker & Co. London, 1841. Fourth edition
Bound in boards stated to have been cut from timbers of the *Royal George*.

1844

157. BOLTON, WILLIAM
A Narrative of the Last Cruise of the United States Steam Frigate "Missouri" from the Day she left Norfolk, until the Arrival of her Crew in Boston, including a full and circumstantial detail of the *General Conflagration* which took place at Gibraltar . . .
Philadelphia, 1844
Barnes Catalogue

158. ELLIS, GEORGE W.
A Poem on the Awful Catastrophe on board the U.S. Steam Frigate "Princeton." Together with a full description of the terrible calamity . . .
Boston, printed by A. J. Wright, 1844. 12 mo., 72 pp.
Barnes Catalogue

159. SMITH, THOMAS W.
A Narrative of the Life of Thomas W. Smith
Boston, 1844
According to bookseller's catalogue, contains the stories of eighteen voyages, five shipwrecks.

1845

160. DARTNELL, G. R.
A Brief Narrative of the Shipwreck of the Transport "Premier," near the Mouth of the River St. Lawrence, 4th November, 1843 . . .
n.p., 1845
Stated by bookseller's catalogue to contain a 9-page list of subscribers.

161. ANONYMOUS
Piratical and Tragical Almanac for 1846
Philadelphia, J. B. Perry, 198 Market St.; Zieber and Company, 3 Ledger Bldg. [1845]
Woodcut—Loss of the Steamboat "Swallow."

162. ANONYMOUS
The Friend, a semi-monthly journal devoted to Temperance, Seamen, Marine, and General Intelligence. 8 pp. an issue
[Honolulu?], 1845–57[?]
Bookseller's catalogue states: "Includes material on whaling, shipwrecks."

1846

163. ANONYMOUS
Naufrages Celebres ou Aventures les plus Remarquable des Marins . . . depuis le 15e Siecle jusqua nos jours. Nouvelle edition
Tours, 1846. 12 mo., 264 pp., portrait, vignette on title

164. DIX, WILLIAM G.
Wreck of the "Glide" with an Account of Life and Manners in the Fiji Islands
Boston, 1846. 122 pp.

1847

165. ANONYMOUS
American Adventures by Land and Sea being Remarkable Instances of Enterprise and Fortitude among Americans. Shipwrecks, Adventures at Home and Abroad. Indian Captivities, &c. In 2 vols.
New York, Harper and Brothers, Cliff Street, 1847. Family Library #174
All the narratives of shipwrecks must be in Vol. II, which I have not seen.

166. GRIEG, ALEXANDER M.
Fate of the Blenden Hall East Indiaman. Captain Alexander Grieg, bound to Bombay, with an account of her wreck and the sufferings and privations endured by the survivors, for six months, on the desolate Islands of Inaccessible and Tristan d'Acunha
New York, 1847

1848

167. ANONYMOUS
An Authentic Account of the Destruction of the Ocean Monarch, by fire, off the Port of Liverpool, and Loss of 176 Lives, with an engraving
Liverpool, William McCall, 1848

168. ANONYMOUS
Destruction of an Emigrant Ship, the Ocean Monarch, by Fire
Liverpool, 1848, reprinted from *Liverpool Journal;* available in Liverpool Record Office

169. LEGG, JAMES HENRY
The Ocean Monarch, a Poetic Narrative, with an original and authentic Account, in Prose, of the Loss of this Ill-fated Vessel . . .
Liverpool, Deighton and Langton; London, Smith, Elder, 1848

The preceding three items are cited in Terry Coleman, *Going to America*, New
York, Pantheon, 1972, p. 267.

1849

170. ANONYMOUS
   The Mariner's Chronicle of Shipwrecks, Fires, Famines, and other
      Disasters at Sea . . . together with an account of the Whale Fishery
   Philadelphia, J. Harding, 1849. 2 vols. in one

171. ENDICOTT, CHARLES M.
   Narrative of the Piracy and Plunder of the Ship "Friendship" of Salem,
      on the West Coast of Sumatra in Feb. 1831; and the Massacre of
      part of her Crew, also, her recapture out of the hands of the Malay
      Pirates
   Salem, printed at the Gazette Office, 1849. Sm. 4to., 20 pp.
   Barnes Catalogue

172. ANONYMOUS
   Perils of the Ocean or Disasters of the Sea
   New York, Murphy, n.d. [1840s?]
Bookseller states: "contains the stories of five ships lost at sea."

1851

173. DUNHAM, CAPTAIN JACOB
   Journal of Voyages (during the War of 1812, etc.) . . . his being cast
      away and residing with Indians
   New York, 1851. 243 pp.
   Barnes Catalogue

174. GILLY, WILLIAM O. S.
   Narratives of Shipwrecks in the Royal Navy between 1793 and 1849.
      Compiled principally from Official Documents in the Admiralty
   London, John W. Parker, West Strand, MDCCCLI [1851]
Contains 38 narratives and a list of shipwrecks in the Royal Navy.

1852

175. ANONYMOUS
   Shipwreck by Lightning. Destruction of Merchant Ships. From the
      "Nautical Magazine" for Nov. 1852
   London, 1852

1854

176. ANONYMOUS
   Emigrant Vessels. Return to an Address of the Honorable the House
      of Commons . . . for Copies of Reports to the Colonial Office, in
      the Six Months ending the 31st day of January 1854, of the loss of
      vessels carrying Emigrants . . .
   House of Commons, 1854. Vol. 46
   Cited in Coleman (see #169), p. 267.

177. ANONYMOUS
     Full Account of the Loss of the S.S. Arctic, with nearly 300 Lives
     Boston, n.d. [1854?]

178. VAN RENSSELAER, CORTLAND, D.D.
     God's Way in the Deep—A Discourse on the Occasion of the Wreck of
          the Arctic . . . delivered at the Presbyterian Church, Burlington,
          N.J., October 25, 1854
     Philadelphia, 1854. 32 pp.

179. WALTERS, R. C.
     A Story of the Wreck of the *Annie Jane,* 1853
     London, Partridge and Oakey, *Ragged School Union Magazine,* April
          1854
This wreck was also described in the *New York Times,* Oct. 13, 1853. Both items are
     cited by Coleman (see #169), p. 267.

1856

180. HOWE, HENRY
     Life and Death on the Ocean. A Collection of Extraordinary Adven-
          tures in the Form of Personal Narratives, illustrating Life on Board
          of Merchant Vessels and Ships of War . . .
     Cincinnati, Henry Howe, 1856. 8vo., 624 pp.
     Barnes Catalogue

181. SHEA, JOHN GILMARY
     Perils of the Ocean and Wilderness: or, Narratives of Shipwreck and
          Indian Captivity. Gleaned from early Missionary Annals
     Boston, Donahoe, n.d. [Preface dated 1856]
Reprints letters describing shipwrecks suffered by Father Lalement somewhere on
     the Canadian coast and by Father Crespel on Anticosti Island. Shea states that
     his version of the latter account is "the whole of the little volume published
     by him [Crespel] at Frankfort, Maine." The title page printed by Shea shows
     that the book was originally published not in Maine but at Frankfort-on-the-
     Meyn in Germany.

1857

182. ANONYMOUS [A Son of the Ocean]
     A Home on the Deep; or, The Mariner's Trials on the Dark Blue Sea
     Boston, Higgins, Bradley & Dayton, 20 Washington Street, 1857
Assorted narratives of exploration, travel, shipwrecks, whaling, naval engagements,
     and piracies, plus 20 poems, 17 engravings.

183. BATES, MRS. D. B.
     Incidents on Land and Water, or Four Years on the Pacific Coast
     Boston, 1857. Plates
Bookseller's catalogue states: "Also shipwrecks."

1858

184. [MOON, H.]
     An Account of the Wreck of H.M.'s Sloop "Osprey," with the encamp-
          ment of her crew and their march across the Island of New Zealand
          . . . by one of her Crew
     Landport, 1858

1860

185. ANONYMOUS
Report of the Master and Wardens of the Trinity House of Port
Adelaide . . . Loss of the "Melbourne" at the Mouth of the River
Murray
Adelaide, 1860. 10 pp.

186. ANONYMOUS
Shipwrecks and Adventures at Sea
[n.p.] Christian Knowledge Society, [1860]

187. ANONYMOUS [Preface signed W. and R. C. (William and Robert Cham-
bers)]
Shipwrecks and Tales of the Sea
London and Edinburgh, 1860

188. ANONYMOUS [By an Old Salt]
The Terrors of the Sea, as Portrayed in Accounts of Fire and Wreck,
and Narratives of Poor Wretches forced to abandon their floating
Homes without Food or Water, thus compelling them to resort to
Cannibalism, with its attendant Horrors
New York, Hurst & Co., 122 Nassau St., n.d. [1860s?]

189. ANONYMOUS
Book of the Sea. A Nautical Repository of Perils and Pleasures, Ad-
ventures, Joys, and Sufferings on the Briny Deep . . .
London, n.d. [1860s?]
Barnes Catalogue

This last item concludes the checklist, but I feel I should mention
one other volume which is perhaps seen more often in antiquarian
bookstores than any book I have listed. W. H. G. Kingston, who
wrote many juvenile novels of the sea, edited an anthology for Routledge in 1873, *Shipwrecks and Disasters at Sea*. This volume contains
22 narratives of wrecks, 1783 to 1871.